GROUP MAGAZINE'S
Best
YOUTH GROUP
PROGRAMS
VOLUME 1

Edited by
CINDY S. HANSEN

Designed by
JEAN BRUNS

Group®
Books

Loveland, Colorado

**GROUP Magazine's Best Youth Group Programs
(Volume 1)**

Cover design by RoseAnne Buerge

Library of Congress Cataloging-in-Publication Data

Group magazine's best youth group programs.

   1. Church work with youth—Handbooks, manuals, etc.
I. Hansen, Cindy S. II. Group (Loveland, Colo.)
III. Title: Best youth group programs.
BV4447.G694   1986   259'.2   86-313
ISBN 0-931529-11-5 (v. 1)

18 17 16 15 14   03 02 01 00 99 98

Printed in the United States of America.

CONTENTS

PART ONE:
SPIRITUAL GROWTH

PART TWO:
SELF-IMAGE

Contents continued

PART THREE:
RELATIONSHIPS 105

PART FOUR:
SPECIAL OCCASIONS

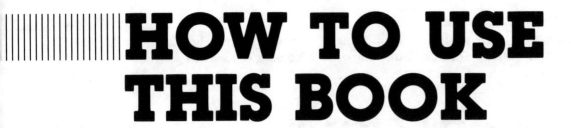

HOW TO USE THIS BOOK

Youth leaders everywhere are concerned about their kids' needs and want to meet these needs. But leaders also have busy schedules and precious little time to prepare creative youth ministry programming.

GROUP Magazine's Best Youth Group Programs (Volume 1) provides youth leaders with 79 chapters packed with creative programs that meet the needs of young people. The programs also are easy to do and require minimal preparation time. The programs are the best Bible studies, meetings and other creative programming ideas from over 11 years of GROUP, the youth ministry magazine. What sets GROUP apart is its practical nature and its desire to equip youth workers with "do-able" programs. The various authors of these articles represent the combined youth ministry experience of decades.

The programs are grouped into four parts that focus on the needs of teenagers.

PART ONE: SPIRITUAL GROWTH

Articles in this part help kids develop their faith with activities such as Bible studies, devotions, parties, games, plays, melodramas and retreats. The activities in this section are fun, effective and help kids grow in their understanding of the Bible and God's love.

PART TWO: SELF-IMAGE

This part offers many meeting ideas and programs that help young people take a look at themselves and develop positive self-esteem. Topics include failure, loneliness, frustration, put-downs, body image and sexuality, priorities and our "special uniqueness" as Christians.

PART THREE: RELATIONSHIPS

This section offers many ideas for helping group members develop friendships and relate to others. Articles cover a whole range of topics: reaching out, ways to say "I like you," preventing suicide, trusting others and friendship. This section also includes ideas for parties, discussions, games, a treasure hunt, prayers, Bible studies and a learning adventure.

PART FOUR: SPECIAL OCCASIONS

Every youth group needs ideas for those special times throughout the year. This section provides group activities for New Year's, Valentine's Day, spring, Good Friday, Easter, summer, back-to-school, Halloween, Thanksgiving and Christmas.

WAYS TO USE THIS BOOK

All of the ideas in **GROUP Magazine's Best Youth Group Programs** can be used with any youth group. Here are some ways to use the programs presented in this book. The ideas can be used "as is" or adapted to fit specific youth group needs.

1. Brainstorm for a weekly series of Bible studies. Develop the studies according to a theme. For example: Offer an eight-week class on spiritual growth. Choose eight studies in the first section of the book and use one each week.

2. Host a holiday hullabaloo. Plan a Santa's Workshop for your group or have the kids sponsor an all-church event. Use "Creative Christmas Cards" and "Santa's Workshop" from Part Four. At other times of the year such as Valentine's Day, Easter or Thanksgiving, combine articles and plan fun get-to-gethers.

3. Cook up an end-of-the-summer barbecue Bible study. Use one of the back-to-school programs listed in the last section of the book, or one of the friendship programs listed in the third section. Have everyone bring meat to grill. Guys bring pop; girls bring chips. Reminisce about summertime fun and look forward to the upcoming year of new friends and new experiences.

4. Latch on to a lock-in idea. Lock-ins are overnight gatherings that usually are held at the church. Plan a lock-in according to a theme or use a program from each of the four sections. For example, you could use "God's Will Game-O-Rama" from Part One, "Being Like Jesus" from Part Two, "A Love Prayer in Action" from Part Three, and a program from Part Four according to the season or holiday.

5. Reach out to others with a retreat. Plan to take your youth group to a cabin, camp area or retreat center. Organize a retreat using any of the programs in the book. Following is a sample "Friendship Retreat" schedule:

Retreat

FRIDAY

6:00 p.m. **Meet at church.** Carpool to the retreat site.

7:30 p.m. **Begin program** (depending on travel time). If you have guitar players in your group, ask them to play for a sing-along. Sing favorite songs, many of which are found in **Songs,** compiled by Yohann Anderson, Songs and Creations Inc., San Anselmo, CA.

8:00 p.m. **Get-acquainted games.** Play "Build a Body" from **Try This One . . . Strikes Again** (Group Books). Give each group member a piece of paper on which is written the name of a body part (head, arm, leg, foot, etc.). When you give the signal, everyone must locate all the others with the same body part. When a group is complete, it should shout out its name.

Then instruct group members to scatter and form complete bodies. The first one to form should shout, "We're number one!" For more competition, have the completed bodies race to cut large body parts from construction paper and create giant people.

Or play "Designer Jeans" also from **Try This One . . . Strikes Again.** Draw a large jean pocket on an 8½x11 piece of paper. Give the group members each a photocopy of a pocket and tell them to write their name on the label and then describe, on the pocket, (emphasizing what the wearer does or feels). Example: Mary Jones Jeans. The kind of person who wears Mary Jones Jeans likes summer more than winter, has long talks with old friends and watches the sunrise alone.

Afterward, ask each person to share his or her designer jeans description. Tell the kids that they all have identified themselves in a positive way. Read Psalm 139 (especially verse 14) and thank God for the "wonder of you."

9:00 p.m. **Together time.** "Friends" (page 149).

10:00 p.m. **Free time.** Pop popcorn, sing songs, play games, etc. For a treasure trove of activities, consult the **Try This One** series from Group Books.

11:00 p.m. **Evening worship.** Read Proverbs 17:17a; 27:6a; John 15:13, and other verses that deal with friendship. Sing songs such as "Friends Like You" from **Songs** (Songs and Creations) and "What a Friend We Have in Jesus."

Gather everyone in a circle and have a "Love Service" as described in **The Best of Try This One** (Group Books). Take a lighted candle and stand in the middle of the circle. Think of one person in the group and without mentioning that person's name, tell why you think he or she would be a good friend. For example, "I think this person would be a good friend, because she is always warm and friendly." Then pass the candle to the person you were describing. That person repeats the procedure. Make sure everyone is affirmed.

Midnight **Lights out.**

SATURDAY

8:00 a.m. **Breakfast.** If served by the retreat center, great. If not, bring supplies to make french toast or pancakes.

9:00 a.m. **Hiking and solitary time.** Give everyone 45 minutes to walk and think of the following three questions:
- What do you appreciate in a friend?
- What are characteristics of one of your close friends?
- Do you show these same characteristics?

9:45 a.m. **Discussion.** Gather in pairs and discuss answers to the questions.

10:30 a.m. **Together time.** "The Portrait of True Friendship" (page 108).

Noon **Lunch.**

1:00 p.m. **Free time.** Hike, take pictures, swim, play softball (or have a snowball fight). Activities depend upon site location and season.

3:00 p.m. **Together time.** Discuss good memories the young people have had with friends. What are special things friends have done for them? What are special things they've done for a friend? As a large group, create a list of special things we can do for friends: send them a "thinking of you" card, call them on the telephone, surprise them with a free ice cream sundae. Next, ask the group members to write their names on slips of paper and drop them in a hat. Have everybody draw a name out of the hat. This is their "secret friend." Tell the members to do a "secret something nice" for that friend during the next week. Use the list of "special things" to get some ideas.

4:00 p.m. **Wrap up.** Encourage each person to answer the following questions:
- What was the best thing that happened to you during this retreat?
- What did you learn about friendship?
- How did you grow closer to everyone in the youth group?
- In the future, how will you use what you've learned on this retreat?

4:30 p.m. **Group prayer.** Gather in a circle and have each person pray for the person on his or her right, thanking God for this friend. Close with a group hug. Pack up and head for home.

We hope the ideas for using this book will be helpful. Have fun adapting, combining or using each program "as is." There are endless ways to use **GROUP Magazine's Best Youth Group Programs.** Youth ministry is made just a little bit easier with all of these creative, helpful programs bound in one book!

A HELPFUL EVALUATION RESOURCE FOR CREATIVE PROGRAMMING

When it comes to creative programming, we'd like to say we enjoy the most innovative, life-changing, faith-energizing programs around. Except that's not always the way it is.

Before reading this book, take a barometric reading of your youth ministry's programming by completing this creative programming weather report. Maybe your group is experiencing a refreshing shower of creativity after a long drought. Or maybe your group's satisfied with its moderate temperatures—never jolted by high or low pressure systems.

Read and evaluate these 50 factors. Then make your forecast for the future. Circle the weather symbol that best describes the following areas of your youth ministry programming. Use this key:

BRIGHT AND SUNNY Right now you're basking in success concerning this program area.	
PARTLY SUNNY You're satisfied; everything's okay—but you could use a creative flash of sunshine now and then.	
CLOUDY AND OVERCAST This area of your programming's been shadowed by downfalls. You wish things were different.	
THUNDERSTORMS Turbulent times describe this area of your programming. Nothing's going right. (You're wondering whether being struck by lightning might not be so bad!)	

Our youth ministry programming . . .

	☀	⛅	☁	🌧
involves young people in the planning process.				
collects group members' needs at least every six months.				
uses surveys, needs assessments and frequent conversation to collect kids' needs.				
meets young people's needs and is relevant to their lives.				
publicizes well in advance so kids know what's coming.				
communicates to the whole congregation what the young people are doing.				
keeps parents informed.				
follows a detailed and organized planning process.				
sets clear and specific goals and objectives.				
anticipates problem areas in the planning stage.				
keeps a backlog of ideas just for last-minute emergencies.				
sparks creative ideas from special seasons and church holidays.				
offers something different each time.				
varies the format of meetings for an element of surprise.				
includes and involves other adults in various capacities.				
collects all necessary supplies in advance.				
checks out the latest and most appropriate resources.				
previews any resource element (film, speaker, record).				
arranges meeting rooms appropriate for its activities.				
flows quickly and smoothly from one activity to the next.				
involves young people in roles of leadership responsibility.				
takes time for one-on-one sharing.				
plans for different group configurations (pairs, small groups, large groups).				
structures community-building activities.				
is consistent with biblical truths.				

	☀	⛅	☁	🌧
approaches biblical truths in new and exciting ways.				
combines experiences for the five senses (touch, taste, hearing, sight, smell).				
does nothing that embarrasses a young person.				
balances activities, discussion and input.				
gives clear and understandable instructions.				
creates an inviting atmosphere as members arrive (music, greeters, action to involve them).				
incorporates, in some way, each person who comes.				
welcomes kids and makes them feel special.				
is Christ-centered and different from any other organization or club.				
allows time for announcements and upcoming events.				
supplies songbooks or song sheets so everyone can read the words.				
begins with activities that include everyone (name tags, icebreakers).				
closes with a meaningful activity (prayer, hugs, song) to wrap up the time together.				
encourages individual and group prayer.				
includes positive and affirming words and actions toward each person.				
unites all the activities with a theme.				
sparks a change or commitment in people's lives.				
stretches kids to think and act as Christians.				
encourages kids to bring friends.				
welcomes newcomers.				
is something kids proudly talk about—at home, at school, at work.				
grows and learns from its mistakes.				
starts on time.				
ends on time.				
evaluates successes and failures regularly.				

A Helpful Evaluation Resource continued

WHAT'S YOUR GROUP'S WEATHER REPORT?

Now tally your symbols.

```
_____  ☀
+  _____  🌤
=  _____  (TOTAL)

_____  ☁
+  _____  ⛈
=  _____  (TOTAL)
```

If you scored 30-50 ☀ and 🌤, good! Celebrate the warmth of relationships and the brilliance of creativity. Do your best to maintain and improve the positive programming you've begun. Say a prayer of thanks for all God's done.

If you scored 30-50 ☁ and ⛈, take cover! But take hope. Stormy times rain great chances to grow and learn. Rise to the challenge. Start gradually. Choose two or three areas of immediate need, then move toward change. With prayer, a commitment to ministry and a relationship with Jesus, predict an exciting change.

FORECAST FOR THE FUTURE

Choose a ☁ or ⛈ ministry area to improve for each of the following time frames. Then make your weather prediction for the future. Instead of consulting The Old Farmer's Almanac, talk with your adult and teenage leaders. Together set specific, measurable and achievable goals to make a change for sunnier weather!

This week:

This month:

The next three months:

The next year:

Now that you have set measurable goals to make a change for sunnier weather, read on for innovative, life-changing, faith-energizing, creative programs to shower on your youth group. Sunny days are ahead with this refreshing resource titled **GROUP Magazine's Best Youth Group Programs**.

PART ONE:
SPIRITUAL GROWTH

1 FAITH

What is faith?

That's a good question. The word "faith" gets tossed around as if everybody knows exactly what's meant by it.

Not so.

No one person knows all about faith. Faith grows in different ways; people live different lives. Yet God continues to work his miracle of a growing faith within each of us.

Help young people wrestle with concerns that surround their faith. Use this Bible study to find some answers to "What is faith?"

1. Objectives—Participants will:
● explore the meanings they give to "faith" and "faithful living";
● be exposed to scriptural references about faith;
● talk about personal aspects or experiences of faith;
● experience learning and working together.

2. Before the Bible Study—Read the entire study including "Other Ideas." Select activities to best meet your group's learning needs and interests.

Choose and prepare the suggested Bible verses so each person will study one reference.

Gather the necessary supplies: Bibles, newsprint and markers.

3. Experiencing Trust and Faith—Lead the following trust games. Focus on faith and trust in action:
● Have kids each choose a partner who's about the same size as they are. Say: Face your partner with your toes almost touching. Hold hands and lean back. Keep your legs and back straight. Support each other with fully extended arms. Relax for a moment, now stand up straight again.
● Tell each pair to choose another pair. Have the four stand close together, facing each other. Say: Join hands with the person on either side, and all four slowly lean back. It can be done!
● Have each foursome choose one person in the group to stand erect with arms at his or her side. Tell the other three to stand behind the chosen person. Have that person, keeping legs and back straight, fall backward. The other three *must* catch the person before he or she hits the ground. Give each person the opportunity to fall backward.
● Have *all* youth group members build a people pyramid. Tell them to be careful and build it quickly.

After the trust games, assemble the whole group and ask: What did you learn about trust from these activities? Which activity was most difficult for you? easiest? Why? Is it easier to trust or be trusted? Explain. Is it easy to believe others will support you?

Why or why not? How do you get others to believe in you and your promises? What did you learn about yourself from these activities?

4. Sorting Out Faith and Feelings—Draw an imaginary line across the room. Label one end "totally disagree" and the other end "totally agree." Read each of the following statements and ask participants to each place themselves at the point on the line that best represents their answer. Ask people to explain their viewpoints.
● Everyone has faith in something or other.
● Seeing is believing—there's no such thing as blind faith.
● It doesn't matter what you believe as long as you're sincere.
● There is only one, true Christian faith.
● All roads lead to heaven; all religious try to reach the same goal.

Continue to explore feelings and thoughts about faith by moving into a more personal realm. Have each person find a partner and discuss these questions: (Display or make typed copies of the questions so everyone can see them.)

How do you feel about the pilot when you're in an airplane? Explain.

How do you feel about the machine or the operator when you're on an amusement ride? Explain.

Do you believe most people? Why or why not?

Do you believe people who compliment you? Why or why not?

Do you believe people who say they love you? Why or why not?

Do you believe people who threaten you? Why or why not?

Do you believe people who tell you their secrets and emotions? Why or why not?

Ask pairs to each share with the whole group one discovery concerning their feelings about faith.

After the discussion, explain that we have faith in many different things, persons or ideas. Trust, belief, hope—all of these are part of faith.

5. Exploring Words of Faith—Next deal with "content" or knowledge about faith. Tell the group members to think of as many words as possible that explain faith. Find a volunteer secretary to write all the responses on newsprint.

When the secretary is ready, encourage participants to call out words about faith. Trust, belief or hope are good words to get the group started.

After the secretary records all the responses, vote on the best four or five words by a show of hands. Leave the word list posted.

Say: When it comes to faith, we can't rely on our own feelings and thoughts. We've got to see what God says.

Faith continued

Prepare Bible verses using one of these two options. Option 1: Print Bible references only (for example, Hebrews 11:1) on separate pieces of paper. Prepare one for each person. Group members will each need a Bible. Option 2: Print whole passages (for example, "To have faith is to be sure of the things we hope for, to be certain of the things we cannot see," Hebrews 11:1) on separate pieces of paper. Prepare one for each person.

Distribute the following references: Matthew 6:31-33; Mark 11:22-24; Luke 8:22-25; John 3:16; Romans 3:22; 10:14; 1 Corinthians 13:2; Galatians 6:10; Ephesians 2:8-9; Colossians 1:21-23; 2 Timothy 2:11-13; Hebrews 11:1; James 5:13-16; 1 John 5:1-4; Revelation 2:10.

Ask each person to study the assigned reference by asking: What does this verse teach about faith? What does this verse say about me? about God? How can this verse become more a part of my daily living?

Have kids report how their verses speak about faith. Have the secretary write key words or thoughts from the reports on newsprint. Reinforce ideas by repeating them or asking questions to clarify.

6. Becoming Faithful People—Help your young people identify faith as a part of life through a Faith Honor Roll. Divide group members into small groups of three or four people. Ask each small group to think of faithful people. Say: You can tell who faithful people are because they live their faith through words and actions. Their lives are examples of Christ's love. Remember, faithful people can include a friend, a family member, a president, a pastor, someone who does small jobs, a denominational leader. They can be living or deceased, local or international.

Have each small group nominate at least one candidate for inclusion on a Faith Honor Roll. When everyone's finished, have each small group describe its candidate and tell why he or she is a faithful person. Ask a volunteer to print the names of all suggested candidates on a large sheet of newsprint. Have the words "Faith Honor Roll" printed at the top in large letters. Leave space on the newsprint for additional names.

Ask: Was it difficult to choose a candidate? Why or why not? How can you tell whether someone is faithful? Are there other characteristics, besides faith, which these people have in common? Explain.

Say: We, too, can be a part of the Faith Honor Roll. Our lives can reflect God's love and be a visible sign of our faith.

Have each person share how he or she can be a more "faithful person." After members share, invite them each to write their name on the Faith Honor Roll.

7. Closing—Have group members join hands. Ask someone in the group to lead a prayer asking God to increase each participant's faith. Here's an example: "Thank you, God for being present in the world and for being with us during this study. Thank you for the gift of salvation in Jesus Christ. Work in us to strengthen our faith and to help us live faithfully. We pray in Jesus' name. Amen."

8. Other Ideas—Depending on the needs of your group, choose one or more of these additional activities to supplement the Bible study experience.

● *Searching for truth*—Select four persons from the group. Ask each of them to tell a story (true or "tall") to the group. Suggest they talk about experiences from school or home, family or friends.

Have the whole group judge which of the four stories, if any, are true. Then reveal which, if any, are true. Ask: How do you decide whether someone is telling the truth? Is it easier to trust others or to doubt them? Explain. Do you think most people trust you? Why or why not?

● *Special "faithful person" guests*—Invite one or more persons to speak briefly, personally, about how faith has affected his or her life. For example, invite a pastor, parent, young person, Bible study leader, youth leader, grandparent.

Take time for questions or requests for further explanations.

● *Faith songs*—Sing favorite songs about faith. For example, "Faith of Our Fathers," and "By Faith I'm Saved."

● *Statements of faith*—Provide statements of faith (creeds, confessions, Psalms, other scripture) which the whole group could read.

● *More questions*—If you feel group members have unanswered questions about faith, supply 3×5 cards. Ask group members to write any other questions they'd like addressed in later discussion.

● *Faith poem*—Read and discuss this poem:
Faith is a friendship begun by the Spirit.
Faith is a window through which we look and see God.
Faith is being one with others—our common unity in Jesus Christ.
Faith is a river, flowing through us from God for others.
Faith is an imagination of how things can be with God.
Invite group members to write their own faith poems.

—Marty Doering

BIBLE PEOPLE

AND YOU

Once upon a time there was a high school Bible class.

Each student diligently studied all the Bible heroes and heroines.

All went well.

Until one day. Some of the students began to argue.

"I could never be as trusting as Noah," decided one.

"It's certain I'll never be as famous as King David," said another.

"Who could ever be as solid as Peter?" wondered one more doubter.

"Impossible. We can't be like those people!" concluded the rest.

The class soon surmised that God must have made "Bible" people differently.

Those Old and New Testament celebrities must have had an "in" with God.

They did everything right.

Or did they?

Noah got drunk.

David fooled around with someone else's wife and killed her husband;

Peter denied that he'd ever seen Jesus.

It wasn't long before the students were disgusted.

Only this time for a different reason:

"Why are we studying these awful, sinful people?"

Then—one, aware of her own sinfulness, whispered,

"Nobody's perfect. Not Noah, Abraham, David or Ruth.

Nobody's perfect—including me."

The discussion stopped.

And the class began to think.

Tentatively, one thinker began:

"Maybe all along we've studied those Bible heroes and heroines

Because they're like us!

Sometimes they're strong and faithful.

Sometimes they're weak and failures."

Buried in the heard-a-hundred-times-before stories came a message:

God loves people.
Not because they're so good.
God loves people.
In spite of the fact they're so bad.
God loves people.

The Bible class was never the same again.

1. Objectives—Use this Bible study to:

● discuss the strengths and weaknesses of 10 Bible people.

● explore participants' own strengths and weaknesses.

● be reminded of God's unfailing love for people.

Bible People and You continued

2. Before the Bible Study—Gather Bibles, 10 3×5 cards, paper, pencils, newsprint, markers.

Skim through the entire Bible study to get an idea of its content and activities.

Involve young people as leaders by finding volunteers for the following tasks:

● *Chart-Maker*—Using newsprint and markers, this person makes two large wall charts. The "Bible People" chart should include 10 blank spaces for Bible names, strengths, weaknesses and how God used each person. Leave enough blank space so answers can be added:

Name	Strengths	Weaknesses	How God used this person

The second chart is the "You" chart. It must contain the following Bible passages: (Individuals will copy this to make personal charts.)

Name	Strengths	Weaknesses	How God uses you
	Romans 8:37-39 1 Cor. 12:7 Ephesians 1:19-20 Colossians 1:27-28	Romans 3:23 Galatians 5:17-21 Ephesians 2:1-3	Romans 12:6-8 1 Cor. 4:1-2 Philippians 2:13

● *Card-Preparer*—This person copies the Bible references on 10 3×5 cards, one Bible person per card. These will be distributed to group members for the "personals" ads. Here's an example of a card:

> Name:
> Personal characteristics:
>   Strengths:
>
>
>   Weaknesses:
>
>
> How God used this person:

Use these Bible references:

Abraham—strengths: Genesis 15:1-6; weaknesses: Genesis 16:1-4; 17:15-19; God used: Genesis 12:1-3; 22:15-18.

David—strengths: 1 Samuel 16:11-13; 17:48-50; weaknesses: 2 Samuel 11:2-5, 14-17; 12:13-14; God used: 2 Samuel 7:8-16.

Jacob—strengths: Genesis 32:7-12, 22-30; weaknesses: Genesis 25:27-34; 27:1-29, 34-36; God used: Genesis 28:10-22; 35:9-12.

Martha—strengths: Luke 10:38; John 12:1-2; weaknesses: Luke 10:39-42; John 11:20-22; God used: John 11:5, 23-27.

Moses—strengths: Exodus 14:13-14, 21-25; 19:1-7; weaknesses: Exodus 3:11; 4:1-17; 5:22-23; 6:1-13; God used: Exodus 3:7-10; 6:2-8.

Noah—strengths: Genesis 6:9-22; 7:1, 17-23; 8:1; weaknesses: Genesis 9:20-29; God used: Genesis 8:1, 15-19; 9:1-3, 8-17.

Paul—strengths: Acts 19:4-8; Philippians 4:11-13; weaknesses: Acts 8:1-3; Romans 7:15-20; God used: Acts 9:20-22; Colossians 1:25-26.

Peter—strengths: Matthew 16:13-19; John 21:15-19; weaknesses: Matthew 26:31-35, 69-75; God used: Matthew 28:19-20.

Rahab—strengths: Joshua 2:8-20; weaknesses: Joshua 2:1-7; God used: Joshua 2:21-24; 6:22-25; Matthew 1:1-17.

Thomas—strengths: John 20:28; weaknesses: John 20:24-25; God used: John 20:29-30.

● *Instruction-Giver(s)*—This person(s) must be acquainted with the Bible study exercises and be able to clearly explain directions to the group.

● *Information-Recorder*—During the group discussions this person records all the information on newsprint.

● *Story-Reader*—This person reads the parable during the devotion time. The story should be rehearsed ahead of time so it can be read with expression.

This Bible study can be facilitated by an adult leader, but it would be a meaningful experience if young people prepared it. Giving young people responsibility not only trains them to become better leaders, but also provides an opportunity for ownership.

3. Who Would You Be?—The *Instruction-Giver*:

● Brings the group together and asks each person to answer aloud: If you could be one person in the Bible, who would you be and why?

● Explains the purpose of the study by saying: This Bible study will help us take a close look at Bible people, explore their strengths and weaknesses, and learn how God used them to accomplish his purpose. It will also be a time to reflect on your own personal characteristics and how God uses you.

4. Bible "Personals"—*The Instruction-Giver:*
● Divides the 10 Bible people cards among the group. (If the group has 10 members, each person gets a card. If it's smaller than 10, some people get more than one card. If the group is larger than 10, form teams, so each team gets a card.)
● Explains how group members are to look up the Bible verses of personal characteristics listed on each card. From this information (and whatever else they know about the person), they should write a "personals" ad about the person named on the card. The "personals" ad needs to include honest information, but must not give the person's name. The object is to write an ad so other group members can guess who it's describing. Have fun with it! Be creative! Here's an example:
(David) Male, likes to dance, sing and play the harp. Occasionally daydreams of women on rooftops.

5. Making Discoveries—*The Instruction-Giver:*
● Brings the group together after the "personals" have been written.
● Facilitates the group guessing game.
The Information-Recorder:
● Writes the correctly guessed names on the "Bible People" chart.
● Fills in the rest of the chart's information as the group brainstorms each Bible person's strengths and weaknesses.
● Encourages group members to use the scripture references on the card to answer how God used each person.
● Makes certain the chart's information is complete.
The Instruction-Giver:
● Breaks the large group into small groups with four members in each.
● Instructs the small group members to answer the following questions:
What surprised you most about each Bible person?
Is it a poor reflection on God when he uses people with "flaws"? Why or why not?
What is the main quality God desires in people?

6. You're a "Bible" Person—*The Instruction-Giver:*
● Distributes paper and pencil to each person.
● Instructs group members to copy the "You" chart displayed on the wall.
● Says: List three personal strengths and three personal weaknesses on your chart. Read the Bible verses listed. Write at least three ways God is using your particular strengths and weaknesses. Jot down key words and phrases from the Bible to complete

your chart.
(The Bible passages in each category can be read individually or as a group.)

7. What You've Learned—*The Information-Recorder:*
● Writes discoveries and learnings from the group on a blank sheet of newsprint.
● Asks the group members these questions:
How has your opinion of Bible people changed?
How has your opinion of yourself changed?
How has your opinion of God changed?

8. Storytime Devotion—*The Story-Reader:*
● Brings the group members together in a circle.
● Reads the parable found at the beginning of this study.
● Invites group members to offer a prayer concern relating to their personal lists of strenghths and weaknesses.
● Encourages group members to take their charts home and refer to them at a later date.
● Challenges members to watch for personal growth and change in the future.
● Suggests group members refer to the "You" chart's Bible passages for support and power.

9. Extras, Optionals, More—Use these suggestions to supplement this Bible study:
● *Bible masquerade*—Transform your Bible study into a party by inviting young people to come dressed as their favorite Bible character.
● *"Guess who" game*—Prepare pieces of paper with one Bible person's name on each piece. Tape one paper on the back of each group member without revealing the name. The object of the game is for young people to guess which famous Bible person they have on their backs by asking other group members questions that can only be answered "yes" or "no."
Add to the challenge. After group members have learned their Bible identity; have them form a chronological line according to when they appear in the Bible.
● *Bible people multimedia*—Encourage a few creative young people to design a multimedia presentation for the entire group. Hunt through old Sunday school filmstrips, flannelgraphs, slides, records and pictures. Be scavengers. The presentation could be shared with the whole congregation as a reflection of your Bible study.
● *For further reading*—Use Frederick Buechner's book, **Peculiar Treasures** (Harper and Row, 1979), as a story resource. This alphabetical tour of Bible characters provides delightful, insightful discoveries about people through whom God worked.
—*Joani Schultz*

3 GOD IS...

1. Before the Bible Study—Gather a pencil, straw, paper, Bible and copy of the "Self-Test" for each person. You also will need a medium-size rubber ball and Kool-Aid in two large containers.

2. Opener—Get the discussion rolling by having the students form a circle. Bounce a rubber ball back and forth to group members. The person who catches the ball must complete this sentence, "God is . . ." Limit the speaking time to one minute. The speaker bounces the ball to another member who adds a comment. Bouncing the ball to the shyer members helps encourage response.

3. God Is—Discuss the kids' various perceptions of what God is like. Is he like a grandfather? a score-keeper? a judge? Say that many people have jammed God into a small, confining box by not understanding what he is really like.

Distribute a "Self-Test" and pencil to each person and let the young people think about how they view God.

SELF-TEST

Circle the picture that describes how you sometimes view God.

The misconceptions we have of God are almost always based on partial truths. To stand on the right track, we need to keep our image of God in balance. Take this self-test and see how you view God. Check the reason you feel best describes how you feel about God:

God is like a loving grandparent because . . .
_____ I'm spoiled by God's love.
_____ I don't think God would ever punish me.
_____ God knows me, and, well, "kids will be kids!"

God is like a cosmic bellhop because . . .
_____ he'll answer all my prayers.
_____ I say, "Thanks, God," once in a while.
_____ I call on him in trouble; he's nice to have around.

God is like a divine watchmaker because . . .
_____ God created all the world and everything in it.
_____ it's up to me to take care of things.
_____ I like to be the one in control.

God is ruler of the "stained glass" slice of life because . . .
_____ my life is lived in sections.
_____ God is Lord—but only at "churchy" things.
_____ *everything* I do couldn't possibly be an expression of love.

God is like a great scorekeeper because . . .
_____ God is watching me all the time to see if I'm bad.
_____ I'll go to hell if I do something bad.
_____ I'm afraid I'll make the wrong choice about something and God will be mad.

—*Tom Glossi*

4. Unearthing Half-Truths—Misconceptions of God are based on partial truths. They aren't all wrong, but they are not total pictures of God either. Choose one person from the group and brainstorm different ideas and conceptions someone could have of that particular person. Talk about why people view people in certain ways. Discuss why it's important to see the person as a whole. Talk about the danger in viewing that person one way—for example, only as a student, or a child, or a manager of McDonald's, etc.

Now read these Bible verses and discuss the perspective of God that they offer. Look for the danger in isolating that from the whole of scripture. Genesis 1:27-28; Deuteronomy 7:9-10; Psalms 30:4-5; 51:3-5; 107:1; 139:1-6; 145:15-16; Jeremiah 11:20; Matthew 7:7-8, 21-23; John 15:1-2; Romans 8:31, 38-39; Hebrews 4:13; James 1:17; 4:12; 1 Peter 5:7 and 1 John 3:1.

5. Our Creed—Ask each young person to divide a sheet of paper into thirds. Title the sections: Father, Son and Holy Spirit. Write all the qualities and characteristics of each person in the Trinity. After everyone has completed the activity, fold the paper and discuss each section separately. What did you learn about God by doing this? What do we gain by knowing God as the Triune God? What quality does each person of the Trinity add to your perception of God?

Close by joining hands and reciting or reading the Apostles' Creed. Begin in a whisper with joined hands at sides. As the creed progresses, gradually speak louder and raise hands for a triumphant AMEN!

6. Refreshments—Play "Glug" from **Try This One . . . Strikes Again** (Group Books). It's best to play "Glug" outside. If you are unable to do this, place several newspapers in the center of the room. On top of the newspapers, place the two large containers of Kool-Aid. Divide into two teams and give each person a straw. Each member dips a straw into the team's Kool-Aid-filled container at the same time and drinks. The first team to finish off their container wins!

4
GOD'S LOVE

In this creative Bible study, young people encounter one particular book of the New Testament. Instead of focusing on verses plucked from here and there, this study focuses on 1 John in its entirety.

The involving activities and discussions bring the words of love to life. They clarify why 1 John delights in the Incarnation—God's love taking human form. And more. They zoom in on how we, too, embody God's love.

PHOTOGRAPHY/DICK KEZLAN

1. Objectives—By studying the book of 1 John, participants will:
- explore what God's love means;
- examine what a Christian's love for other people means; and
- find ways of expressing God's love to others.

2. Before the Bible Study—Encourage each person to read the book of 1 John before the Bible study begins. Suggest that group members read a chapter a day for five days.

Gather supplies: Bibles, newsprint, markers, slips of paper, pencils, a hat or basket, and a ball of clay or Play-Doh for each person.

3. The Shape of Our Lives—Begin by handing each person a lump of clay. Have group members form the clay in a shape that expresses the kind of shape their life has been in lately. (For example, someone might mold a shape that goes in many directions to represent busyness; someone might create a happy face for feeling good.) Have members tell the reasons for their clay shapes.

Say: We *talk* a lot about God's love, but how do we really know it? Let's take a closer look at one entire book of the Bible, 1 John. In this book, we'll discover the shapes God's love takes in our world.

4. The Shape of God's Love—Divide the group members into pairs. If your group is smaller than 12, assign more than one set of verses per pair; if there are more than 12 members, assign verses more than once.

Give each pair one of the following Bible passages: 1 John 1:1-4; 2:1-6; 3:1-10; 4:7-10; 5:1-12; 5:13-21.

Have the pairs read the Bible passages and select key words from them. Then have pairs shape their clay in a way that tells the whole group what their particular passage says about God's love and the shape it takes for us. (For example, the pair with 1 John 3:1-10 could create clay family members holding hands.)

Have pairs use the key words from their passages to create a "title" for their clay creations. (For example, the clay family could be titled "God's loving children.")

Have pairs write their titles on pieces of paper to be displayed with their clay shapes. Display all the sculptures and titles. Have members mingle around the "art gallery" and comment on the works of art and their meanings. Then gather the group members together and discuss. Ask: How do these clay shapes make you feel? How do they express God's love? Are the shapes all alike? different? What does that say about God's love? What difference does each shape of God's love make in your life?

5. The Shape of Our Love—Say: 1 John not only tells us about God loving us; it covers how we love God too. Instead of focusing on God's action, let's explore our actions of love.

Assign the same pairs new passages: 1 John 1:5-10; 2:7-17; 3:11-24; 4:11-21. This time tell them to shape the clay to express how God wants us to love him. (For example, a pair with 1 John 3:11-24 could create a clay heart linking two clay figures.)

Have group members sit in a circle and place all the clay shapes in the center. Ask: What do these sculptures say about our love for God? Are we always able to love God the way we want to? Why or why not?

As a large group, make a list on newsprint of all the things normally thought of as "sin." Then list what 1 John would list as sin. See especially 1 John 1:6, 8-10; 2:4, 9, 22-23; 3:4-6, 8-9; 4:20; 5:17. Are both lists the same? Why or why not?

Have each person choose one of the following statements. Then have each person complete "I would respond to this statement . . ." and "1 John would respond to this statement . . ." Discuss answers.
- You don't have to like certain people; just try to get along with them.
- The important thing is just accepting other people.
- You can love without liking them.
- A loving person must be Christian.

6. Love Takes Shape—Have each person silently think of someone he or she finds difficult to love. Have each person tell why this person is hard to love—without giving names. As a large group, list on newsprint as many practical ways as possible to *love* the people. (For example, praying, saying something good about the person, listening to try to understand the person better, etc.)

Now it's time to shape up your group's love. Put the names of each person present in a hat or basket. Have members draw a name (not their own) from the hat. Instruct them to use their clay to shape a "love sculpture" for the person whose name they drew. Say: The sculpture should express something you love about that person, why that person is especially lovable, or how much you love him or her.

7. Closing—Go around the group and have group members, one by one, give the sculptures to their recipients. They can add a few loving explanations and hugs. Have fun loving one another! Let everyone take home his or her "love sculpture" gift.

Close with a circle prayer. Ask all participants to pray a prayer of thanks for someone who's been God's love for them.

—Nancy Going

5 FRUIT PUNCH

For the 14th year in a row, Melissa Crunch, GROUP Magazine poster maker and part-time cement finisher, is making extra money with her fruit juice stand in beautiful, downtown Dust City, Colorado.

In her free time, Crunchie, as her friends call her, is studying the fruit of the Spirit passage in the Bible. The verses go like this:

"But the fruit of the Spirit is love, joy, peace, patience, kindness, goodness, faithfulness, humility, and self-control; against such there is no law" (Galatians 5:22-23).

A Christian's life shows certain special qualities. Like a tree that gives good-tasting fruit, our lives show signs of what's happening to us spiritually. Use these exercises as a self-discovery process to explore how these fruit are evident in your life.

You've probably read these verses several times. But what do they mean to you? For each of the fruit listed below, jot down what each means to you . . . in your life. For instance, to you, "self-control" might mean "not passing on gossip whenever I hear it."

To me, each of these words means...

Joy
Goodness
Patience
Love
Peace
Kindness
Faithfulness

FRUIT JUICE STAND

ILLUSTRATION/JEAN BRUNS

chairs. Have each person choose a different fruit to be called. Everyone should try to remember each other's fruit-names. Have one person stand in the middle of the circle and call out two fruit-names. The people with those fruit-names should exchange chairs without allowing the middle person to sit down. The middle person's objective is to sit in an empty chair. After the exchange, whoever's left in the middle calls out the fruit-names for the next round. Another option: Call "fruit basket upset!" and everyone must trade places.

4. Fruit Punch—Distribute different colors of fruit-flavored Life Savers. Divide into discussion groups by matching flavors. Then work through the "Fruit Punch" exercises below. Discuss answers.

5. Closing Prayer—Have small groups choose one fruit of the Spirit for each person that best describes that person's life. Everyone must agree on one fruit per person.

One by one, close with a prayer thanking God for each person in the group. Include the fruit of the Spirit that's shown in his or her life.

6. Fruit Salad Snack—Create a giant group fruit salad by cutting up your fruit and adding whipped cream. Make it and eat it!

The Big Squeeze

How well are you doing in each of these areas? Shade in the graph according to how well you feel you're doing in each of these areas:

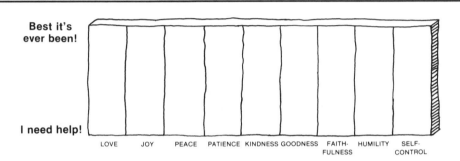

Best it's ever been!

I need help!

LOVE   JOY   PEACE   PATIENCE   KINDNESS   GOODNESS   FAITH-FULNESS   HUMILITY   SELF-CONTROL

The Fruit Pie Supreme

Choose the two areas from "The Big Squeeze" where you rated yourself the highest. Write them here:

Now's a good time to celebrate the great things God's given you. Try this: Plan a simple party in your mind to celebrate the two areas you just chose. Thank God for them.

Fruit Salad

Write the two areas where you rated yourself the lowest in the blanks on the left:

Area #1	
Area #2	

Now jot down ideas to the right of each area on how you can become stronger. If you need some help thinking through your two areas, try these verses:

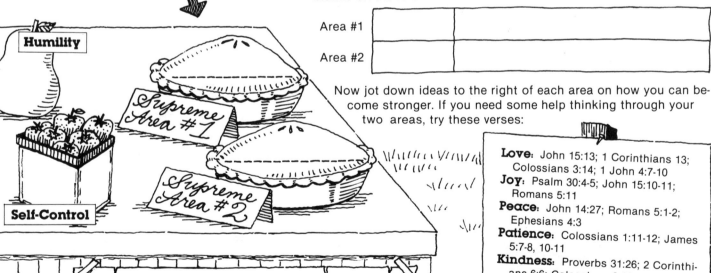

Humility

Supreme Area #1

Supreme Area #2

Self-Control

Love: John 15:13; 1 Corinthians 13; Colossians 3:14; 1 John 4:7-10
Joy: Psalm 30:4-5; John 15:10-11; Romans 5:11
Peace: John 14:27; Romans 5:1-2; Ephesians 4:3
Patience: Colossians 1:11-12; James 5:7-8, 10-11
Kindness: Proverbs 31:26; 2 Corinthians 6:6; Colossians 3:12-13
Goodness: Romans 15:14; 2 Thessalonians 1:11-12; 2 Peter 1:5
Faithfulness: 2 Thessalonians 3:3-5; James 1:2-4; 3 John 5
Humility: Proverbs 22:4; Ephesians 4:2; 1 Peter 5:5
Self-Control: 2 Peter 1:6

Fruit Offering

Write a prayer asking God to help you in the areas needing improvement. Close with thanks for the areas where you see the fruit of the Spirit!

DOES GOD MAKE A DIFFERENCE?

1. Before the Bible Study—Gather a pencil, Bible and copy of the "Self-Quiz" for each person. You also will need bowls, spoons and all the makings for ice cream sundaes.

2. Under the Influence—Say the following to the group members: Imagine someone who's drunk. His speech sounds slurred, barely understandable. He can't walk without weaving or stumbling. Liquor has taken over. The person is "under the influence."

As Christians we're called to be "under the influence" too. Not of alcohol, but of God. Ephesians 5:18 says, "Do not get drunk with wine, which will only ruin you; instead, be filled with the Spirit." Instead of too much wine controlling your speech and actions, God wants *the Spirit* to control you.

There are lots of times when you're not thinking about God. But in a way you are. Being filled with the Spirit means letting God control all your thoughts, words and actions—in everything you do. Being controlled by God *does* make a difference!

3. Quiz Time—Have your kids take the following self-evaluation. Have them mark a dot on each continuum above the letter that best represents how they'd respond in each circumstance.

SELF-QUIZ

1. A "nerd" is looking for a place to sit in the school lunchroom. You: invite the person to join you. A B C D E ignore and make fun of the person.

2. You need a good grade on this test and suddenly realize you can see the smartest kid's test paper. You: look only at your own paper. A B C D E copy the smart kid's answers as fast as you can.

3. Your teacher asks you and your friends to be quiet. You: settle down and listen. A B C D E shout out a wise-crack.

4. You returned late from a party your parents told you not to attend. You: apologize and tell the truth about where you were. A B C D E lie about where you were.

5. Your sisters or brothers really bother you. You: try to understand and not aggravate them. A B C D E pick on them, attacking their most sensitive issues.

6. Your parents ask you to do something you don't want to do. You: obey them and do it. A B C D E refuse and say "Absolutely not!"

7. Your parents disapprove of your new friends. You: listen and try to understand what they're feeling. A B C D E say "It's my life and I'll do what I want!"

8. You're at work and your friend asks to make a secret long-distance phone call. You: don't allow it because it's against the rules. A B C D E say "Go ahead; I'll cover for you."

9. Your boyfriend/girlfriend pressures you to "go all the way." You: say "No, I don't feel it's right." A B C D E do it to keep from breaking up.

10. Your friends want to sneak into an "R" rated movie. You: say no and suggest a more appropriate show. A B C D E go along with the crowd.

11. Your friends want you to get drunk with them. You: say no. A B C D E say yes and join the party.

12. The people you hang around with use God's name in vain—a lot. You: tell them why it bothers you and ask them to stop. A B C D E find yourself swearing too.

		A	B	C	D	E	
13. You get up in the morning and look in the mirror. You:	are glad you're you.	A	B	C	D	E	wish you were somebody else.
14. Some classmates win a school election, make the team or succeed in some other area. You:	congratulate them and are happy.	A	B	C	D	E	resent their accomplishments and make nasty comments behind their backs.
15. It's Sunday morning and time to get ready for church. You:	look forward to growing in your faith.	A	B	C	D	E	decide to sleep in and watch television.
16. You overhear a group gossiping. You:	stick up for the person being talked about.	A	B	C	D	E	join in the conversation.
17. You're having such a good time that you're tempted to break your curfew. You:	leave and get home on time.	A	B	C	D	E	stay out late.
18. You haven't studied for a test. You:	take the test anyway and suffer the consequences.	A	B	C	D	E	skip class.
19. You discover some people are spreading lies about you. You:	forgive them and go on.	A	B	C	D	E	blow up and hold a grudge.
20. You got to work a few minutes late. Later your supervisor asks when you got in. You:	tell the actual time you arrived.	A	B	C	D	E	tell the time you should have been there.

4. Scores—When the kids are finished, have them connect the dots and see how much God fills their everyday life. Have them shade in the left side, for example:

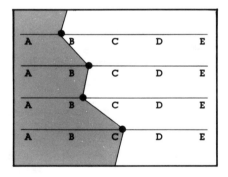

Say to the youth: If the space on the right is larger, it's evident God's controlling you more and more. If the opposite is true, check the areas that need improvement.

Were you surprised to find so many decisions God can influence? Being filled with the Spirit shows. When God controls, love takes over. "Your life must be controlled by love, just as Christ loved us and gave his life for us" (Ephesians 5:2a).

5. Words, Actions and Thoughts—Tell the group members that God's loving influence controls our words, actions and thoughts. Look up and discuss the following verses: Ephesians 4:29; James 2:17; Galatians 5:23b; Romans 12:2.

6. Select-a-Scene—Use the Self-Quiz for a creative activity. Write each statement on a separate sheet of paper. Have members each draw a statement and role play their response. Do some role plays with actions only—no words; then do words only—no actions. Have the group members talk about how God did or didn't make a difference in their roles.

7. Closing—Have everyone read together Romans 12:2, "Do not conform yourselves to standards of this world, but let God transform you inwardly by a complete change of your mind. Then you will be able to know the will of God—what is good and is pleasing to him and is perfect." Pray that God will fill every moment of the students' lives so that they are "under his influence."

8. Game Time—Eat refreshments in an unusual way with this "Ice Cream Special" from **Try This One . . . Strikes Again** (Group Books). Create one sundae for each couple. No skimping on those gooey toppings. Now, the race begins. Have each couple lie on the floor in a straight line on their backs with their heads touching. Place their ice cream sundaes and spoons beside their heads. Each person has to feed the sundae to the person whom his or her head is touching. All heads must remain flat on the floor. The first couple to consume their sundae (with more inside them than on them) wins the race!

—Joani Schultz

7

20 CREATIVE BIBLE STUDIES

Pack your traveling clothes, grab your Bible and get ready for an adventure. You are about to take a scriptural journey using the experiential method of Bible study. The following ideas are short road maps that lead to an understanding of scripture by experiencing it. Get with other leaders and imagine how each idea would work with your youth group. Dream a little. Then pick an idea and expand it into a complete session. Study Bible commentaries and consult resources that will help you grasp the passage to be studied. Then tell your young people to get ready for an exciting adventure. Try one. It's worth the risk.

1 CARDBOARD ARMOR
Read Ephesians 6:10-18.

Using pieces of thin cardboard (or heavy grocery sacks or bags), scissors and string, have everyone make his or her own armor. Instruct each person to leave off one piece of armor.

Once everyone's armor is in place, use scraps of paper to wad into "stones." Give each gladiator five "stones." The object is to try to hit the opponent's unprotected spot before he or she hits yours. Pair off and begin the battle.

Afterward, discuss which areas, if any, were the most vulnerable and the importance of having *all* the armor. Discuss the different pieces of armor and why they are important.

2 YOUTH GROUP MURDER
Read Matthew 5:21-24.

Bring in different newspaper accounts of assault and murder. Meet ahead of time with two young people. During the meeting, have them get into an argument with each other. One pretends to stab or strangle the other. The "murderer" rushes from the room while the "murderee" lies lifeless on the floor. Sit back for a minute and let the rest of the group react.

Then call the "murderer" back and debrief. Why did Christ compare anger with murder? In what ways are the two similar? different? How should Christians deal with angry feelings?

3 CHILDREN
Read Matthew 18:1-5.

Bring three or four youngsters between the ages of four and seven to spend time with your group. Sing a few songs and play a few simple games. After the children leave, debrief. Why do you suppose Christ said what he did about children? What childlike qualities should Christians have?

4 BLIND STUMBLE
Read 1 John 2:9-11.

Blindfold everyone in the group. Have people hold hands as you lead them around for at least 15 minutes. Why is not loving compared with darkness? How are not loving and darkness similar? different? How are Christians supposed to love?

5 PAPER TOWEL VISION
Read 1 Corinthians 13:11-12.

Use a camera (without film), paper towel tubes or empty pop bottles as viewers. Have people look through a viewer and describe how the view is narrower than without it. Discuss how this narrower view relates to the scripture. What things do you give up as you grow older? What things would become clearer if you were perfect? Why doesn't God give Christians perfect vision?

6 NICKEL GIVEAWAY
Read James 2:14-17.

Give four nickels or dimes to each person and head out to a mall or shopping center. Have each person give one nickel to four people and observe how the people react. Return and debrief. What is faith? How does handing out money relate to the scripture? How do you put faith into action? What are some problems with putting faith into action? What are ways we can express our faith?

7 CAGED RULES
Read Matthew 18:21-22; Mark 9:35; Luke 12:15; John 7:24; 13:34; 14:15; 2 Corinthians 13:7.

Take five minutes and brainstorm as many rules people have to keep as possible. Pass around a bird cage, a policeman's badge—anything having to do with rules and restrictions. Discuss which rules you dislike the most. Discuss the purpose of rules—and what would happen if there were no rules. Should Christians follow rules that seem outdated and ridiculous?

8 NEWSPAPER CLIPPINGS AND LOVE
Read Matthew 5:43-48.

Pass around newspaper clippings of stories of world tension, especially those between the U.S. and other countries (i.e., arms buildup, military skirmishes, international threats). Discuss what would happen if we took this passage literally. Next, hand out pictures of different people. Have everyone assume those people are our enemies. Imagine why they're enemies and in what ways we are to love them.

9 STRING MAZE
Read Mark 4:2-9, 14-20.

In a different room, build a maze using string, gravel, two-sided tape, wet sponges and cookies. Lay the maze out something like this:

Blindfold people before they enter the room. Once inside the room, have them get on their hands and knees and follow the string (one at a time). The object is to make it to the good soil—the cookies. Explain that they are to stop once they get caught in the gravel, sticky tape or wet sponges. Have people describe how they felt. Then discuss the types of soil in the scripture where the seeds fell, the results and how each can be applied today.

10 SALT
Read Matthew 5:13.

Serve unsalted popcorn and wait for reactions. Then salt the popcorn. Compare the salted and unsalted versions of the popcorn. List ways Christians can be "salt" in the world.

11 FOOT WASHING
Read John 13:4-17.

Before reading the passage, bring in a wash pan with water and a towel and start washing feet. Note people's reactions. Have people describe how they felt as their feet were being washed. Compare reactions to the disciples' reactions. Discuss the point Jesus made. What can we learn from this experience?

12 SORE FEET, SIN AND FORGIVENESS
Read Psalm 5:4; Romans 5:12.

Have each person write on a 3×5 card where he or she has sinned or come up short when it comes to living the Christian life. Each person is to fold the card four times and place it in his or her shoe.

Plan some activity that calls for action such as volleyball, a crazy relay or whatever.

After the activity have people compare the feeling of the card in their shoe with things that aren't right in their life. Discuss how sin and guilt affect people.

Read Acts 10:43; Matthew 26:28; 1 John 1:9 and discuss how forgiveness should free us from sin and guilt.

Have everyone remove the cards from their shoes. Have a brief ceremony where you burn or tear up the cards.

13 DOUGHNUT AND JUICE COMMUNION
Read Matthew 26:26-29.

Bring in doughnuts and juice. Eat and drink. Discuss why Jesus used bread and wine as objects to be used to remember him. Also ask your group why they think Christians use the cross to remember Jesus when Jesus wanted bread and wine to stand for him. Compare and contrast the symbols.

14 BALLOON JOY
Read Psalm 92:4; James 1:2.

Give a balloon to everyone and ask them not to inflate them, but to have fun bouncing them in the air. Compare the lifeless balloons to how they feel when they're depressed. Then inflate the balloons and have everyone bounce them in the air. Compare the differences being filled with air makes. Compare the lively balloons with being filled with joy. Where does joy come from?

15 KNIVES, FORKS AND ORDER
Read 1 Corinthians 12:12-31.

Serve a simple meal, maybe vegetables and crackers. Give knives, forks, spoons and plates to different group members. For instance, give six spoons to one person, five forks to someone else, and so on. There are enough utensils for each person in the group. Tell everyone that no one can start eating till each person has a knife, fork, spoon and plate. Upon a signal, everyone is to start handing out what they have. The situation will probably be chaotic. Compare the situation with the scripture passages. Discuss why order is necessary and how different talents and gifts should all work together.

16 COAT HANGER MOBILES
Read 1 Corinthians 13:4-7 or Galatians 5:22-23.

Use magazines to find pictures of people and situations that illustrate the characteristics mentioned in the passage. Use coat hangers, string and pictures to make a personalized mobile. Starting at the top of the mobile, place the picture of the characteristic where you feel you are the strongest and so on, until the weakest characteristic is on the bottom of the mobile. For each characteristic, discuss things people can do to become stronger.

17 PAPER AIRPLANES AND HOPE
Read Romans 5:2-5; 15:4.

Have everyone write different hopes and dreams they have for their personal or spiritual lives. Names are optional. Fold the paper into airplanes and fly them. Have everyone retrieve an airplane (not their own) and read it out loud. Briefly discuss the different hopes and dreams and how the passages relate to them.

18 ROOM-SIZED EVALUATION
Read Romans 5:6-11.

Designate one corner of the room to stand for material things, one corner for social relationships, one corner for mental strengths, and one corner for physical abilities. The center of the room stands for the verse itself. Discuss what the passage means in light of personal and spiritual priorities. Have kids stand nearest the corners they think best show their priorities. The goal is to be as near the center as possible. Discuss different things people can do to move closer to the center of the room.

19 GOD AND THE WALL
Read 1 John 4:8; Hosea 13:7-8; Jeremiah 3:12-13; Luke 22:39-44; Philippians 2:5-8.

Paper one wall with sheets of newsprint or butcher paper. Divide into teams. Ask each team to come up with a misconception about God on the wall or illustrate it in some manner. Then have teams switch locations. Have each team come up with scripture and explanations and ways to dispel the misconception the other team wrote on the wall.

20 TEARS AND TAPE RECORDERS
Read 2 Corinthians 12:8-9; 1 Peter 3:3-4.

Ahead of this session, have some young people tape record people in the church as they describe their saddest or most trying moments.

Play the tapes for the youth group and have members list ways they can help in sad times.

—Gary Richardson

ANYBODY HERE KNOW RIGHT FROM WRONG?

8

1. Before the Bible Study—Gather a pencil, Bible, 3×5 card and copies of the handouts for each person. Invite an elderly person, parents, young adults and high school kids to take part in a panel on "gray areas."

2. Bible Study—The following verses give principles for making decisions in those gray areas: Luke 12:37-48; Romans 12:2, 10, 18; 1 Corinthians 6:12, 19; 10:31; 2 Corinthians 6:14; Galatians 6:10; Colossians 4:5-6; 1 Thessalonians 5:22; 2 Timothy 2:22. After

reading the verses, make a list of principles that help determine right from wrong.

3. Gray Area Panel—Distribute the 3×5 cards and pencils. Have the youth write one situation or activity in their life that doesn't seem to have a clear right or wrong answer. Gather these questions and ask them one at a time to the panel members. Discuss how being a Christian helps or hurts making decisions between right and wrong. Then allow all participants to work through the next exercises:

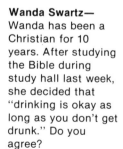

THE ALL-STAR YOUTH GROUP

This article is dedicated to the following people who are in the process of making tough decisions. Take a minute now to meet the latest all-stars:

Wanda Swartz—Wanda has been a Christian for 10 years. After studying the Bible during study hall last week, she decided that "drinking is okay as long as you don't get drunk." Do you agree?

"Lips" Lonigan—People call her "Lips" because she makes fun of almost everyone she knows. When her Christian friends tried to talk with her about it, she said, "How can you be so stupid? Look at all the times Jesus made fun of the Pharisees." Do you agree with her?

Muffy Whitaker—Muffy lives for parties. She can't wait till Saturday nights when everyone gets together and has a fantastic time. There's beer at the parties, but she never drinks anything. Her parents found out about the drinking and won't let her go to any more parties. Muffy thinks her parents are wrong. What do you think?

Kip Smith—Kip and his youth group occasionally attend R-rated movies as a group. After the movie, the group goes to someone's house and discusses the movie from a Christian perspective. Even though he learns a great deal about how being a Christian relates to everyday life, Kip doesn't feel right about seeing films that contain dirty language or sexually explicit scenes. What should he do?

Winfred Tulane—Winfred's friends have called him "33" ever since he broke the school record for continuous, non-stop listening to records (his whole summer vacation and the first four days of the new school year). Since becoming a Christian, "33" isn't so sure about listening to records that contain suggestive lyrics. Do you agree with him?

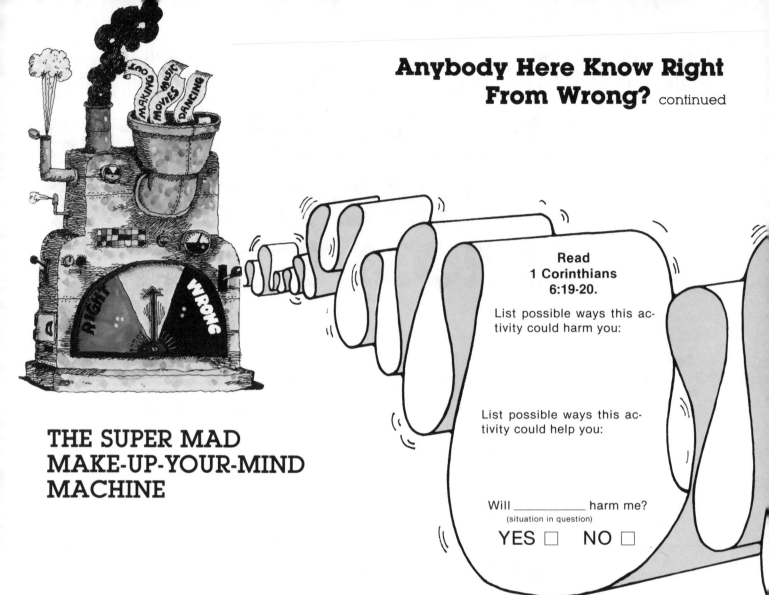

THE SUPER MAD MAKE-UP-YOUR-MIND MACHINE

Read
1 Corinthians
6:19-20.

List possible ways this activity could harm you:

List possible ways this activity could help you:

Will _____ harm me?
(situation in question)

YES ☐   NO ☐

Deciding what's right and what's wrong in some situations isn't easy.

Pick an issue or situation that gives you the hives when it comes to determining what's right. (Or, pick a situation from the "All-Star Youth Group" section.)

Then let this machine help you grind out your thoughts.

Name of activity or situation in question

_____

(For instance, "Is it okay to tell off-color jokes?")

ILLUSTRATION/JARED LEE

4. This Is Great! This Is Stupid!—Using one side of the room for "This Is Great!" and the other side for "This Is Stupid!" work through the statements under this next exercise:

THIS IS GREAT! THIS IS STUPID!

Check the box that best describes the way you feel about each of the following statements.

	THIS IS GREAT!	THIS IS STUPID!
1. There is nothing wrong with most activities as long as they don't hurt anyone.		
2. What's right for me is right for me and what's right for you is right for you, even if we don't agree.		
3. People should let their consciences be their guide.		
4. The only way to live a Godly life is to stay away from anything that could be considered sinful.		
5. I should base all my right/wrong decisions on whether or not not it expresses love for the other person.		

**Read
1 Corinthians
6:12.**

List possible ways this activity could control you:

Will _____ master me?

YES ☐   NO ☐

**Read
1 Corinthians
10:31.**

List the ways this activity glorifies God:

List ways this activity doesn't glorify God:

Does _____ show God off?

YES ☐   NO ☐

5. Closing—End the Bible study with a prayer asking God for help and strength to make responsible decisions.

**Read
Philippians 4:8.**

What things go on in my mind as I take part in this activity?

Take notes on those thoughts here:

Based on those types of thoughts, should I take part in this activity?

YES ☐   NO ☐

Based on my answers from this machine should I take part in this activity?

YES ☐   NO ☐

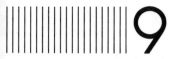

9

GOD'S WILL
Game-O-Rama

This series of three learning games is designed to help your young people learn a basic process in determining God's will. The benchmarks in that process are God's Word, prayer, circumstances and consultation with other Christians.

"God's Will Game-O-Rama's" three games build on that process from the maze "Find Your Way Thru" to "After High School Express" to "The Marriage Puzzle." Play the games in that order, if possible. Consider expanding your session to at least two hours. A "God's Will Overnighter" would make a great format for this study.

Divide into groups of four. Have people stay in those groups through all three games.

Give one copy of "God's Will Game-O-Rama" to each person.

Read through each of the games carefully. Test-play them with other leaders. Be sensitive to areas where your young people may need your help.

The rules and guidelines for each game are self-explanatory. For "Find Your Way Thru," be sure everyone refers to "The Road Map." You might want to mark those places on the maze and brief your kids once the game begins. For "After High School Express," make sure your kids understand which squares are to be used to change directions.

Have fun as you and your group members discover God's will!

This maze will help you find a framework for deciding God's will in everyday situations.

OBJECT: To travel from Crazy Al's Drive-In to Little City Bridge.

TO PLAY: Begin at Crazy Al's and find your way to Little City Bridge. Begin by yourself. At different points in the maze, you will be asked to do things with your small group.

Along the way, you'll encounter different places (i.e., The Good Book Nook) that refer you to The Road Map. Find that entry in The Road Map and follow directions.

MATERIALS: A pencil and a copy of this game for each person.

FIND

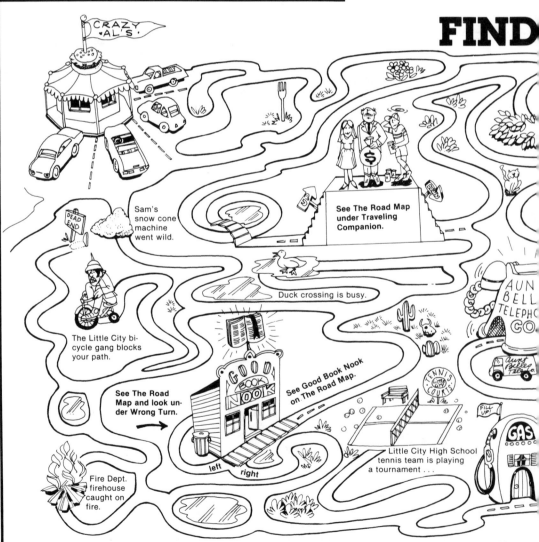

CRAZY AL'S.

DEAD END

Sam's snow cone machine went wild.

See The Road Map under Traveling Companion.

Duck crossing is busy.

AUNT BELL TELEPHO CO

The Little City bicycle gang blocks your path.

GOOD BOOK NOOK

See Good Book Nook on The Road Map.

TENNIS COURTS

FILL UP!

GAS

See The Road Map and look under Wrong Turn.

left   right

Little City High School tennis team is playing a tournament . . .

Fire Dept. firehouse caught on fire.

THE ROAD MAP

Begin your adventure at Crazy Al's Drive-in, in the upper left-hand corner of the maze. DO NOT READ THE ROAD MAP AT THIS TIME! At different points, signs on the maze will direct you to "The Road Map." Find the proper heading and follow the directions given there.

TRAVELING COMPANION

Choose one of the following "little" decisions you need to make as a traveling companion for the entire trip.

-who to date
-handling problems and conflicts
-what classes to take
-how to spend money
-whether to attend a party where there's beer

THE GOOD BOOK NOOK

Circle the number that best describes how often you consult the Bible when it comes to making decisions.

Always		Sometimes		Never	
1	2	3	4	5	6

If you scored yourself:
1-3, take the right street
4-6, take the left street

WRONG TURN

The Bible is the prime source for finding God's will.

You'll never find God's will for your life, even in the little areas unless you spend time studying and reading God's Word. Go back to The Good Book Nook and try the other street.

GAS

God's will is revealed in his Word. Here are some Bible passages that can help you find God's will.

Who to date
1. Proverbs 22:24
2. 1 Corinthians 7:32
3. 1 Corinthians 13:4-7

Handling problems
1. Isaiah 26:3-4
2. John 16:33

3. Philippians 3:13, 14.

Which classes to choose
1. Matthew 25:14-30
2. Romans 12:6-8
3. 1 Corinthians 12:4-11

Spending money
1. Deuteronomy 14:28-29
2. Proverbs 28:22
3. Matthew 6:1-4

Booze party
1. Psalm 104:15
2. John 2:6-11
3. 1 Corinthians 6:19

Read the verses that accompany your traveling companion. Then move on down the road.

continued on page 38

YOUR WAY THRU

ILLUSTRATION/LAUREL WATSON

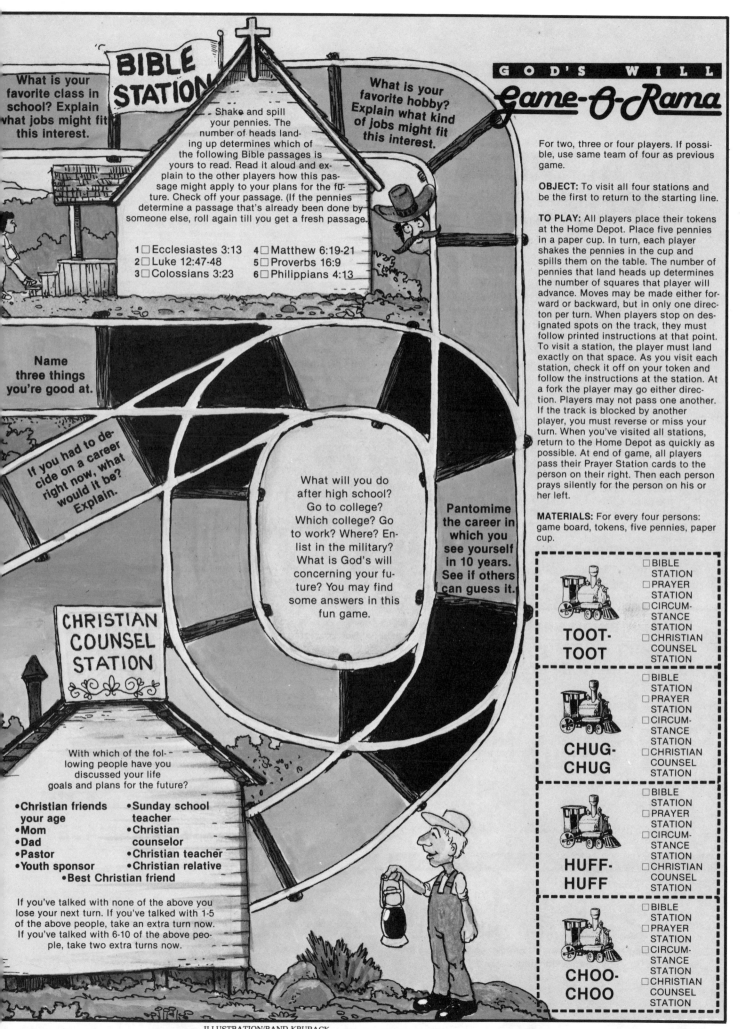

BIBLE STATION

What is your favorite class in school? Explain what jobs might fit this interest.

Shake and spill your pennies. The number of heads landing up determines which of the following Bible passages is yours to read. Read it aloud and explain to the other players how this passage might apply to your plans for the future. Check off your passage. (If the pennies determine a passage that's already been done by someone else, roll again till you get a fresh passage.)

1 ☐ Ecclesiastes 3:13   4 ☐ Matthew 6:19-21
2 ☐ Luke 12:47-48   5 ☐ Proverbs 16:9
3 ☐ Colossians 3:23   6 ☐ Philippians 4:13

What is your favorite hobby? Explain what kind of jobs might fit this interest.

GOD'S WILL
Game-O-Rama

For two, three or four players. If possible, use same team of four as previous game.

OBJECT: To visit all four stations and be the first to return to the starting line.

TO PLAY: All players place their tokens at the Home Depot. Place five pennies in a paper cup. In turn, each player shakes the pennies in the cup and spills them on the table. The number of pennies that land heads up determines the number of squares that player will advance. Moves may be made either forward or backward, but in only one direction per turn. When players stop on designated spots on the track, they must follow printed instructions at that point. To visit a station, the player must land exactly on that space. As you visit each station, check it off on your token and follow the instructions at the station. At a fork the player may go either direction. Players may not pass one another. If the track is blocked by another player, you must reverse or miss your turn. When you've visited all stations, return to the Home Depot as quickly as possible. At end of game, all players pass their Prayer Station cards to the person on their right. Then each person prays silently for the person on his or her left.

MATERIALS: For every four persons: game board, tokens, five pennies, paper cup.

Name three things you're good at.

If you had to decide on a career right now, what would it be? Explain.

What will you do after high school? Go to college? Which college? Go to work? Where? Enlist in the military? What is God's will concerning your future? You may find some answers in this fun game.

Pantomime the career in which you see yourself in 10 years. See if others can guess it.

CHRISTIAN COUNSEL STATION

With which of the following people have you discussed your life goals and plans for the future?

• Christian friends your age
• Mom
• Dad
• Pastor
• Youth sponsor
• Sunday school teacher
• Christian counselor
• Christian teacher
• Christian relative
• Best Christian friend

If you've talked with none of the above you lose your next turn. If you've talked with 1-5 of the above people, take an extra turn now. If you've talked with 6-10 of the above people, take two extra turns now.

TOOT-TOOT
☐ BIBLE STATION
☐ PRAYER STATION
☐ CIRCUMSTANCE STATION
☐ CHRISTIAN COUNSEL STATION

CHUG-CHUG
☐ BIBLE STATION
☐ PRAYER STATION
☐ CIRCUMSTANCE STATION
☐ CHRISTIAN COUNSEL STATION

HUFF-HUFF
☐ BIBLE STATION
☐ PRAYER STATION
☐ CIRCUMSTANCE STATION
☐ CHRISTIAN COUNSEL STATION

CHOO-CHOO
☐ BIBLE STATION
☐ PRAYER STATION
☐ CIRCUMSTANCE STATION
☐ CHRISTIAN COUNSEL STATION

ILLUSTRATION/RAND KRUBACK

GOD'S WILL Game-O-Rama

THE MARRIAGE PUZZLE

Should you get married? Or should you remain single? If you do choose to marry, does God have a particular mate in mind for you?

These are important but difficult questions. You may find some answers by learning to detect God's will. The following puzzle may help you push toward that goal.

Work this puzzle by yourself. But remain in your group of four. When all four persons have successfully completed their puzzles, exchange insights. What did you learn? How are you closer to finding God's will concerning marriage?

OBJECT: To form a triangle using some or all of the pieces below.

TO PLAY: Look over the numbered possible indicators of God's will. Select the ones you would trust to help find God's will for your life concerning marriage. Do the required activity in each of the indicators you choose. Then cut out the corresponding pieces. WARNING: One or more of the puzzle pieces below may not fit in the puzzle. That type of puzzle piece may correspond to an unreliable indicator of God's will. After the game your leader can help explain unreliable indicators of God's will.

MATERIALS: For each player a copy of this game and a pair of scissors.

LEADERS: You'll find the solution on the following page.

Before making any decision concerning marriage, I would . . .
[select any that are applicable]

1 ASK GOD

Before making any decision about the prospect of marriage in my future I'd talk with God. So far, I've asked for God's guidance on:

☐ who to date   ☐ who to marry
☐ how to date   ☐ when to marry
☐ marriage vs. singleness   ☐ why to marry

God reveals his will to us when we talk frequently with him in prayer.

TAKE PIECE #1

2 CONSIDER SINGLE-NESS AND THE BIBLE

Before deciding to marry or not, I'd check out what the Bible says about the single life.

Read Matthew 19:12. I've considered not marrying because:

☐ I was born that way   ☐ others made me that way
☐ because of the kingdom of heaven

Read 1 Corinthians 7:7. Do your gifts equip you better for:

☐ single life or   ☐ married life?

Read 1 Corinthians 7:32-35. Place an X on the line showing how you would balance your time and devotion between a spouse and the work of the Lord.

God _____ spouse

How does the position of the X affect your feelings toward remaining single or marrying?

God sees great value in both singleness and marriage. The single life is not second rate. Jesus was a single adult.

TAKE PIECE #2

3 ACT ON FEELINGS

God usually speaks to me through my feelings.

Briefly describe a big issue or decision in your life:

_____

When I think about this issue I feel: (check any that apply)

☐ uneasy   ☐ superior   ☐ bubbly
☐ funny   ☐ lonely   ☐ tense
☐ inferior   ☐ happy   ☐ angry
            ☐ depressed

Based on these feelings, I think God's will is:

_____

TAKE PIECE #3

4 ANALYZE WHAT HAPPENS

Sometimes I can see God's will in the things that happen around me.

But analyzing circumstances requires great care. Common sense must rule. Assess the following circumstances.

	a sign of God's will	unsure	no sign of God's will
You get sweaty palms every time you see a certain person	☐	☐	☐
After praying for a life mate, a special person calls on the phone	☐	☐	☐
You like to be alone	☐	☐	☐
Your pastor's marriage fails	☐	☐	☐
Your steady date continually says he (or she) loves you	☐	☐	☐
You don't get along with your date's parents	☐	☐	☐

TAKE PIECE #4

5 CONSIDER MARRIAGE AND THE BIBLE

Before making any decision about marriage, I'd see what the Bible says about it.

Read Matthew 19:4-6. Place an X on the line showing where you assess your desires now in regard to the independence the single life provides as compared to the cooperative "oneness" of marriage.

cooperative
"oneness" _____ independence

Read 1 Corinthians 7:8-9. How strong are your desires for the opposite sex?

burning   slight
desire _____ desire

Read Ephesians 5:21-33. How ready are you to submit yourself to a spouse?

ready _____ unready

Marriage is God's invention. It is good when rooted in God's planning.

TAKE PIECE #5

6 TELL GOD TO LEAD

When I really want to know God's will, I set up a situation for him to show me his wishes. Here's a good example:

☐ 1. Pray.
☐ 2. Allow God to speak to the situation. Close your eyes, open the Bible randomly and put down your finger somewhere on the page.
☐ 3. Determine how this particular verse applies to the present situation in question.
☐ 4. Act on the situaion, according to this verse.

God works in mysterious ways.

TAKE PIECE #6

7 SEEK ADVICE OF OTHER CHRISTIANS

I use the spiritual maturity of other Christians to help me find God's will.

On the following decisions, would you lean toward the advice of other Christians, or more toward your own intuition?

Whom to date:		Considering marriage or singleness:
listen only to myself	**decide by what others think**	
		Deciding whom to marry:
The problem of lack of dates:		Deciding at what age to marry:

TAKE PIECE #7

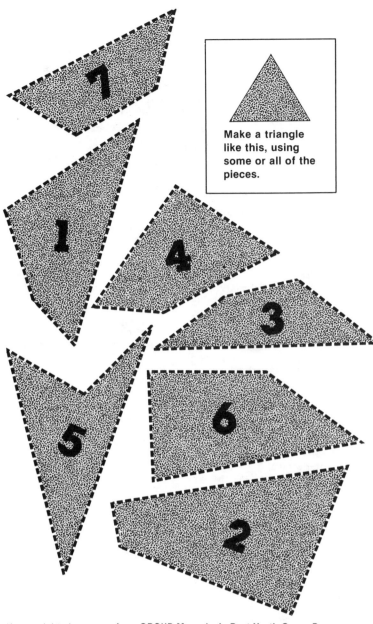

Make a triangle like this, using some or all of the pieces.

(A copyrighted resource from **GROUP Magazine's Best Youth Group Pro-grams**. Permission granted to copy this handout for local church use only.)

THE SOLUTION

"The Marriage Puzzle" could be the most difficult of the three games, especially if someone gets the wrong puzzle piece. If someone gets stuck, don't be quick to run to the rescue. If the youth have all the correct pieces, help them (if they need it) get started toward the solution of the puzzle. Here's how the pieces are to fit together:

If someone has a wrong piece, help him or her determine which piece is wrong—and why.

Wrong Piece #3: "Act on Feelings." While feelings sometimes are valid indicators of God's will, they are highly vulnerable to many things: fatigue, health, diet, peer pressure, emotional state, the weather, and so on.

Relying on feelings to determine God's will can be highly dangerous. It is difficult to determine which feelings are God-sent and which are normal fluctuations of day-to-day living. When our feelings and God's Word do not match, the Christian needs to go against his or her feelings and follow God's Word. Such a process lets the person control the feelings instead of letting the feelings control the person.

Many of God's great leaders experienced feelings other than "peace" as they followed his will. Have your group read about those people in Exodus 3:7-14; Jonah 1:1-17; Acts 14:19-22.

Wrong Piece #6: "Tell God to Lead." We've all heard stories of people who have been guided miraculously as they read Bible verses they chose at random. But random verse-reading in order to find God's will is actually testing God and asking him to be a magician. Have someone read Matthew 4:5-7 and compare this passage with that of treating God as a magician.

GOD'S WILL
Game-O-Rama

continued from page 33

AUNT BELLE'S TELEPHONE COMPANY

Circle the statement that best describes you:

a. I pray for everything, including which toothpaste to use.

b. I pray about everything that's important to me and not much else.

c. I usually pray especially hard when I want something.

d. I pray often, like talking with a close friend—at different times and often.

e. I pray most when I'm in trouble or have problems.

If you circled a or b, take the left street.

If you circled c or e, take the center street.

If you circled d, take the right street.

SNYDER'S SWAMP

Prayer is an important part of finding God's will. But it is much more than just using God as a celestial Santa Claus. Prayer is talking with God as you would a close friend—you praise him and worship him and let him take control of your life as you get to know him. Return to Aunt Belle's Telephone Company and try again.

LICORICE SHERBET

Find a sheet of paper and write a letter to an expert in the area of your "little" decision. Explain your concern and your doubts.

Now address the letter to God. Should prayer be like this letter? Is there anyone who knows more about your desires and decisions than God? Continue.

ROLLER CITY

What percentage of the time do you carefully evaluate the things going on around you as possible indicators of God's will? Choose a number between 0 percent and 100 percent of the time.

If you scored yourself 76 or above, take the left street. If you scored yourself 75 percent or below, take the right street.

SOAPS

Not everything that happens is an indicator that God is trying to tell you something. But it is always best to be aware of how you handle situations, how you relate to people and how circumstances change at different times in your life. Go back to Roller City and try another street.

BRIDGE OUT

You are to be commended for praying for everything. Sometimes, though, God gives a basic outline in his Word, then the rest is up to you. Your time might be better spent in not asking God for so much, but in praising and worshipping him in your prayers. Return to Aunt Belle's Telephone Company and try again.

MOLDY ARCHES

You are on course. As you enjoy the grease burgers, burned fries and syrupy Cokes, evaluate one of the following circumstances. (If you're playing this game alone, choose your topic and think it through.) What are different things you learn from the circumstance? Based on the information you have, as well as what you read into the situation, what would you do next?

D.D. (Whom to date) For weeks now, you get that electric feeling everytime you're close to D.D. You've spent days trying to get D.D. to notice you. Now, finally, you two get to know each other. One afternoon, in English class, he

(or she) asks you out. But the date is something else. You hardly talk or even look at each other—there's not much to say. You breathe a sigh of relief when the date is over. How about it? Should you date D.D. again? Is God telling you to look for someone else? What would you do?

You're a creep! (Problems and conflicts) Joe/Josephine is your close friend. At least you thought you were good friends. But lately, he (or she) has been acting strangely toward you. One afternoon at school, you see Joe/Josephine standing in the hall talking with some people you barely know. You walk to him (or her) and say hi. He (or she) takes one look at you, frowns and says loudly, "Get lost, creep!" What would you do next? Should you drop him (or her) immediately. Punch him (or her) out? Should you concentrate on finding new friends? or what? What do you think God would want you to do?

Trig or Thumb Tack Painting? (Which class to take) The last grading period is almost over and you need to decide which classes to take next time around. Unlike most times, you have a great choice of classes to take. Some are tough; others are easy. You want to keep your grade point average up, but you also feel you want to learn some things in the tough courses. When it comes to taking classes, how do you know which classes God wants you to take? What criteria do you use in deciding which class to take?

A Who Concert or World Relief? (How to spend money) You finally get that part-time job you wanted and you're feeling pretty good about your financial situation. You get your first big paycheck. Then, oddly enough, your youth group session is on world hunger and you leave feeling guilty about your affluence. What should you do? What

percent should you budget for the church? for recreation? for clothes? for world hunger? should you save? How do you determine how much you should keep for yourself and how much you should give away?

Beer or Bibles? (Going to a party where alcohol is served) For weeks, the topic of conversation among your friends has been this Saturday night's party at Rod's house. You'd planned all along to go. But this afternoon you hear from different people that beer will be plentiful. You doubt the party will get out of hand, but you're not sure if you should go where there's alcohol. What should you do? You realize that Jesus wouldn't have been scared away. You also understand what Jesus said about overdoing drinking. What do you think is God's will in this situation?

WANDA SUE'S WATER SLIDE

You've almost made it through Little City. But first, check the statement that best describes you:

When I try to determine God's will, I . . .

☐ try to think it through myself.

☐ try not to let my friends know what I have in mind. I drop hints and see how they respond.

☐ talk to anyone who'll listen: adults, kids, dogs.

☐ talk mainly to Christian friends and adults whom I trust.

Get with three or four Christian friends. Together pick one of the areas where it's sometimes difficult to determine God's will (who to date, handling problems, what classes to take, how to spend money, whether to attend a party where there's booze). Every person in your group has one minute to give his or her opinion on the topic. Think carefully about what you'd say. If there's more time, discuss another topic.

THE WHINERS

Have you ever met a whiner? You'll find whiners in every family and every group of friends. They usually say things like:

"I don't wanna watch that TV show."

"Hamburgers again?"

"Why do we have to go shopping?"

Another thing about whiners: They reproduce like bunnies. Take a couple of whiners, put them in a room of people and the whiner population shoots right up.

Although we sometimes think we have plenty of reasons to whine, God wants us to do just the opposite. Instead, he wants us to be winners.

A winning attitude involves relying on God during life's ups and downs. A winning attitude is strengthened through prayer and reading God's Word.

This Bible study will help group members replace whining with winning attitudes.

1. Objectives—Participants will:
- compare physical hunger with spiritual hunger;
- list five principles regarding spiritual growth; and
- list four practical steps to feed themselves spiritually.

2. Before the Bible Study—Do the following:
- Schedule the study during lunch or dinner so participants will be hungry. Allow 2½ hours for the entire study.
- Arrange to use the church kitchen for the first half of the study. Students will need to use the stove, cooking utensils, plates and silverware for their meal.

The Whiners continued

● Ask students to bring their Bibles and 50 cents to the meeting.

● Ask several parents to drive young people to a nearby grocery store. They will leave for shopping after the opening part of the study and shop only 20 minutes.

● Gather tape, newsprint, magazine pictures of food and the song by Keith Green, "So You Wanna Go Back to Egypt?" on the album of the same name, available from your local Christian bookstore. You'll also need writing materials, a marker, plastic spoon, paper plate, cup and several three-inch strips of paper for each student.

3. The Meal—Form a circle. Show magazine pictures of food and ask the young people to tell what they're most hungry for.

Divide the class into groups of four. Give each group a paper and pencil. Explain that you're giving them a chance to do something about their hunger. Ask each group to prepare a grocery list and decide how to use each person's 50 cents for food.

Have the groups carpool to the grocery store and buy the items on their lists. After 20 minutes, return to the church kitchen to prepare and eat the meal.

Afterward, gather in a circle to discuss feelings and observations. Ask: Did you work as a team or as individuals? Explain. Did you combine the money to get a better deal per person? Why or why not? What could have gone better during your planning? Did feelings of hunger cause complaints? negative attitudes? whines? grumpiness? Explain. Once you had eaten, did you feel better? Compare physical hunger and spiritual hunger. What are similarities? differences?

Say to the group: Whining is nothing new. People have been doing it for years. Back in Moses' time, there were at least a million whiners—the Israelites. They were physically hungry and uncomfortable in their desert wanderings. They were fed up with the desert life. They despised the monotonous landscape and the unbearable heat. Worst of all, they had to spend all this time with other grumbling families.

Many times during the desert years, the Israelites whined, grumbled, complained and stopped following God. They were spiritually hungry. We're going to look at some of the Israelites' mistakes so we can avoid making the same mistakes when we go through desert times in our own lives.

4. The Israelites' Mistakes—Ask a young person to read Exodus 16:3. Notice that the Israelites looked back to the "good old days" instead of trusting God for present-day troubles. Play Keith Green's song, then ask: What are some "Egypts" (good-old-day memories) that we often run back to? (For example,

last year's youth group was always more fun.)

Have another youth read Exodus 16:6-8. Point out that the Israelites were upset about being in the wilderness; they blamed Moses and Aaron for their lack of food. Ask: What are some of the things we gripe about? Do we tend to blame leaders, coaches, teacher or parents when things go wrong? Give examples.

Ask a group member to read Exodus 16:11-12. Notice that manna wasn't enough. The Israelites complained and God gave them quail to eat. Ask: When God blesses us, do we complain and ask for more? Why or why not? How do we fail to notice our blessings? When do we forget to thank him?

Say to your group: The Israelites blamed Moses for their problems and quickly forgot the blessings along the way. The same situation and feelings happen today.

5. Lessons to Learn—Assign a young person to read the following youth leader's story:

Scott was a leader in my youth group. He came to me one Sunday and said, "I need to tell you something privately." We stepped into a nearby corner and Scott said, "I hate to tell you this, but I'm not growing spiritually." Immediately I wanted to punch out his lights. What a wimpy, weak excuse to make! I controlled my clenched hand and let him continue: "I'm just not getting fed spiritually."

"So what are you telling me?" I asked.

"Well, I've decided to go to another church," he replied.

I must admit I was hurt and angry. Sure, I felt rejection, but worst of all, I felt like a failure. I kept asking myself, what did I do wrong?

Divide in pairs and discuss the following questions: Do you think the youth leader failed? Why or why not? What should the youth leader do? Did Scott do the right thing? Why or why not? How could this situation have been avoided? How could the youth leader teach Scott to feed himself spiritually and not to rely on being spoon-fed?

Have a young person write the following five spiritual-growth lessons on newsprint:

● Spiritual food (God's Word) is necessary for spiritual growth (1 Peter 2:2).

● Providing the food is God's responsibility (John 6:35).

● Providing the spoon (or the utensils) is the leader's responsibility (Deuteronomy 6:6-7).

● Eating daily is your responsibility.

● Complaining is a result of spiritual hunger.

Divide into five groups and assign each group one of the spiritual-growth lessons. Instruct them to create role plays for their lessons. Search the kitchen, nursery, or other church areas for props such as

Why can't our leader make this more exciting?

spoons, rattles and paper sacks to aid in the presentations.

For example, a role play for the first lesson could be: Two kids are kneeling on the floor, heads down, ignoring two closed Bibles in front of them. Two others are kneeling down in a similar fashion, but they are reading their Bibles. Each time the readers turn a page, they grow taller until at last they're standing up straight, on tiptoe.

Role play the lessons. Then ask: What do each of these lessons tell us to do when we're spiritually hungry?

Say: The following are four tips to maintain a regular, healthy spiritual diet. If we follow these tips, we can be spiritually-fed winners—not spiritually-hungry whiners.

6. How to Feed Yourself—*Eat daily.* Very few of us simply forget to eat a meal. As in our meals, we need to set a regular time to ingest God's Word.

Distribute a paper plate and marker to each person. Have members write on the plate a specific time each day they'll sit down for a meal of God's Word.

Eat early. We need to develop the practice of eating before we're starved. Spiritual food should be an everyday priority—not as a duty, but as an enjoyable activity.

Give each person a cup and several slips of paper. Have young people look up the following verses and choose the ones most satisfying to their spiritual hunger: Deuteronomy 31:8; Psalm 9:1; 27:1; 34:19; 2 Corinthians 4:8-10; Galatians 5:22-23; Ephesians 1:18-19; Philippians 4:4-8, 13; Colossians 3:2; 1 Thessalonians 5:16-18; 2 Thessalonians 3:3; Hebrews 11:1; 13:6.

Have each person write one verse per slip of paper and place them in the cup. Say to the members: Every time you feel a physical hunger pang, reach into the cup, pick a verse and read it. Use physical hunger as a reminder to feed yourselves spiritually as well as physically each day.

Eat it when it's fresh. Like some of the Israelites, we Christians sometimes live on yesterday's manna—the verse memorized last summer, the sermon heard last year, etc. God's Word was meant to be ingested when it's fresh and exercised immediately.

Give the young people a fresh way to view scripture. Have everyone read Psalm 119:59-60. Then, have them rewrite the verses in their own words on their plates. An example of a rewrite of these verses: "I thought of the things I was doing and decided to look to You for guidance. I quickly and eagerly decided to listen and obey You."

Underneath the rephrased versions of the verses, have young people write a prayer concerning the scripture. For example: "Always help me look to you, God, and keep your commandments."

Have the young people save their plates as a reminder of how they can add a fresh perspective to familiar scripture.

Be involved with other believers to get better utensils. By fellowshiping, learning and worshiping together, we develop tools to help feed ourselves.

Give everyone a plastic spoon and ask: In what way has our youth group given you tools to feed yourselves? How have you enabled others to feed themselves? Pass the tape to each person. Have young people tape the spoons to their paper plates as a reminder of their responsibility to feed themselves the Word.

7. Closing—Ask participants to keep their plates, cups and spoons as reminders to daily feed themselves God's Word.

Join hands in a circle. Tell young people that God wants us to have positive winner attitudes, not whining ones. Winner attitudes happen through daily prayer and feeding on God's Word. And his Word makes us strong. Christ's strength is our strength through daily troubles.

Have everyone close their eyes as you read 2 Timothy 3:14-17 as a blessing.

—*Tim Smith*

Devotions should be a time to get nearer to God. Trouble is, sometimes devotions tend to be fairly predictable and somewhat dull.

Following are 10 fun Bible-centered ideas for devotions. Ideas range from holidays to bike trips. Use these in your regular group meetings or on a rainy day when your other plans are washed out.

1

GOD'S WORD

1. Each person is given an 8½×11 sheet of paper.
2. On the top left side, each person writes words or phrases that refer to two of his or her favorite Bible stories. On the top right side, each person writes positive words that relate what God is trying to convey through the stories.
3. On the bottom left side, each participant writes two recent significant events in his or her life. On the bottom right side each person writes positive words that relate what God might be trying to tell them through the events.
4. Close with everyone reading the positive messages they receive from God's word. String the papers together, write the messages on balloons, or shout them in celebration.

2

A NEW LIFE

This devotion is done in two parts, one several weeks before Easter and the other at Easter time.

Part 1

1. The young people decorate a shoe box, plastic food-storage container or rust-proof container with symbols of a new life: butterfly, flowers, Easter pictures or words such as ''Alleluia.'' Fill the box with symbolic items such as promise verses.
2. Read the account of Jesus' death and burial. Take the box and bury it in the church yard.
3. Have people share the meaning of Jesus' death and why he had to die. They can share things in their lives that need to die so that they can be new in Jesus.
4. Members can offer prayer for each other's needs.

Part 2

1. The group returns to the place where the box is buried.
2. Read the account of the Resurrection, then dig up the box. Sing joyful Easter songs.
3. Take the items out of the box and use them to decorate your youth room or another area in the church such as the pastor's office.
4. Share ways in which Christ's Resurrection gives hope to conquer death. Read to the group Ephesians 1:17-20; 2:1-10. Explain they now possess the same power that raised Jesus from the dead. Have the group repeat after you: ''I now possess the same power in me that raised Jesus from the dead. Alleluia.'' (Repeat several times.)

GROUP DEVOTIONS

3

FRESH BREATH

1. Uphill struggles can be breathtaking when on a bike trip. This devotional can help you and your group catch your breath the next time you're on a bike trip. Pull the bikes safely off the road and have each person share a time when he or she felt empty, flat, depressed, needed air or life. Ask the kids: What happened? How were you helped?

2. Read John 20:19-22 and Revelation 21:1-7.

3. Explain that Jesus breathed his spirit into the disciples at a time when they, too, felt exhausted. Discuss what it means to be made new in Christ.

4. Take time to give each other a fresh breath of air by making affirming statements about one another. The leader can name a person in the group, make an affirming statement, and then the others can follow suit.

5. Take time to help each other pump up deflated tires and check tire pressure.

4

THOUGHTS WORTH WEARING

1. Read Colossians 3:5-14.

2. Place a trash can in the center of the room. Divide into groups of four to six. On separate sheets of paper, the participants write items that they have put off, burdens they want to unload and other concerns. They then wad each piece of paper and throw it into the trash can.

3. Provide each person with a large sheet of newsprint or newspaper. Have them cut a hole in the paper, poncho-style. They then decorate their ponchos with symbols and words to express the qualities that should be "put on" by a person in Christ. The young people then can model their ponchos.

4. Instruct the young people to pair up and pray that their partner will have the strength to "put on" the desired qualities written on the ponchos.

5

ALPHABET THANKSGIVING

1. Use this devotion any time, anywhere. Just ask your group to go through the alphabet and share things they are thankful for from A to Z (or things that describe God's love or reasons to praise God). For example, someone could be thankful for God who's "Always there." Someone else could thank God, "Because he cares," and so on.

2. Let this be a litany by cuing the people to yell their responses at the same time. You can make a game from this idea by instructing the person whose turn it is to repeat all the things the group mentioned before his or her turn.

6

UNBOXING THOUGHTS

1. Young people have a lot to say, but sometimes have trouble saying it. You can help the kids with this idea. Label various boxes "Burden," "Joy," "Help," and so forth.

2. The young people then can anonymously write their concerns and joys on paper and drop the notes in the appropriate box. Group members then draw from the boxes, read the notes, and the rest of the group responds through rejoicing, sharing, caring and solving. This can be done monthly or weekly.

3. Pray for each concern. Make sure this is done anonymously, unless the people feel the need to reveal themselves.

7

BRACE YOURSELF

1. Make a tradition of celebrating the removal of teeth braces.

2. Schedule a special gooey party. Everyone brings chewy, gummy candy and other food that the person was not able to eat. Let the young people gorge themselves.

3. Make buttons that say, "Smile, God loves you." Share how important it is to smile, rejoice and be happy in the Lord.

4. Divide into medium-size groups and give each group five minutes to express through motions, songs or acting the following phrases based on Philippians 4:4-7:

(1) REJOICE, REJOICE
(2) IN YOUR LIFE IN THE LORD
(3) BE GENTLE, BE GENTLE
(4) DON'T WORRY, DON'T WORRY
(5) ASK GOD FOR WHAT YOU NEED
(6) GOD'S PEACE KEEP YOU IN CHRIST JESUS.

8

RAINBOWS AND PROMISES

1. Read Genesis 9:8-17.

2. Explain to your group that a rainbow isn't just color that splashes across the sky; it is also a sign of God's promise and love. We need to open our eyes and look for the rainbows God gives us in our daily lives.

Divide your group into teams of six to eight people. Hand out newsprint and laundry markers. Then have the teams make a banner, drawing symbols or writing words that show some of the rainbows God gives us daily. Have the teams share their banners with the entire group.

3. In closing, give everyone a piece of string. Instruct each participant to tie a bow on his or her index finger. Explain that the rainbow was one way God reminded himself of the promise he made to us, and now the string is a reminder of God's promise to us. Ask each person to share a promise or word from God that's especially meaningful to him or her. Close by singing a favorite group song.

9

RAINY DAY DEVOTION

1. "Don't Rain on My Parade" (or picnic or outing or volleyball game) is a well-known old song. Rain does fall and many times we experience disappointment. Divide your group into pairs. Have one person tell about a recent disappointment in his or her life or about a time when he or she "got rained out." Then ask the second member of the pair to do the same.

2. Read Romans 5:1-5. Instruct the pairs to discuss ways in which the passage relates to what they've been telling each other.

3. Discuss with the entire group positive things that can be learned from disappointments. What good things does rain provide?

4. Say something such as, "Go out, run in the rain and thank God for his renewing, refreshing gift. Let the rain fall on your face. Then come back in, dry each other off and pray for your partner."

10

FRUIT OF THE SPIRIT

1. Read Galatians 5:22-25.

2. Divide into groups of four. Each group should decide which fruit of the Spirit its members would like to develop. The groups have five minutes to develop a pantomime on the desired trait(s).

3. Gather the groups; each group presents its pantomime. The others try to guess which trait is being acted out.

4. After all pantomimes have been presented, members pair up and discuss strengths and weaknesses.

5. The partners then pray, giving thanks for their strengths and praying for weaknesses.

—Lee Hovel

12

HEY GOD, REMEMBER ME?

1. Before the Bible Study—Gather a pencil, Bible and copy of "Communicating With God" for each person. You also will need newsprint, markers, pipe cleaners, yarn, paper clips, Popsicle sticks and other "junk."

2. Relationship Sculptures—As kids arrive, ask them each to create a sculpture from the junk to symbolize their relationships with God.

Sit in a circle with all sculptures in the center. Have members guess what each sculpture means. See how accurate the guesses are. As a leader, be sensitive to the happy relationships, but be especially in tune with the kids who express hurting ones. Keep the focus on positive ways to help kids grow in their relationship with God.

3. Best Relationships—Ask each person to complete these sentences: "I pray to God when . . ." and "I feel uncomfortable praying when . . ."

Have everyone think of the "best" relationship he or she has. On chalkboard or newsprint, have the group list qualities that make for good relationships. Go back over the list and circle all the qualities that enhance communication.

4. God Talk—Say to the group members: Prayer is talking with God. Communicating with God need not be different from any other relationship. Just think of your best friend. You know you can go to your friend for anything—anytime. Jesus wants that same "best friend" attitude when it comes to prayer. As your forever friend, God is happy when you let him know about your expectations, gratitude, sorrow or other special needs.

Distribute pencils and copies of "Communicating With God." Use these exercises to help the kids discover their present communication commitment with God and what they can do to strengthen and improve it.

COMMUNICATING WITH GOD

Telephones are a vital tool for communication. Which telephone best describes how you view your prayer relationship with God?

I usually call my friends for these reasons:

1.

2.

3.

I usually pray for these three reasons:

1.
2.
3.

You can communicate with God just like a best friend. Read this reminder of that friendship promise in Romans 5:10-11.

Three places I can pray are: (Circle three)

Use these prayer starters anytime, anywhere. They can be the beginning of a communication process that shares the whole you.

I praise you for . . .
I'm sorry because . . .
I'm thankful for . . .
I need . . .
Someone else needs . . .

Use the following passages to help you spark a close talk-time with God.

Psalm 100:1-3
Psalm 51:3-4
Psalm 100:4-5
Psalm 50:15

Now it's time for a personal prayer contract. Take this seriously and watch your God-relationship grow!

A Commitment to Communicate
I will pray not only when I have a problem, but also when I

_____

_____

Signed, _____

Date _____

5. Discuss—Talk about the exercises. What makes communication great? How do the qualities listed earlier (see step 3) compare to the relationship you have with God? Which are most difficult for you and God? Which are easiest? Why is it sometimes difficult to communicate with God?

6. Deepening a Relationship—Brainstorm ways to build a deeper relationship with God. List them. Ask each person to choose one thing that he or she will do to strengthen that God-relationship. Close by having group members pray for hope, strength and the ability to meet their personal goals.

13

IF I ONLY HAD MORE FAITH

1. Before the Bible Study—Gather a pencil, Bible and copy of "My Faith" for each person. You also will need mustard seeds, clear contact paper, markers, paper and scissors.

2. Faith and Mustard Seeds—Bring mustard seeds to this meeting. Begin by having your group close their eyes. Place a mustard seed in each person's hand. Allow time to reflect on the tiny gift you've given them. While their eyes are still closed, read Matthew 17:20. Then ask kids to explain how their faith is like that seed.

3. Agree or Disagree—Create a continuum line across the room designating one end "agree" and the other end "disagree." Read the following statements. Have kids stand along the continuum at the spots that best illustrate what they think about each statement. Ask volunteers to explain why they chose to stand where they did.

● Most people worry that they don't have enough faith.

● You can do anything. Nothing will be impossible for you.

● Unless faith is used it isn't any good.

● You make the decision whether or not your faith will grow.

4. Discuss—Talk about different ways to help faith grow; for example, find Christian friends, read the Bible, worship regularly, give time and talents, pray and trust, etc. Ask the young people to think of other ways.

Ask: Which of the ways to help your faith grow do you feel best about doing? Which do you struggle with the most? What kinds of things are you doing presently in each area?

Next have participants draw a mountain. Inside the mountain write and complete: "The greatest concern I have right now is . . ." Beside the mountain, answer: What's the greatest obstacle in conquering that concern? How do you think God can use that concern for your personal growth? What three things can you do to overcome this obstacle? Read the following Bible passages and talk about ways you can put them into action: Matthew 6:25-34; Romans 1:17; Hebrews 11:1; James 2:14-26.

5. Personal Faith—Now that everyone has read and discussed the article, have the young people complete the following activities and help them think about their own faith life.

MY FAITH

My faith is most like . . .

Describe a time when you felt your faith was really strong. Then describe a time when you felt your faith was really weak.

Compare both times. What made them different? Was it the place? the time? the people? the circumstance? Are there ways you can avoid times of weak faith? How? Are there ways you can keep your faith strong? How?

Read the account of old Abraham and Sarah's faith in Romans 4:18-21. What can you learn from the way they used their faith?

A Faith Checkup

	always	some-times	never
Do I take responsibility for my faith?			
Do I surround myself with Christian friends?			
Do I get involved in the Bible through personal devotions?			
Do I participate in a weekly Bible class?			
Do I worship regularly?			
Do I give myself away by doing things for others?			
Do I pray and trust God will support me?			
Do I look for results of faith in my relation-ships?			

Look at your faith checkup. What areas need the most improvement? Think of one thing you can do this week to move you into faith action.

Make sure your goal meets these requirements:

1. Is it possible and realistic?

2. Is it specific and measurable?

3. Is it something you have complete control over?

Write your goal here:

6. Bookmark Making—Provide clear contact paper, markers, paper, scissors and more mustard seeds. Have each person make a bookmark. Instruct them: Cut contact paper into strips 6 inches by 1½ inches. Write the words "Faith moves mountains" on paper. Place the words and mustard seeds between sheets of clear contact paper. This creates a durable Bible bookmark.

7. Pray for Mountain-Concerns—Stand in a circle and place all bookmarks in the center. Using the bookmarks, form the shape of a mountain. Have each person share one mountain-concern in his or her life. Join hands and pray for each person.

SEEDS FOR SPIRITUAL GROWTH

What happens when you suggest doing something more "spiritual" in your youth meetings?

Do your kids . . .

• yawn because they imagine a carbon copy of Sunday morning worship?

• envision a complex conglomeration of meaningless motions and religious mumbo-jumbo?

• wave goodbye to fun with a one-way ticket to stuffiness?

If you're tired of yawns and faulty perceptions when it comes to spirituality, try these

ILLUSTRATION/ROSEANNE BUERGE

49

Seeds for Spiritual Growth continued

10 innovative ideas for enhancing spiritual growth in your group!

A "SPIRITUAL" DEFINITION

Have group members each write down the words or phrases that they immediately think of when they hear the word "spiritual." Instruct members to fold their papers when they finish, so they can't see their list. Now have each of them write a careful, well-thought-out definition for the word "spiritual."

Have them unfold their papers when they're finished and compare the two responses. Discuss: What do these responses reflect about spirituality? Is it joyful? sad? serious? intellectual? inconsistent? Explain. What does spirituality mean to you personally? When and where are you "spiritual"? Think of some person, place or thing that is "spiritual" to you.

As a group decide on a definition of "spiritual."

WHAT SPIRITUAL SHAPE ARE YOU IN?

Have group members describe how they look on the outside by molding clay or shaping pipe cleaners. Then have them model how they feel about themselves on the inside. Ask: What are the differences in the two models? How would you change the two models if your "spiritual battery" was at "full charge"? How do you go about charging your spiritual battery or keeping it charged? How does worship charge your battery? prayer? certain music? long walks? being with a certain person? Right now what would be the best way to "jump start" your spiritual battery? What can we do about "charging your battery" as a group? How can we charge the group's spiritual battery? Could the group use a jump start or a little boost? Explain.

SPIRITUAL BATTERIES

Keep up with your group's "spiritual charge" by

creating "spiritual batteries" out of posterboard. Include movable meters to indicate the level of charge. Post all the batteries and have members indicate their "spiritual battery charge" when they arrive at the youth group meeting and when they leave.

How about a large group battery or a sponsor battery too?

SPIRITUAL IMAGING

Imaging is a powerful, non-threatening way to get in touch with spirituality. Use the following guided meditation as part of a youth meeting or worship time.

Say: Close your eyes and relax. You don't have to do anything but be here right now. Take a couple of deep breaths. Feel how good it feels to breathe and be alive. Now, imagine deep inside your body, a tiny burning coal. It's not hot, but it's giving off a tiny light. What color is the light coming from your coal? Now, imagine that every time you take a breath it's the breath of God coming into your life. And every time you breathe that small coal gets a little brighter, and the light gets a little stronger. Keep breathing in. Keep watching that light grow brighter and brighter until it fills your whole body—until there's no darkness anywhere. Only light. When everything is bright and warm and clean just enjoy that feeling. Remember that feeling. Now, say thank you to the Spirit, the breath of God, that has filled you with all that light. Do it silently. Say whatever comes to you, and when you've finished open your eyes. Remember God is light.

SPIRITUAL "GUESS WHO"

Have each group member complete the following sentence on paper: I feel closest to God when I am . . .

Have a sponsor collect the responses and read them to the group. Have group members guess which person's response they are hearing. Following the exercise, discuss and ask: Were there any surprises? Why or why not? Who do you think has a spiritual style similar to yours? What new ideas did you discover about drawing closer to God?

GETTING "INTO" BIBLE STORIES

Choose a Bible story to "get into." The prodigal son (Luke 15:11-32), the good Samaritan (Luke 10:30-37), Jesus with the Pharisees (Matthew 12:1-14) or Jesus before Pilate (John 18:28-40) works well.

Have each member select a character from the story and decide what that character felt—about God, other people in the story, himself or herself. Then, one at a time, have each member "model" those feelings to see if the group can guess which Bible character is being portrayed. Follow up by asking whether everyone agrees with the portrayal of that character's feelings.

Also use Bible stories to explore spirituality by using some of the relaxation ideas mentioned earlier. Read a passage and have individuals ask themselves silently: "What is the Spirit of God saying to me?" Or, "God, what do you want me to hear?" Build a variety of discussion or worship experiences around this participatory scripture reading by designing special prayers and opportunities for personal sharing.

SPIRITUAL LIGHT

This worship-oriented experience is best done outside at night, but works well inside too. Give each group member a small candle. Explain that the candle will represent spiritual light. After group members light their candles from a central "Christ candle," instruct them to walk alone, silently, as far from the light as they can while still being able to hear clearly.

When they have scattered across the yard or sanctuary and the individual lights seem small against the darkness, gather the group members together again around the "Christ candle." Then read a portion of scripture. (Matthew 5:14-16; John 1:1-9 or 1 John 1:5-7 is appropriate.) Discuss the contrast of their small lights in the dark with the gathered body of light. Put this in the context of both corporate and individual spirituality and worship. Touch on the joy of being in touch with God's Spirit in the quiet darkness and the gathered community of light.

SPIRITUAL COLLAGES

Ask group members to think of the most "spiritual" person they know. Now, provide old magazines, scissors, glue and posterboard—have each person make a collage of this person. Tell members to find pictures and words to describe how the "spiritual" persons act, how they treat themselves and other people, how they feel about God, and so on. When finished, discuss the collages in small groups. See if any common denominators of the "spiritual person" appear.

Another idea: Have each group member design a collage of his or her own spiritual life, and then create a collage of the life of the most spiritual person he or she knows. Discuss how members view their own spiritual lives, how they see the other persons' and what the differences are.

SPIRITUAL LIFE "EXCUSES"

Instruct each person to list reasons "Why I don't have time for spiritual body building." Illustrate this by having each person draw a pie graph. Then have them divide the pie into sections showing where their time is spent.

Or have individuals list all the things they do during a day and see where "spiritual body building" falls.

A third way to look at the time allotted for spiritual growth is to see who can come up with the most absurd, crazy and irrelevant reasons for not having time for God. Responses such as "I have to walk my guppy" or "My lint collection needs grooming" would qualify. Talk about what stands in the way of growing spiritually.

SPIRITUAL TOP 10

Challenge your group members to come up with a "Spiritual Top 10"—a list of the 10 most powerful and sure-fire ways of growing closer to God. Don't be satisfied with simple answers such as "pray" or "go to church." Look for spiritual power or meaning in any activity. For example, stretch their spiritual images by suggesting that the plant in their bedrooms can remind them of their own spiritual growth, nourishment and dependence on God; or suggest that a reassuring touch from a friend can help them remember God's presence.

Next have members rate their personal investment in each of the "Top 10" on a scale of 1 to 10. Evaluate how members feel about where they stand. Then encourage them to set practical, measurable goals for developing the areas of needed improvement.

—*Jim and Melissa Smith-Farris*

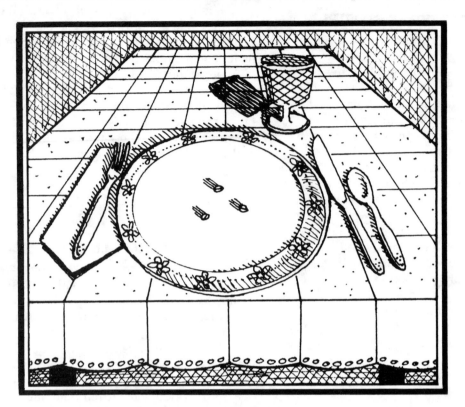

4 HUNGER EXPERIENCES

There's nothing happy, exciting or spiritually enriching about world hunger. It's a difficult topic.

Still, world hunger doesn't go away. And it does no good for us to ignore it. Christians need to be informed about the problem; awareness is the first step to finding solutions.

Dare to take your group into areas where the answers don't come easily. Struggle together with an issue that seems bigger than life.

When you explore world hunger with your group, don't pound the terrible facts into them or make them feel guilty about their economic status. Rather, gently introduce this problem with experiential learning methods. This will help group members retain the information longer, and also challenge them throughout their lives to seek answers.

Here are four ideas for you to use. Three are learning/awareness experiences, and the fourth is a suggestion for action.

ILLUSTRATION/JEAN BRUNS

1

HUNGER MEAL

While not a new idea, a hunger meal is still a highly effective way to help participants be more aware of the world hunger situation.

Announce that group members should not eat dinner before coming to the youth group meeting; a meal will be served. Publicize the topic of hunger for the meeting, but don't give any more details about the meal.

Designate specific tables or place settings as First, Second or Third World. According to the size of your group, use these ratios: one member in Group 1 (First World); three in Group 2 (Second World); and six in Group 3 (Third World).

Set the First World table (or place settings with flowers and a cloth tablecloth; the Second World table can have a paper tablecloth, but no flowers; and Third Worlders get a bare table in the corner.

Group members receive the meal that corresponds to their "world": First Worlders get meat, vegetables, bread, butter, dessert, and a drink with ice or milk; Second Worlders get a vegetable, bread, and a drink or milk; Third Worlders get water (only one glass), a starchy vegetable such as rice or potato, and no butter.

After group members have been eating for about five minutes, announce that there is plenty of food left for the First Worlders and they may "have as much as they want." All other countries, however, may not go to get any more food. Hopefully the First Worlders will realize that they can get food for their hungry neighbors too.

When the meal is over, debrief the experience. Discuss what happened and how each "world" felt. Ask how this could be used as a learning experience and applied to real life.

2

LEARNING WITH MEDIA

Play the song "Children of Sanchez" by Chuck Mangione (on his album **Children of Sanchez** by A&M Records).

Pass out lyric sheets and have group members discuss the song in small groups. Give each group a copy of these questions: What things does the singer say are more important than bread or food? Why? When could food really be more important? How can love and understanding (sixth verse) help a person thrive? What is meant by "every child belongs to mankind's family"? What are our responsibilities to the family? What is the hunger that is in the eyes of the children in the fourth verse? If you could condense this song into one statement, what would it be?

Challenge group members to create a slide show about hunger and caring, which could be shown to the whole congregation along with a special report about the group's studies and concerns.

Some suggestions for songs to use in a slide show are "Children of Sanchez," "American Fast Food" by Randy Stonehill (on his album **Equator** by Myrrh Records), and "He Ain't Heavy, He's My Brother" by Neil Diamond (on his album **Rainbow** by MCA Records).

3

PAPER PLATE PERSPECTIVE

Here's a creative way for group members to visualize the breakdown of control of resources in our world.

Give each group member a paper plate with instructions to divide it into thirds with a pencil. Tell the group that the plate represents all of the Earth's resources, not just land. Ask each member to draw six faces (or circles) on two-thirds of the plate, and explain that out of 100 people, these six represent the First Worlders. Then tell the group members to draw 94 faces on the other third of the plates. These represent the Second and Third Worlders.

Ask: How do you feel being one of the six people? How do you think the other 94 people feel? How do you think they feel toward the six? How can we stop them from feeling this way?

Now instruct group members to color in the faces of two of the six and 34 of the 94, and tell them these are the people who are suffering from malnutrition. Discuss why some in the two-thirds are suffering.

4

"DEAR CONGRESSMAN . . ."

Write letters to your U.S. congressman concerning certain bills or decisions dealing with hunger relief. Keep up to date on this information by contacting Bread for the World, 802 Rhode Island Ave., NE, Washington, D.C. 20018.

When a letter needs to be written, send a special newsletter to group members (and congregation members). Explain the specific reason for the letter and what group members should request. Include your U.S. congressman's address, which you can get by calling the editorial office of your local newspaper.

If group members would prefer not to have the responsibility of writing letters on their own time, call occasional letter-writing meetings.

—*Sam Halverson*

16

MOO, MEOW AND OINK

Take your group back to the time of Noah for an unforgettable creative worship experience.

This spectacular event involves everyone and illustrates that all Christians are a part of the body of Christ.

Imagine this: As the colorful story of Noah and the ark is told, we hear the loud sounds of all the animals, we see huge storm clouds float across the auditorium, lightning flashes, thunder roars, and rain actually splats upon the worshipers.

"Moo, Meow and Oink" is most effective when done with a large gathering. Use it at a regional youth rally, retreat or conference.

The animal noises are provided by the worshipers, each according to the month in which they were born. Thunder is created by stomping of feet. Simply flash the lights in the room to create lightning.

Clouds are simulated with huge six- to eight-foot weather balloons. They're available from Edmund Scientific (101 E. Gloucester Pike, Barington, NJ 08007; 1-800-222-0224). The balloons are inflated with a vacuum cleaner or hair dryer. They're very lightweight and they float and bob much like fluffy clouds. You'll need at least five or six balloons for the proper effect. We used 24 balloons at GROUP's National Christian Youth Congress—with a crowd of 2,500 people. The balloons will burst if they touch a sharp object on the ceiling or wall. So, urge your worshipers to be gentle. If any balloons do pop, simply work this into your narration, mentioning something about cloudbursts.

Rain is created by squirt guns. Station several people with squirt guns throughout the crowd. When the narrator mentions rain, fire the squirt guns into the air.

Plan your creative worship gathering in a big room with a high ceiling.

Provide an adequate sound system for your narrator.

Here's the script:

Narrator: Before me, believe it or not, are all the creatures in the world. And some of you don't even know who you are. So I'm going to help you out. And I need you to help me out too. I'm the narrator for this story—the story of Noah and the Ark. But you are the characters in the story. That means you have speaking parts. Don't worry—it's pretty simple stuff.

Here's what I need. I'll assign you a character according to the month in which you were born. Then, whenever the name of your animal is mentioned, you stand and sound off with that animal's noise. Ready?

January—**DOG**
February—**CAT**
March—**OWL**
April—**LION**
May—**PIG**
June—**COW**
July—**CHIMPANZEE**
August—**SHEEP**
September—**COYOTE**
October—**HORSE**
November—**FRUIT FLY**
December—**KANGAROO** *(hop around)*

Now, there are a couple of other things I need from you. In the story, we'll talk about thunder. You can make thunder by stomping your feet. And when we talk about clouds, I'll need your help in carefully moving the clouds across the sky. Clouds are pretty fragile. So you'll really need to be careful. One more thing about the sounds you're helping with: When I go like this (cut throat motion) you need to stop the noise so the story can continue. Well, I think we're ready to start the story.

Many years ago there was a man named Noah. Noah was quite a guy. After he was 500 years old, he became the father of Shem, Ham and Japheth.

At about this time, God became very angry with the way things were going on the earth he created. The world was filled with corruption and violence. The people were always thinking and doing evil things. God had had it up to here. He—was—mad . . . at everybody but Noah.

Noah was a good guy. He respected God and lived a clean life. So God called to Noah: "Noah! Noah!" Noah looked around. At first he thought it was his wife. His wife had sort of a low voice. "Noah! Up here!" Now God had Noah's attention.

"I have decided to destroy all people, for the earth is filled with crime. I want you to make a big ark of gopher wood. Make it with many rooms and cover it inside and out with tar.

"Soon I will bring a flood of waters upon the earth, to destroy all flesh. Everything that is on the earth shall die. But I will establish my covenant with you. You shall come into the ark—you, your sons, your wife with the deep voice, and your sons' wives."

At first this sounded pretty good to ol' Noah. But then God went on: "Oh, Noah. It won't be just you and your family. I want you to bring along two of every living creature."

Noah was an obedient man. So he began doing everything that God commanded. As you might imagine, Noah's neighbors were quite amused when this old man began building a huge boat, and started bringing in every animal imaginable. But that didn't bother Noah.

Two by two he loaded the animals onto the ark. First came the dogs (pause after each animal to allow noises), then the cats, then the owls, then the lions, then the pigs, then the cows, then the chimpanzees,

then the sheep, then the coyotes, then the horses, then the fruit flies and finally the kangaroos. When all the animals were loaded, they made a noise that could be heard for miles (all animals sound off). Soon darkness covered the sky (turn out most of the lights).

Then huge clouds began coming in from the north. (Push weather balloons gently over crowd.) They rolled slowly across the sky. First one, then another. Soon the skies were filled with clouds. Never before had anyone seen clouds like these. They were big clouds, filled with moisture.

Soon it began to lightning (turn lights on and off rapidly) and thunder (stomp feet).

The animals became frightened and began to cry out (all animals sound off).

Then came the rains (shoot squirt guns into air). It rained for 40 days and 40 nights. The rains continued and filled all the streams and rivers and lakes and oceans. Finally the entire earth was covered with water.

After 40 days the rains stopped (stop squirt guns). And the clouds began moving back to where they came from (push balloons back). Gradually the skies began to clear. The big rainclouds separated and disappeared, allowing the sun to shine. And the waters that covered the earth began to recede.

When it was safe, Noah opened the door of the ark and began releasing the animals. First came the chimpanzees (pause after each animal), then the cats, and the dogs, then horses, and the lions, then the owls, and the sheep, then the coyotes, the pigs, and then two, no, three, no, five, no a dozen, no . . . countless fruit flies and of course the kangaroos. All of the animals were overjoyed to get out of the ark . . . which had become a bit overwhelming for even the pigs' noses.

Noah and his family and the animals all went forth to live a happy life as they replenished the earth.

What a great story! It's one of my favorites. It's a fun story, but it's full of all kinds of subtle meanings. Notice how God took great care to be sure to protect the survival of all the different species of animals? He didn't just let giraffes on the ark, or anteaters, buzzards or iguanas. He wanted all these and thousands more. God loves diversity. He loves variety. Imagine what a drab world this would be if there were only frogs. No . . . the beauty in our world comes from the great and colorful variety of creatures and things around us.

The body of Chirst is like that. Here in this room, we come from many different backgrounds, some wealthy, some not so wealthy, we come from big towns, little towns, big families, little families. What a beautiful ark we have here. *One body in Christ.*

Some of us are tall, some short, some black, some white, some heavy, some light. Some of us are shy, some not; some beautiful, some plain; some are good at sports, others are good at cooking. What a beautiful ark we have here. *One body in Christ.*

Some of us worship God one way, others praise him another way. Some of us spread the Good News with our mouths, some of us spread the Good News with our actions. What a beautiful ark we have here. *One body in Christ.*

Just like the creatures in the ark, we are all different. But that diversity creates a kaleidoscope of beauty. To take any element away would shrink the rainbow. One body in Christ. All different—and glad for it. In the ark, lions didn't try to be sheep. Pigs didn't try to be owls. No, each was happy being himself.

What a great lesson! I want to be me. Nobody else. I want to be me . . . a part of the body of Christ.

—*Thom Schultz*

A PRAISE PARTY!

1. Before the Party—Choose three young people to be the "Psalm Readers." Assign them their parts and explain that each portion read will be echoed by the rest of the group. By using appropriate expression and tone of voice, group members can echo not only the words, but also the mood of each Psalm.

Gather these supplies for the party: newsprint, markers, eyebrow pencils, damp cloths, yellow crepe paper streamers (one, six- to eight-foot strip for every other person), and refreshments.

2. A New Song—Sing some of your group's all-time get-everybody-going songs. Then have Psalm Reader One begin the echo-cheer:

Psalm Reader One: Psalm 100:1-2 (shouted, cheer-leader-style).

(For example)
Sing to the Lord (group echoes)
All the world! (group echoes)
Worship the Lord with joy; (group echoes)
Come before him with happy songs! (group echoes)

Next divide the group in half for creating some of your own "happy praise songs." Give both groups newsprint and markers. Assign one group the tune (a round) "Are You Sleeping?" and the other group, "Row, Row, Row Your Boat." Give them 10 minutes to compose their new songs. Have them write the words large enough for all to see.

Come back together and have each group teach the other its song. The most fun will be dividing the group in half to sing songs as rounds.

3. A Prayer for Forgiveness—With an eyebrow pencil, mark a "blotch of sin" on each person's cheek. Tell them it represents the darkness of their sins. Ask group members to each silently pray for something in their life that needs cleansing. Have everyone close their eyes during the Psalm.

Psalm Reader Two: Reads Psalm 51:2-10 (softly, reflectively, again as an echo reading).

After the Psalm, have members use a damp cloth and "wash away" each other's "sins."

4. A Time for Thanksgiving—Give every other person a length of bright yellow crepe paper. Have the group members form a circle. Go around the circle and have one person holding a length of crepe paper, tell something he or she is thankful for. After saying that, have that person toss one end of the streamer to someone across the circle who doesn't have a streamer. Repeat the action until everyone has shared. By this time a bright yellow sunburst will be created.

Ask the group to create a slow-moving circle sunburst-dance while the Psalm Reader leads the echo cheer. Have fun! Experiment with raising and lowering the streamers in a flowing pattern.

Psalm Reader Three: Reads Psalm 150:1-6 (shouted, cheerleader-style with an echo).

5. A Time for Celebration—Make your Praise Party complete by creating a favorite food together. How about ice cream sundaes with lots of toppings, or submarine sandwiches with lots of ingredients?

PSALMS MELODRAMAS

Anger, love, fear, compassion, depression, excitement. All are part of a teenager's world. All are also part of the many emotions reflected in the Psalms.

Delve into the Psalms with your group. Show teenagers a God who loves and doesn't abandon his people in the midst of difficult emotions. Let them learn through history's drama of God and people in relationship. Let your young people see for themselves how God is still their God when they struggle with confusing emotions.

Use your imagination to make the message of the Psalms relevant in your group member's lives. The Psalms lend themselves to rhythmic, responsive-reading and dramatic renditions, and more. Experience with your group meaningful, creative celebrations centered on the Psalms.

Here are some ideas to get you started.

PSALM 51

This is a Psalm of confession and absolution. King David wrote this after the prophet Nathan confronted him with his sin of adultry with Bathsheba. David is trusting in the cleansing action of Yahweh's grace and mercy. Sin always separates, and David feels the pain of separation. Only if Yahweh washes away his sins will David be able to rejoice and proclaim God's greatness. One of the key lines of this Psalm is "Be merciful to me, O God, because of your constant love."

Divide group members into four groups. *Each* of the four groups has a verbal and visual action to say and do one right after the other *every time* the key line, "Be merciful to me, O God, because of your constant love," is read. In order, the groups' instructions:

Group 1: Members stand and huddle together in an area apart from the larger group. They shout together "SIN! SIN! BAD! BAD!" They run back and sit down.

Group 2: Members stand and with their hips and arms make the motion of a washing-machine agitator. They say together "GUSH! GUSH! GUSH!" They sit down.

Group 3: Members stand and pretend they are clothes hanging on a clothesline to be dried by the sun. They stretch out their arms and say together "UMM! UMM! MIGHTY FINE!" They sit down.

Group 4: Members stand and wave their arms above their heads. They say together "PRAISE THE LORD! PRAISE THE LORD!" They sit down.

Have each group practice its part individually. Then have the four groups practice their parts back-to-back so the minidrama will move quickly.

Read the Psalm, adding the key line (which is the first part of verse 1) after verses 5, 9, 13, 17 and 19. Every time the groups hear "Be merciful to me, O God, because of your constant love," they act out their short drama of God's cleansing action.

PSALM 98

This is a Psalm of praise to the sovereign God. To think of God's power and might makes us as human beings seem unimportant. Yet verse 3 reminds us that God kept his promise to the people of Israel with constant love and loyalty. God chooses his people, delivers them with a great victory and rules the world. God says yes, we do belong to him and he keeps his promise.

This Psalm is paraphrased to fit a four-beat rhythm. Group members maintain the rhythm by snapping their fingers while a leader reads the paraphrase to the rhythm in a singsong manner. The finger-snapping is interrupted when the whole group says and claps at the appropriate place: "And God said YES (clap, clap)! I choose (clap, clap)! You're mine (clap, clap)! YES! YES!" Then group members continue snapping their fingers to rhythm while the leader reads another section of the Psalm.

Here is the paraphrase with the group's responses:

(Group members begin snapping fingers. The leader reads:)
Sing a new song to the Lord;
He has done wonderful things!
By his power and holy strength,
He has won the victory.

(Group members say and clap:)
"And God said YES (clap, clap)! I choose (clap, clap)! You're mine (clap, clap)! YES! YES!"

The Lord announced his victory;
He made his power known.

He kept his promise to the people
With constant love and loyalty.
All people everywhere
Have seen the vict'ry of our God!

(Group members say and clap:)
"And God said YES (clap, clap)! I choose (clap clap)! You're mine (clap, clap)! YES! YES!"

Sing for joy to the Lord;
Sing all the earth;
Praise him with songs and shouts of joy!
Sing praises to the Lord;
Play music on the harps!
With trumpet and with horns,
Shout with joy before the Lord.
For he is king!

(Group members say and clap:)
"And God said YES (clap, clap)! I choose (clap, clap)! You're mine (clap, clap)! YES! YES!"

Roar, sea, and all creatures in you;
Sing, earth and everyone!
Clap your hands, O ye oceans;
Hills sing together.
Sing with joy before the Lord,
Because he comes to rule the earth!
He rules the people of the world
With justice and with fairness.

(Group members say and clap:)
"And God said YES (clap, clap)! I choose (clap, clap)! You're mine (clap, clap)! YES! YES!"

PSALM 136

This Psalm perhaps was used antiphonally. It deals with God's great works in creation, the Exodus, the wilderness wanderings, the conquests of Canaan, and other occasions of deliverance.

Have group members sit side-by-side (on chairs, pews or on the floor) to form one straight line. The person seated farthest to the right stands and runs to a lectern in the front of the group. On the lectern, have a photocopy of this Psalm with the beginnings and endings of the verses (and parts of verses) marked. Also have a pencil on the lectern. The first person reads the first part of verse 1. Then that person marks with the pencil where he or she stopped

reading, runs to the place on the far left of the group and squeezes into the row. Meanwhile the other group members say the response and lean to the right as if they were in a bus making a sharp left turn.

The group response after every reading is "For his love enduuuuuures forever." During "endures," group members lean to the right; on "forever," group members spring back to normal position.

The next person on the right runs up and reads the first part of verse 2, runs back to the left side, and sits down while the other group members respond.

Repeat in this manner until the Psalm is completely read.

PSALM 73

This Psalm is for people who are in the pits and angry with God. The beautiful message is that God does not abandon his people even when they are angry at him. God's presence even through pain and struggles is one thing that the wicked do not have. After doing this Psalm, talk about God's presence in the midst of pain and suffering.

Have group members sit in a circle. Hand out pencils and paper. Tell each group member to write down a time he or she felt anger toward God or thought God was unfair. For example, "Bill cheated and got an A and I studied hard for that test and only got a C" or "My dad's company folded and he's without a job."

Begin the Psalm with a leader reading verses 1-3. Then the leader sounds angry and reads verse 4, following which two or three other leaders say in unison an angry tone "And another thing, God . . ." The group member sitting to the right of the leader should read his or her sentence written on the paper. The leader continues sounding angry and reads the first part of verse 5; the other leaders say in unison in an angry tone "And another thing, God"; and the next group member to the right reads his or her sentence.

Continue until the leader reads the verses and parts of verses through verse 14, even if some group members must read their sentences more than once. Or, continue until all the group members have read their sentences, even if the leader must backtrack and read verses (and parts of verses) 4-14 again.

The leader reads the remaining verses of the Psalm in a softer and more thoughtful voice.

PSALM 150

This simple Psalm emphasizes that we should praise God with every gift. People are like instruments in an orchestra; they're different. But when they praise God together with their different gifts there is a beautiful sound of harmony, a harmony of God and his people.

The leader should raise his or her arm to signal the group members to shout together "Praise the Lord!" The Psalm begins and ends with this shout. Divide the group members into six sections to determine which sounds they will contribute to the reading:

Section 1: the sound of the trumpets.
Section 2: the sound of the harps.
Section 3: the sound of the drums. This section may also dance.
Section 4: the sound of the flutes. This section is joined by the sound of the harps.

Section 5: the sound of soft cymbals (group members whisper "crash").
Section 6: the sound of loud cymbals (group members shout "crash").

Practice having everyone shout in unison "Praise the Lord!" at the leader's signal. Let each section practice its sound.

This may be done two ways: (1) After the leader reads about each sound, the corresponding section contributes its sound for a few moments, then stops. (2) After the leader reads each sound, the corresponding section adds its sound and continues it until the leader's signal at the end for everyone to shout "Praise the Lord!" The leader should pause for each sound to be added, then continue reading, preferably with a microphone.

Whichever way it's done, the leader should read the Psalm with strength and zest.

—*Dick Hardel*

PART TWO:
SELF-IMAGE

19
BEING LIKE JESUS

Jesus Christ was and still is the example of a person who could reach out to others. His humanness allowed him to see the suffering and pain of others; his God-ness empowered him to do something about it. Wherever Jesus went, he saw other human beings who needed to be touched in loving, caring, forgiving, healing ways. When people hurt, he healed them. When people strayed from God, he called them back in a spirit of loving reconciliation. When people lost hope, he gave them life.

As a human, Jesus provides the example of the type of person we can be. He's the model of someone who lived—and died—for others.

Use this Bible study to challenge your group members to see Jesus' example and say, "We can do that too!"

1. Objectives—The participants will:
● play a game that reveals 10 Bible people.
● discuss Jesus as a human being who cared for other human beings, and as God who could help human beings.
● see Jesus as a good role model and a good friend.
● receive affirmation concerning ways they themselves reflect Jesus' qualities.

2. Before the Bible Study—Gather the following materials:
● a Bible for everyone in the group (or have participants bring their own).
● a pencil and a piece of paper for each participant.
● a chalkboard and chalk or newsprint and markers.

Begin by carefully reading this Bible study so you'll be familiar with it and will feel comfortable leading it. Look through the scripture passages in the "I'm Touched" section. You'll need two passages for each small group of four or five members. Using this guideline, estimate the number of groups you'll have and the number of scripture passages you'll need. Then select the particular passages you want to use.

Appoint a group leader for each small group who can keep the discussion moving.

3. Making Introductions—Begin by having participants say their own name and one quality of Jesus that means the most to them. For example, Jesus is a friend, or Jesus is always ready to give.

Then say: We're going to explore the characteristics of Jesus and how we can be more like him. But first we're going to look at a few Bible people who were good and not-so-good examples of what it means to imitate Jesus.

4. Name That Person—Divide the entire group into two teams to play "Name That Person"—similar to "Name That Tune." Have each team select one person to be the captain. The captain's only responsibility is to speak for the group. Play begins by flipping a coin to determine which team starts the bidding. From that point on, the teams alternate the privilege of starting the bidding. The captain of the team who won the toss says something like, "We can name that person in five clues." Five is the most any team can bid. The bid then passes to the other team who can either bid lower or say, "Name that person!" The leader then gives the number of clues the winning team bid. The team members then discuss the answer

"Name That Person" Clues

Answer: Judas Iscariot

This person . . .

Clues:
1. was in conspiracy with the chief priests and elders of the people.
2. received thirty pieces of silver for a certain job.
3. gave Jesus a kiss.
4. hanged himself.
5. betrayed Jesus.

Answer: Mary (mother of Jesus)

This person . . .

Clues:
1. said an important "yes."
2. had a cousin named Elizabeth.
3. had a nephew, John the Baptist.
4. was visited by an angel.
5. had a husband named Joseph.

Answer: Jesus

This person . . .

Clues:
1. was Jewish.
2. argued with the Pharisees.
3. could tell a great story.
4. cured many people of various illnesses.
5. got lost in the Temple once.

Answer: Paul

This person . . .

Clues:
1. was a Jew.
2. wrote several letters to various people.
3. traveled with a man named Timothy.
4. persecuted Christians.
5. was blinded during a conversion experience.

Answer: The astrologers (or three kings or wise men or magi)

These people . . .

Clues:
1. were looking for Jesus.
2. received a message in a dream.
3. went to see Herod.
4. followed a star.
5. brought three famous gifts.

Answer: John the Baptist

This person . . .

Clues:
1. told the people to reform their lives.
2. lived in the desert.
3. wore clothes made of camels' hair.
4. ate locusts and wild honey.
5. dunked people in the Jordan River.

Answer: Joseph (father of Jesus)

This person . . .

Clues:
1. had a father named Jacob.
2. got a message from the angel of the Lord in a dream.
3. almost broke up with his fiancee.
4. was a carpenter.
5. had a wife named Mary.

Answer: James and John

These people . . .

Clues:
1. were two of Jesus' followers.
2. were in a boat when Jesus called them.
3. were fishermen.
4. abandoned their father and his boat to follow Jesus.
5. had a father named Zebedee.

Answer: Matthew

This person . . .

Clues:
1. cheated others.
2. had dinner with Jesus—which upset the Pharisees.
3. gave up his sinful way of life to follow Jesus.
4. was a tax collector.
5. had one of the Gospels named after him.

Answer: Peter

This person . . .

Clues:
1. was a fisherman.
2. and his brother were followers of Jesus.
3. had a brother named Andrew.
4. was also called Simon and Cephas.
5. denied Jesus three times.

Being Like Jesus continued

among themselves. If they give a wrong answer or don't know, the other team gets a shot at it. The team who gets it right gets one point and the other team gets zero. If neither team gets it right, nobody gets any points. The team with the most points at the end of the game wins.

After the game is over, discuss with the whole group: What did you discover about these Bible people? about yourself? How does Jesus make a difference in people's lives?

5. I'm Touched—Next say: We just met some of the people in Jesus' time. Now we're going to explore times in Jesus' life when he reached out to certain people. While we do the next activity, focus on Jesus' qualities and how they affected the people around him.

Divide the group into small groups of four or five members. Give each group two of the suggested passages to read and discuss. Write the discussion questions on newsprint for all to see. Have one person from each group be the "secretary" who jots down all of the group members' responses.

Use these questions:
● Who was touched by Jesus in this story?
● Why do you think Jesus reached out to these persons?
● How were they touched by Jesus?
● How do you think they felt?

Use these scripture passages:
● Matthew 8:1-4 (Jesus heals a man)
● Matthew 9:9-13 (Jesus calls Matthew)
● Matthew 14:13-21 (Jesus feeds 5,000)
● Matthew 15:29-31 (Jesus heals many people)
● Matthew 20:29-34 (Jesus heals two blind men)
● Matthew 28:1-10 (The Resurrection)
● Mark 2:1-12 (Jesus heals a paralyzed man)
● Mark 4:35-41 (Jesus calms a storm)
● Luke 5:17-26 (Jesus heals a paralyzed man)
● Luke 7:1-10 (Jesus heals a Roman officer's servant)
● Luke 7:11-17 (Jesus raises a widow's son)
● Luke 19:1-10 (Jesus and Zacchaeus)
● Luke 24:13-35 (The walk to Emmaus)
● Luke 24:36-53 (Jesus appears to his disciples)
● John 2:1-12 (The wedding at Cana)
● John 13:1-17 (Jesus washes his disciples' feet)
● John 19:25-27 (Jesus on the cross)
● John 20:24-29 (Jesus and Thomas)

6. Preparing Skits—After the discussion, have each small group choose one of its assigned passages as the theme for a skit. In the skit, the group members should pretend to be people of Jesus' time discussing what had just happened in the passage. For

example, if a small group chooses the story of Zacchaeus (Luke 19:1-10), group members could pretend to be Zacchaeus and his family cleaning up after Jesus' visit and discussing what Jesus did there.

Have each small group present its skit, read the Bible passage and give answers to the questions for that particular passage. Have one young person record on newsprint all the answers to the fourth question, "How do you think they felt?" Have other group members add how they might feel.

7. What Does This Mean for Me?—If the total group is larger than 10, do the following discussion in small groups of five or six members. Throughout the discussion, focus on Jesus as a role model; someone whom we can imitate. *Use these questions:*
● Which of the passages studied appeals to you most? Why?
● If you had been living in Jesus' time, do you think you'd be a close follower of Jesus—or someone who wanted to get rid of him? Why do you feel this way?
● How do you see Jesus right now? As a friend, a high-and-mighty God, or something else? Why do you think you see him that way? How would you like to see Jesus? What keeps you from doing that?
● List on newsprint some specific things in Jesus' life that would be good for us to imitate. Why did you choose these things? Do you think people today try to imitate Jesus? Why or why not?

8. Name That Person—Again!—Close the discussion and say: Jesus set an example for us. Sometimes we fall short, but many times we do share his qualities with others. As a way to remind us that we're imitators of Jesus, we're going to play "Name That Person" again, only this time using our group members.

Give directions for the closing experience. Have participants each write their name on a sheet of paper. Shuffle all the papers; then exchange names. Make sure no one gets his or her own name. Instruct group members to each write three "clues" about the person whose name they drew. The clues must illustrate how that person is like Jesus. For example, this person welcomes strangers into this group, takes time to listen, and isn't afraid to give good hugs! Suggest they refer to the list of Jesus' qualities created earlier in the discussion.

Have the group form a circle. Then one by one, have each person read all three clues for the "mystery" person. Have the whole group "Name That Person." After the group has guessed (whether right or wrong), the clue-writer gives the person the paper with the qualities. A hug would be appropriate too!

9. Closing—Close with a prayer asking for strength to be more like Jesus.

—*Patrick Mulcahy*

20
I'M SPECIAL

1. Before the Meeting—Gather a pencil and copies of the article and handouts for each person.

2. Reading—Read "I'm Special" aloud or choose a volunteer who can read this brief article with enthusiasm and feeling. Have volunteers read the following scripture verses aloud and explain what makes us special, according to the passage. The verses are Genesis 1:26-31; John 3:16; 1 Corinthians 1:26-31; Ephesians 1:4-5, 2:4-9; and 1 Peter 2:9.

I'm Special

I'm special. In all the world there's nobody like me.

Since the beginning of time, there has never been another person like me. Nobody has my smile. Nobody has my eyes, my nose, my hair, my hands, my voice. I'm special.

No one can be found who has my handwriting.

Nobody anywhere has my tastes—for food or music or art. No one sees things just as I do.

In all of time there's been no one who laughs like me, no one who cries like me. And what makes me laugh and cry will never provoke identical laughter and tears from anybody else, ever.

No one reacts to any situation just as I would react. I'm special.

I'm the only one in all of creation who has my set of abilities. Oh, there will always be somebody who is better at one of the things I'm good at, but no one in the universe can reach the quality of my combination of talents, ideas, abilities and feelings. Like a roomful of musical instruments, some may excel alone, but none can match the symphony sound when all are played together. I'm a symphony.

Through all of eternity no one will ever look, talk, walk, think or do like me. I'm special. I'm rare.

And, in all rarity there is great value.

Because of my great rare value, I need not attempt to imitate others. I will accept—yes, celebrate—my differences.

I'm special. And I'm beginning to realize it's no accident that I'm special. I'm beginning to see that God made me special for a very special purpose. He must have a job for me that no one else can do as well as I. Out of all the billions of applicants, only one is qualified, only one has the right combination of what it takes.

That one is me. Because . . . I'm special.

I'm Special continued

3. Do-It-Yourself-Mystery-Me-Word Kit—Allow only about two minutes for this exercise to be completed. Then spend 10-15 minutes having individuals share their mystery words with the group. If any of the words are the same, have the group compare the kids. If you are thick-skinned enough, let your group come up with your personal mystery word.

DO-IT-YOURSELF-MYSTERY-ME-WORD KIT

Place the letter of the item in the boxes below for each part of the kit that most nearly fits you. See what crazy word those letters form. Compare your special word with those of your friends. And you thought you were all alike!

1. The Nose Mart
B. K. L. T. V.

2. Madame French's Handwriting Shack
A. *Now is* E. *Now is* O. *Now is* U. *Now is*

3. Joker Jake's Laugh Barn
(S.) Belly-laugher (M.) Titterer (P.) Snorter (L.) Guffawer (C.) Giggler

4. Lou's Eyes Cream Parlor
O. I. E. A.

5. Shady Shep's Favorite Color Shop
red D. yellow G. green K. orange N. purple R. blue W.

Here's me:

1. NOSE: ☐
2. HANDWRITING: ☐
3. LAUGH: ☐
4. EYES: ☐
5. MY COLOR: ☐

Your personal mystery word →

4. You're Unique! You're Special! You're You!—Allow only a couple of minutes for everyone to complete this exercise. If your group members know each other fairly well and feel comfortable with each other, divide into groups of four or five and have people guess how each other responded. If your group members don't know each other very well, divide into smaller groups and spend about 15 minutes where each person shares some of his or her responses.

YOU'RE UNIQUE! YOU'RE SPECIAL! YOU'RE YOU!

Read quickly through the following list. Use an X to identify those traits that are the real you. Use a ✔ to indicate the traits you'd like to have.

- ☐ have cute dimples
- ☐ people can trust me
- ☐ usually say the right things
- ☐ talk a lot
- ☐ wear striped socks
- ☐ friendly
- ☐ laugh a lot
- ☐ afraid of the future
- ☐ depend on others a lot
- ☐ independent
- ☐ like 40% Bran Flakes
- ☐ waste time
- ☐ don't understand myself
- ☐ use Close Up toothpaste
- ☐ trust myself
- ☐ trust others
- ☐ pick my nose in public
- ☐ daydream a lot

- ☐ wear dirty underwear sometimes
- ☐ usually say the wrong things
- ☐ life scares me
- ☐ like to be around people
- ☐ watch cartoons
- ☐ have talents no one knows about
- ☐ like being intelligent
- ☐ often get embarrassed
- ☐ cry at sad movies
- ☐ say stupid things
- ☐ have pretty eyes
- ☐ like being a jock (jockette)
- ☐ people like to be around me
- ☐ sing in the shower
- ☐ spiritually mature
- ☐ listen well

ANIMAL CRACKERS

If I were an animal, I'd be a (circle one):

5. It's Me!—Allow about five or six minutes for your kids to complete this exercise. In groups of four, have each person give his or her answers. In the larger group, you might want to find out who had the same answers and who had the most "difficult" answers for each question.

6. Closing—Have everyone think of different people in the group. Then list as many positive traits of different people in the group as possible. People don't have to mention names. Close with a large group prayer. Thank and praise God for his creativity in making each person.

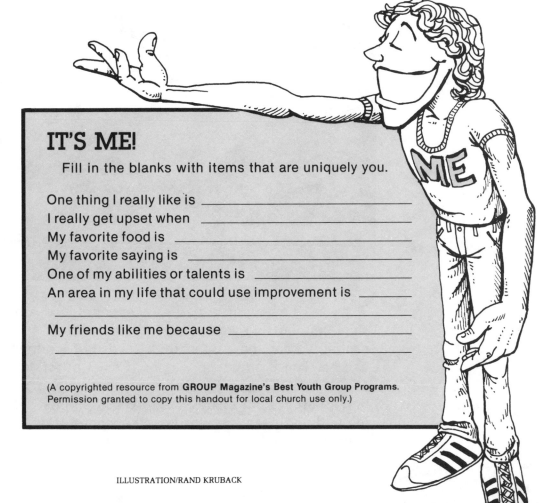

IT'S ME!

Fill in the blanks with items that are uniquely you.

One thing I really like is _____
I really get upset when _____
My favorite food is _____
My favorite saying is _____
One of my abilities or talents is _____
An area in my life that could use improvement is _____
_____
My friends like me because _____
_____

ILLUSTRATION/RAND KRUBACK

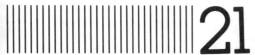

21
ENCOURAGE ME

If you've ever had a bad day, encountered a problem that completely baffled you, or just found yourself sad or depressed, you probably know how important a word of kindness and encouragement can be. Those on whom we count most often do not uplift us as much as we need. The responsibility for encouraging, however, belongs not only to others but also to ourselves. We must take the first step by being willing to say the words and respond in ways that model encouragement.

PHOTOGRAPHY/RON MEYER

1. Objectives—Use this Bible study to:
- explore how God values and supports us as his people;
- recognize the need for encouraging each other; and
- experience the power of praise with each other.

2. Before the Bible Study—Gather newsprint; markers; pencils; chalk and chalkboard or overhead transparency supplies; a copy of Philippians 1:3-8 for each person; an envelope for each person; Bibles; masking tape; and enough 3×5 cards so that each person will have one card for every other person in the group (for example, if there are 10 participants, each will have nine cards).

Read through the Bible study and think through the discussion questions.

Write the five questions from section four on newsprint, chalkboard or overhead transparency.

3. Role Play—This opening activity is designed to examine how people respond when given praise and encouragement instead of disapproval and negativism.

Ask four people who are spontaneous and comfortable with the group to help you with a role play. Choose one of the two following role plays or make up one of your own.

Do the role play twice, each time with different people. The first time, the "initiator" should present his or her situation and then respond as honestly and normally as possible to what the "responder" says. The responder should be positive, helpful and encouraging.

The second time, the responder should be negative, critical and discouraging, while the initiator reacts again as he or she normally would in such a circumstance.

4. Encouragement From God—Say: If we are to encourage others, we must value ourselves. We must believe that what we say and do has an impact on others. It is God's love, proven and demonstrated in Christ, that gives us our worth and our example. The Bible is God's Word of encouragement. It reminds us who we are and what we're capable of doing as God's children.

Read these scripture references and use the discussion questions that follow.

Isaiah 43:1-7—This passage talks about belonging to God. In what way is it encouraging to know we belong to God?

1 Peter 2:9—Restate this passage using descriptive words to replace "chosen race," "king's priests" and "holy nation." Choose words such as "God's personal friends." How does being chosen for something important make you feel?

1 John 3:1a—Being in God's family is like having the ideal parent. Describe God as the ideal parent. How would the ideal parent bring up children to encourage and uplift others?

Tell your group: Encouragement comes more easily when we like and respect the people we are supporting. But Jesus demonstrates the need to build up those around us, no matter who they are or how we feel about them.

Divide members into groups of four or five. Give each group a Bible. Ask each group to read either Luke 19:1-10 or John 8:1-11. Hand out large sheets of newsprint and markers. Display the following ques-

---

Role Play 1: Sarah

Initiator: Sarah, a high school student. She comes home from school after flunking her biology exam. She feels terrible. She'd studied a little, but not as hard as she should have. She'd also gone to a movie with friends the night before the test. Sarah is normally a B or C student. Her next test is in two days.

Responder: Sarah's mother.

Role Play 2: David

Initiator: David, a member of the high school football team, which just lost an important game. The team didn't play very well, but David feels particularly bad because he fumbled a ball that the other team recovered to score the winning point. David wants to quit the team. He goes over to his best friend's house after the game.

Responder: John, David's best friend. John has just returned from watching the game.

When the role plays are completed, ask the following questions.
- How did the endings of the two role plays differ?
- What words did you hear that sounded the most helpful? harmful?
- Is it ever helpful to be negative or discouraging? If so, when?
- What's the difference between being a negative or critical person and being honest?
- Think of a time when someone discouraged or intimidated you. How did you respond?
- When you are with positive people, do you act and talk differently than when you spend time with negative people? Explain.

Encourage Me continued

tions (which you've already written on newsprint, chalkboard or overhead transparency). Each group should select one person to record answers to each of these questions.

- What words or actions helped build up the person to whom Jesus spoke?
- Why was what Jesus did or said encouraging?
- In both situations, Jesus encouraged people whom others put down. What risk did he take in doing so?
- What risk do we take when we encourage other people?
- What changes may have taken place in the life of this person as a result of his or her encounter with Christ?

Have group members get back into the large group. Ask one member from each small group to explain his or her group's scripture reading, and then have that group's "recorder" share answers with the large group.

After all groups have reported, ask group members to think of times when their lives were changed because someone took time to encourage them. Be prepared to tell about an experience from your own life. Have several others share if they're willing.

5. Encouragement From Paul—Say: The apostle Paul also realized the importance of positive and encouraging words. Many of his letters began with inspiring and heartening words.

Hand out pencils and copies of Philippians 1:3-8. Instruct the group members to silently read the passage and underline words or phrases that they would find particularly supportive had the letter been sent to them by a personal friend.

Ask several people to tell the words they underlined and why they found them important.

Based on this study and individual experience, define the word "encouragement." Write the group's definition on chalkboard or newsprint.

Brainstorm a list of encouraging words to use to support and care for each other. (Include ideas such as "You look nice," "Good job!" and "Nice work!")

Explain that encouragement takes the form of both words and actions. Ask: How should we act to build up each other? List the answers.

Read Colossians 3:12-16. Compare the scripture reference with the action ideas just listed. Should anything be added to the group's list? Ask: Why is it important for encouragement to be more than words?

6. Encouragement From Friends—In this part of

your Bible study, you will put encouragement into action.

Hand out packs of 3×5 cards to group members. Each person needs a card for every other person in the group. Also, make sure group members still have pencils. (To save time, if your group is large, you may wish to do this in groups of 10 young people.)

Give one envelope to each person. Tell each person to write his or her name on the envelope and tape it on the wall with all the others.

Tell group members to write the name of each other group member on a 3×5 card; one name per card.

Have your kids write words of praise or encouragement on each person's card. They should make each card as personal as possible. Words of praise can include anything from how the person looks to comments about his or her character or faith.

When people have finished filling out the cards, they should place them in the proper envelopes. At the end of the meeting, everyone may take his or her own envelope, go somewhere, read and enjoy!

7. Closing Devotion—Hand out Bibles. Ask the group members to turn to Psalm 91. Ask one person to read the passage, or have the whole group read it together. Then have group members silently go back over the psalm and each select one passage that they think would be especially helpful for them to remember at a "down" time in their lives. Ask them each to share the passage they chose with someone else and explain the reason for their choice.

8. Enrichment Experiences—Here are additional ways your group members can practice praise and encouragement.

- Special letters: Have group members each choose a friend or family member and write a letter saying how much they appreciate him or her.
- Secret pals: Put everyone's name in a hat. Let each person draw a name. For a given amount of time, each person will be responsible to give encouragement and kindness to that "secret pal."
- Psalm search: Have each person choose a different psalm and copy verses that have words of comfort and help. The passages could be put on post cards, stationery or note cards.
- Adopt grandparents: Get names of people from the local rest home and give them to your young people. Have your kids write letters to and visit their "adopted grandparents" who are often lonely.

—Paula Mott-Becker

22

ADVENTURE CAMPING

One mistake and I'm dead. I tried to force that sick thought from my mind. I needed all the concentration I could muster.

"You can do it!" my friend yelled. Over the past two weeks, I'd grown to trust my life to my new friend's judgment.

The time for action was now. There could be no turning back.

The sweat from my palms flooded the fingers of the thick leather gloves I wore to protect my hands from the rappelling rope.

I backed up to the edge of the 90-foot cliff, hooked my boot heels over the edge and leaned backwards into the thin air.

Between short, shallow gasps of air, I heard my friend shout more encouragements: "Don't be afraid! Just lean back and jump!"

I leaned back more till I started to fall. I jumped. Backwards. Off the cliff.

After that half-jump, half-fall, my confidence grew with each bounce off the side of the cliff. I was a little sad to reach the bottom.

My friend's first rappelling trip off the cliff was quick and smooth—much more daring than mine.

My new friend, who helped me make it through the challenging two weeks of camping, hiking and rappelling was named Wendi. She was 13 years old and a freshman in high school. But she helped me more than any skilled cliff climber could ever do.

Adventure Camping continued

ADVENTURE CAMPING IS ADVENTURE

It doesn't really matter how old you are, whether you're a crusher of a guy or a petite, pixyish girl. What counts is what's inside you. Some people call it character. Others call it guts. Whatever you call it, adventure camping brings it out.

"Adventure camping" isn't a good description of this character- and friend-building experience. There's much more to adventure camping than just camping. Actually, adventure camping includes such different heart-pounding activities as rappelling, rock climbing, spending time alone in the wilderness, solving a number of "impossible" problems, river rafting, backpacking, and a bunch of other creative challenges.

The Institute for Creative Living in Cleveland, Ohio, includes several stress-inducing and friend-making challenges in its program. These "initiatives," as director Marcia Mauter calls them, include such sweaty palm activities as getting a group of people over a 14-foot wall, walking balance beams, figuring out how to get a tire over a 14-foot stump, crossing pesky wire bridges and getting the entire group onto a small elevated platform.

In fact, Bob Kobielush, director of leadership development for Christian Camping International, says adventure camping includes such activities as experiencing a totally different culture (i.e., spending a weekend in the inner city if you live in a squeaky clean suburb).

THE MYSTIQUE IS THERE

Ask almost anyone who's ever been weak-kneed on a rock climb, staggered through a grueling backpacking trip or spent a sleepless night alone in the wilderness. There is an almost mystical quality about adventure camping.

Although the "mystical" formula varies from situation to situation, there are common ingredients in the life-changing recipe. "The key is to isolate people from the environment they're used to and place them somewhere new," says John Yates, National Coordinator, Christian Wilderness Leaders Coalition. "Add to that new environment the responsibility of solving new challenges as a group: how to cook a meal in the rain, how to climb a mountain, how to get your group over an unfriendly obstacle."

Then add to that recipe spiritually mature, skilled leaders who are committed to talking with individuals about how God relates to their lives.

The result: personal development, spiritual growth and adventure.

All types of interesting discussion just seems to happen in adventure camping situations. "We talk about our relationship with ourselves, our friends, our enemies, our parents and most of all with God," says Ellen Strickland of Camp Id-ra-ha-je, a Christian adventure camp in Colorado. "We talk about girls, guys, goals and our group. We even talk about fears and victories and, well, some very personal things."

YOU'LL NEVER FORGET THIS EXPERIENCE

Being a group member and facing unique situations in an alien environment sets the stage for memorable events. Recalls Bob Kobielush: "One guy who had deformed arms came to our camp. We didn't know his handicap was so severe until he showed up to meet his cabin buddies—a group of high school athletes. Everyone, including me, thought we'd made a terrible mistake by making him stay in that cabin.

"His cabin buddies didn't have much to do with him. His arms were so deformed that his elbows almost touched in front of him. And the guys in his cabin had to include him in everything they did.

"As it turned out, the athletes learned more about dealing with their own handicaps than they did about competition, softball or camping. Being with the 'handicapped' guy was a life-changing event, not only for the athletes, but for the staff members too."

Another adventure camping memory-maker is the emphasis on the group. "The individual and the group are more important than any of the activities," says John Yates. "And a group accomplishes only what its members want to. If they rock climb, they rock climb because they want to. If they go up to a mountain peak with the rest of the group, they go because they want to go. Whether we make it up a mountain isn't really important. What's important is that we work together and that we can accomplish things as people in fellowship together."

ADVENTURE CAMPING CHANGES THINGS

One of the most fantastic changes adventure camping makes in people's lives is in the way they learn to view others. "Many people are basically into themselves—they don't care much about other people," says Ellen Strickland. "It's quite a healthy slap for the most selfish, self-confident person to find out that he or she needs the group's support and encouragement."

And that change usually doesn't take place during the adventure itself. The experience gives the person a different pair of glasses with which to see other

I never really thought about it much. But I sure learned a lot about some of the girls on our backpacking trip last month.

The hike up to the summit started out kind of tense. I really didn't want the girls to come. They'd just slow us down.

I like girls—uh, I mean I *really* like girls. But not when they hold you back. I didn't want to have to carry a girl down from the summit. I was wrong.

At first, a bunch of us guys started out fast. We hadn't been at the summit very long when the girls came tromping along.

I tell you, I've found out that the girls just don't give up. They may not be as strong as most guys, but they don't quit. I guess I really have a lot to learn about girls.

—Tim, 15

I learned so much about God on the camping trip. How can anyone go on a week-long camping outing in the mountains and not come away believing in God?

My leader gave me Bible verses that let me get to know God better. And our late night talks under the stars, well, I'll never forget that week. Never.

—Delores, 14

It bothers me a lot to say this: I'm shy. People often misunderstand my shyness and think I don't care about anyone. I really do care, mostly. It's just that I don't know how to show it.

I almost didn't go on the rafting trip. But my parents and friends talked me into it. Boy, am I glad they did.

We'd just started the trip when we hit a terrible set of rapids. The only way we kept the raft upright was for everyone to not panic and paddle together. We did it!

Later on, we got into a crazy water fight and about drowned each other. Even though I got the worst of it, it wasn't so bad.

Near the end of the trip, we pooled our soggy sack lunches. It was the best food I ever tasted. I also made a lot of friends . . . ones I'd known for years . . . but didn't really know till the raft trip.

—Ben, 14

I'll never forget the 24-hour "solo" that I did at the end of my two-week camping and backpacking trip. I knew when I signed up that I'd have to be alone. And I guess I thought about it all through the two weeks. As my solo time got closer, I became obsessed with wondering if I could make it through the day and night by myself. Totally alone.

When the day came, I left my tent, sleeping bag and food with the rest of the group. My leader gave me the physical boundaries of my "territory" and a Bible.

I experienced fright, cold, loneliness, tears. But you know something? That was one of the most valuable times in my life. I learned unbelievable things about myself and about God.

Want to know what I learned? Do you have two or three days to listen?

—Linda, 17

people. And that new perspective eventually changes attitudes and behavior. Having a different vision of who you are makes a fantastic difference in your life.

WHERE TO START

You probably remember at least one time when a hiking, camping or biking trip touched you like nothing else could. You can create adventure camping situations to touch other people's lives.

But planning a successful adventure camping experience isn't as easy as planning a weekend retreat or even a denomination-sponsored church camp. Life can get pretty tricky any time a group of unpredictable people venture into new and alien situations.

If you're thinking about designing your own adventure outing, there are at least four critical things to keep in mind:

Adventure Camping continued

Use Professionals. Whomever you choose to handle the skilled needs of this special ministry must have special training. He or she must know exactly the goals of the outing, what has to happen to meet those goals and the dangers and problems involved.

The leaders also need to know first-aid and emergency treatment as well as such details as food preparation, transportation schedules and how to handle everyday group tensions. The world's greatest rock climbing leader could cause his outing to fizzle if he's also the world's worst organizer.

Don't Skimp On Equipment. Don't take shortcuts when it comes to buying, renting or borrowing equipment. Get in touch with other people who've successfully completed an experience similar to the one you're planning. Borrow their equipment. Purchase good Army surplus materials. Don't forget to check with rental outlets for large or expensive pieces of equipment.

Planning. This event must be planned carefully, with attention to details. Don't assume things will happen automatically. Your checklist should include these areas:

- ✓ What are your goals?
- ✓ What kind of people are you taking? Do they have any special needs?
- ✓ Develop a step-by-step plan
- ✓ Assign responsibilities
- ✓ Adequate insurance coverage?
- ✓ Obtain proper equipment
- ✓ Budget okay?
- ✓ Transportation schedules
- ✓ Physicals
- ✓ First-aid and emergency training
- ✓ Permission forms
- ✓ Everyone know rules and punishments?
- ✓ Have enough help?
- ✓ Are professionals lined up for the special events (rappelling, rock climbing, etc.)?
- ✓ Follow-up on all people, programs and planning

Take a Dry Run. Once everything has been planned, get all the youth and adult leaders together and take a dry run through the entire outing. Of course, the dry run takes extra time. But it's absolutely necessary.

PEOPLE AND PROGRAMS

Unless you have solid resources and skilled professional leaders, you may wish to use one of the hundreds of existing adventure camping organizations.

If you're interested in knowing more about adventure camping, you can become a member of the Wilderness Leaders Coalition and receive a quarterly newsletter and a listing of Christian camps by joining Christian Camping International, P.O. Box 646, Wheaton, IL 60187.

You can also receive a comprehensive listing of camps and wilderness experiences from the American Camping Association, Bradford Woods, Martinsville, IN 46151.

—*Gary Richardson*

MORE IDEAS FOR ADVENTURE CAMPING

1. Free Information—Check the addresses on the last page of the program. You can receive plenty of information by writing to these organizations.

2. Try It—Don't let the lack of experience keep you from trying an adventure camping trip. Part of the mystique of adventure camping is the risk of trying something new. Go ahead. Grab some mystique.

3. Homemade Adventure Camping—Try a weekend version of adventure camping. Set up the following simple obstacles. Then divide into teams of five or six and turn the teams loose on the following course. Debrief afterward. Get some construction trade guys in your church to help you set up the course.

The wall: Make an imaginary wall by stretching a rope between two trees about five feet above the ground. The objective is to get the entire team over the rope without touching it or any other part of the wall.

The platform: Suspend a 3-foot square piece of plywood about five feet off the ground. (Use heavy plywood, chains and heavy eyebolts.) The object is to get the entire team onto the platform.

Rope bridge: Check the **Boy Scout Handbook** for directions on constructing a rope bridge. Get the ropes and have the teams construct the bridge. Then have fun crossing it.

The gorge: Place two platforms about 12 feet apart. (Plywood placed solidly on two sawhorses for each platform works well.) Give each team two 2-by-6 boards which are 8 feet long. The object is to get the group from one platform to the other using only the two boards and the team's ingenuity.

---

23 WHAT IS REAL?

"Real isn't how you are made. It's something that happens to you."

Teenagers struggle to define their identity. They often respond differently when they're with friends, with parents, with teachers and with the youth group.

But if it weren't for relationships with others, people would have *no* identities. Because it's in community that personalities develop; that people can know who they really are.

The key, then, to "being real" is through open, caring, vulnerable relationships with others and with God. This study will help your group members see that key.

What Is Real? continued

1. Objectives—Group members will:
● define what it means to be real; and
● look at specific ways to be real.

2. Before the Bible Study—Prepare enough copies of the discussion questions so that each member will have a copy.

Write the 10 verse references from Romans 12:9-18 on the tops of 8½×11 sheets of paper, one reference per sheet.

Gather the following materials:
● Artificial and real flowers (enough for half of the group members to each have an artificial flower and the other half to each have a real flower), and a safety pin for each member.
● Two blindfolds, 10 wax fruit, enough real fruit for each group member to have one, and four large fruit baskets.
● **The Velveteen Rabbit**, by Margery Williams, filmstrip and cassette (from Contemporary Drama Service, Box 7710, Colorado Springs, CO 80933), filmstrip projector, extra bulb, cassette player. If you decide not to use the filmstrip, you can order the children's book from Running Press, 125 South Twenty-Second Street, Philadelphia, PA 19103.
● Newsprint, markers, Bibles and pencils.

3. Greeting—As young people enter the meeting room, safety-pin on each a single-flower "corsage." Pin a real flower on the first group member, an artificial one on the next, and so on, so that half of the group has real flowers and the other half has artificial flowers.

Welcome group members to this study on "being real."

4. The Fruit Basket Game—For this crowd-breaker relay, divide kids into two teams: the real-flower team and the fake-flower team, according to their flower corsages.

Place at the far end of the room two baskets, each filled with five wax fruit and half of the real fruit. It's best if you've refrigerated the wax fruit, as well as the real fruit, prior to the game.

Have the team members line up behind each other, with the front members facing the fruit baskets at the far end of the room. Place an empty fruit basket behind each team and tell kids that the object of this game is simply to fill their empty fruit baskets. Put blindfolds on both front team members.

Choose one adult sponsor to stand between the teams and tell them which fruit to get next, as they are ready. The sponsor should have a list of the fruit in each basket. (For example: wax banana, real banana, real orange, real grapes, wax apple, real apple, etc.)

The game begins: The sponsor yells out "wax banana" and the two front, blindfolded team members run to the baskets, find the wax bananas, return and place them in their team's empty basket. (If they got a wrong fruit, they must go back to the first basket and try again.) They remove the blindfolds and place them on the next team member in line and the game continues. The sponsor keeps each team informed of which fruit it needs to get next.

The team that collects all its fruit first wins.

5. The Velveteen Rabbit: What Is Real?—Gather the group members to sit together and view the filmstrip. If you don't use the filmstrip, read the children's book.

Hand out the discussion questions, and pencils, so each member has a copy on which to jot down thoughts.

Follow along in the filmstrip reference script and be prepared to stop the projector at these points: after frame 17; after frame 26; after frame 38; and, of course, at the end. If you choose to read the story, check the following filmstrip directions and stop reading at similar places in the book.

Discuss the following questions as a whole group at the appropriate times:

FILMSTRIP DISCUSSION QUESTIONS

● **At first stop:** The horse says, "Real isn't how you're made. It's something that happens . . . and it takes a long while." What do you suppose he means by this? Do you agree? Why or why not?

He also says, "By the time you are real, most of your hair is loved off and your eyes drop off and you are very shabby. But these things don't matter because when you are real, you can't be ugly except to people who don't understand." Explain. When are some times you've felt that people didn't understand you, didn't see the real you?

● **At second stop:** As the velveteen rabbit's coat became more and more shabby, and his tail came unsewn, and the pink on his nose rubbed off, he became more and more real. What are some painful things you've experienced that have helped you become more real?

When the boy called the velveteen rabbit real, the rabbit felt that he was. But what actually made him real? Could he have achieved "realness" by himself, sitting alone on the nursery shelf? Or was it only in relationship with the boy that he got his identity? Explain.

● **At third stop:** Even though the velveteen rabbit was certain he was real when he was with the boy, he didn't feel real when he was with the wild rabbits. Why?

He sat still and tried to hide the fact that he had no hind legs. When are times you've felt you had to hide your real self from others because you feared they wouldn't accept you?

● **At end:** The good fairy told the velveteen rabbit that, before, he had been real to the boy but now he would be real to everyone. List the people with whom you feel the most real. Who are the people who know you the best and still love you, in spite of your "shabby coat, unsewn tail and rubbed-off nose"?

Think of people you know who pretend to be somebody they're not. Describe the type of relationship you think they have with the people they try to impress. (For example: using put-downs, having to wear the "right" clothes.)

Now describe the type of relationship between friends who are honest and real with each other. (For example: willing to risk showing true feeling, not needing to be "perfect.")

What does it mean to "be real"?

6. Romans 12:9-18: How to Be Real—Tell group members that one way to think of "being real" is being honest in our relationships with other people and with God.

Divide group members into small groups of three or four. Give each group newsprint and markers. Hand out the 10 verse reference sheets among the groups. (If there are two groups, give both five sheets; if there are four groups, give two groups three sheets and two groups two sheets; etc.)

Have the small groups think about "real" people they know and list on newsprint characteristics of those people and their relationships with them.

Next have small group members read Romans 12:9-18. Instruct the groups to discuss the verses listed on the sheets they were given, and to brainstorm specific ways to live out those verses. They should list ideas for each verse on its reference sheet. (For example: Verse 9 says: "Don't just pretend that you love others: really love them. Hate what is wrong. Stand on the side of good." Ideas might be: Give a friend half of your sandwich if she forgot her lunch; Really listen when a friend tells you about a problem; etc.)

When small groups have finished listing practical applications of their verses, gather together the whole group. Discuss the lists of "real" characteristics, and then the specific ways to be real that relate to the Bible verses.

Ask: What are ways to be real in our relationship with God? (For example: prayer, Bible reading, worship, fellowship, etc.) Remind group members that God is at work within them (Philippians 2:13), and that "being real," like for the velveteen rabbit, is a lifelong process—an exciting one.

7. Closing—Close with a prayer for the courage to be vulnerable, close, honest—*real*—in relationships with people and with God.

Invite group members to munch on the fruit—or make a fruit salad together, if time permits!

—*Cindy Parolini*

24

HOW'S YOUR BODY IMAGE?

1. Before the Bible Study—Gather a pencil, Bible, copies of the handouts, sheet of paper and crayon for each person. You also will need masking tape.

2. Bible Study—Ask the youth to read these Bible passages and explain how they apply to self-image: Psalms 8:5-6; 139:1-4; Matthew 18:12-14; 22:39; Romans 5:6-8; 8:1-2; Ephesians 2:4-5, 10; Philippians 4:13; 1 Peter 2:9.

3. Mirror Factory—Use "The Mirror Factory" to help your group clarify how they feel about their bodies. Use "Try Perfect Body Soap" to help your young people take steps toward making their bodies more likeable. Discuss the exercises when the kids are finished.

THE MIRROR FACTORY

By age 17, the average person has spent nearly a year and a half looking in the mirror. That information comes from the GROUP Magazine world-famous research team.

When the research team isn't busy researching or washing windows at Walt's Wonderful Supermarket, they design exercises to help people take a look at themselves—both their good and bad sides.

They've designed this exercise for you. For each of the following areas, check the box under the face that best describes how you feel about yourself.

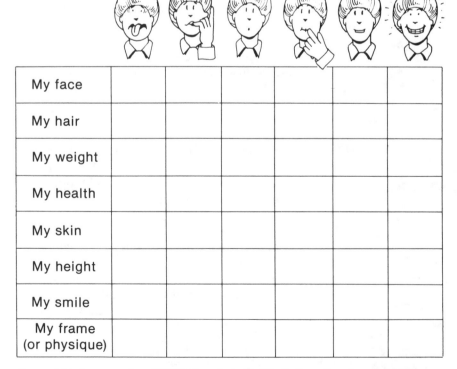

My face						
My hair						
My weight						
My health						
My skin						
My height						
My smile						
My frame (or physique)						

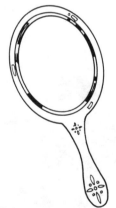

Of all the faces you checked, which two personal traits did you least like? Write those two traits in this mirror.

Which two personal traits did you rate the highest? Write those traits in this mirror.

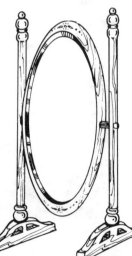

Be happy for those strong areas. If you'd like to start doing something about those bad areas, work through "Try Perfect Body Soap."

ILLUSTRATION/LAUREL WATSON

TRY PERFECT BODY SOAP

GROUP Magazine scientists have invented a soap that's guaranteed to give you a more perfect body.

The key to this soap, according to Sylvia Swart, GROUP Magazine scientist and chocolate shake expert, is to carefully follow the directions above each of the following blank soap wrappers.

Fun Stuff

What activities do you enjoy, or would like to try? Write them here:

Exercise

If you're not already involved in a consistent physical activity, what are two things you can begin doing now to give your body some exercise? List them here:

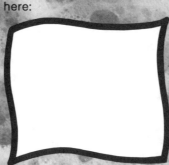

Friends

List the names of three people who are close friends or who you think would make close friends. Once you have *close* friends who care about you, ask them to evaluate your body, your personality—everything about you. They can help you feel better about yourself. Write three names here:

Change!

Write three things that you can start doing, stop doing, or change that will affect the way you see yourself. (For instance, stop eating fatso chips, see a dermatologist, get better-fitting clothes, and so on.) Write your ideas here:

Toss!

The rest is simple. Unwrap the soap, hold the Perfect Body bar carefully as you walk to the nearest wastebasket. Then drop the bar of soap into the wastebasket and save the wrappers you just completed. Use them as guides to help you start working toward a body you can live with.

4. Crummy Commercials—Divide into teams of three or four. Ask each team to come up with a parody of a commercial that includes bad things commercials say about people to get them to buy their product. Each group picks one person to take the brunt of the commercial. For instance, one group may pick a guy to be the "star." His team sets up a situation where they tell him he needs certain products (deodorant, teeth whitener, mouthwash, shampoo and so on). Let the groups come up with their own list of products. If any get stuck, give them a few of these topics of TV commercials: body odor, bad breath, yellow teeth, slippery dentures, nasal spray, athlete's foot, iron poor blood, split ends, jock itch, zits, age spots, weight control.

After 10-15 minutes, have the teams meet together and act out their commercials. Discuss the influence the media have on how we like or dislike our bodies.

5. Self Sheet—Tape a sheet of paper to each person's back and give each person a crayon. The object is for the group to mill around and write something positive about each person on the sheet of paper, without signing their names. Possible graffiti might be: "Great eyes," "Wild smile," etc. After the signing has stopped, have everyone remove their sheets and read the positive things people wrote about them.

6. Closing—Ask the young people to form a circle and hold hands. Close with a silent prayer—everyone thanks God for the person on his or her right.

25

SAYING YES TO YOUR SEXUALITY

1. Before the Meeting—At the top of a chalkboard or newsprint write the words "sex" and "sexuality." Write each "Feeling Okay Quiz" statement on a slip of paper and place all 10 in the same envelope. Make a copy of Psalm 139 for each person. If possible, provide helpful books on sexuality and related topics. You also will need a pencil, chair and copy of the article for each person.

2. Opener—Begin the meeting by playing the game "Wink 'n Run" from **Try This One . . . Too** (Group Books). Seat all of your girls in a circle. Leave one chair open. Now a guy stands behind each chair. The guys put their hands behind their backs. The object is for the guy standing behind the empty chair to get a girl into his chair. He does this by winking at one of the girls. That girl tries to run to his chair. The guy behind her chair tries to stop her by quickly putting his hands on her shoulders. If he's not fast enough, he winks to try and lure a girl to his chair. After a while, switch and put the guys in the chairs and let the girls do the winking.

3. Jumping In—Have everyone sit together and brainstorm examples of the words "sex" and "sexuality." List all ideas on the chalkboard or newsprint.

Write down everything that's suggested. Then briefly discuss the difference between sex and sexuality.

4. Role Modeling—Divide group members into groups of four or five. Have each group take one or two "Feeling Okay Quiz" statements from the envelope. Allow 15 minutes for each group to plan a role play to represent each statement. For example, for body language, the guys could imitate how girls walk, sit or act; the girls could show how guys appear to them.

5. Read the Article—Read and discuss the following article. Have each group member complete the "Feeling Okay Quiz." Make sure you talk about specifics of *where* to get information, *how* to assess values and *what* influences our behavior.

6. Discuss—Ask the kids these questions after they finish the quiz. What did you learn about yourself concerning sexual information? values? attitudes? behaviors?

7. A Celebration—Read Psalm 139 responsively, alternating the verses between the leader and the group. End with a large group hug!

YOUR SEXUALITY

Many young people have questions about their sexuality. To find answers, it's important to know what's meant by "sexuality."

First of all, sexuality is much more than two sets of genitals coming together. It's a new mother breast-feeding her baby; or a two-year-old watching his father shave and wanting to try it too; or Joe, a normal, healthy guy, looking at Sally and getting turned on. You become a sexual being at the moment of your birth, and remain one until you die. Sexuality determines your maleness and femaleness, and influences every aspect of your life. Your

sexuality is what makes you a unique and special person. And it's important to feel good about your "sexual" self.

Feeling good about yourself and your sexuality comes from having an understanding of where you've been and where you are now. Take a few minutes to complete the following quickie quiz; then look at some tips on handling the problem areas.

For each statement, put an "X" on the spot that best describes you:

Feeling Okay Quiz

Can we talk about something else?	I feel okay.	I have absolutely no problem.	
●————————————●————————————●			Information

1. I know the right words, not just slang, in talking about sex. (For example, penis, vagina, clitoris, orgasm.)

2. I can talk to my parents about my sexual feelings, and I ask them questions about sex.

3. I have some understanding of what the Bible teaches about sexuality.

4. My church does a good job of helping me with my problems and questions about sex.

5. I have taken time to sort out my sexual values. (For example, I know if, where and when I might be willing to engage in heavy petting or other sexual activity.)

6. My personal values relate to those of my parents.

(right margin bracket: Values & Attitudes)

7. On a date I can talk to him or her about my sexual limits; I listen to what he or she is saying to me.

8. I'm aware of what "body language" messages I'm sending: the way I sit, stand and walk.

9. Knowing people judge by appearance, I dress in appropriate clothes; I choose from current fads and styles, but still reflect the real me.

10. Even though I may hear them all day in school, or at the movies, or even at home, I avoid using profanity or the common four-letter words.

(right margin bracket: Behavior)

Now look at your answers. Count the number you checked "okay" or "no problem." Rate how you feel about your sexuality:

8-10: Yes, I'm comfortable with my sexuality!

4-7: Maybe I need to take a look at myself.

0-3: Help!

An Equation for Saying Yes to Your Sexuality

Notice how all the quiz statements point to a formula for feeling good about yourself and your sexuality. Here's the formula:

Good information helps you formulate healthy **attitudes and sound values** which lead to wise choices in your **behavior** (actions).

● **Find good information.** There are plenty of places to gather information about sexuality. Check your church, local library or local Christian bookstore for books on sexuality; talk to your mom or dad; initiate a sex education course at your church.

● **Form positive sexual values.** Make smart media decisions. The movies, videos and popular music today are aimed at you—the money-spending teenage market. Hold on to sound beliefs. Look to Jesus, to your parents, and to your beliefs in your own ability to make right choices.

● **Be aware of your behavior.** Face it, whether you like it or not, people judge you by what they see and hear. Your behavior is simply a reflection of what's going on in your head.

Remember: Good information + strong values + honest behavior = a person who can say "I'm free to be me, free to live in Christ!"

—*Barbara Nelson*

DO YOU EVER FEEL LIKE A NOBODY?

1. Before the Bible Study—Gather newspaper, newsprint, Bible, string, tape, yarn, scissors, construction paper, markers, a candle and matches. Number slips of paper one through seven. On each slip, write one of the following verses: Genesis 1:27, 31; Jeremiah 1:4-5; 1 Peter 3:3-4; 1 Timothy 4:12; Job 32:9; Psalms 111:10; 119:99. Write the "What to Do" list on newsprint and post it on the meeting room wall.

2. Nobodies—Divide your kids into small groups and give them newspaper, string, tape, yarn, scissors, construction paper, markers, etc. Tell them to make one of their group members into a "nobody" (they might give him or her crazy facial features, an extra arm, etc.). Vote on the best-looking nobody.

Ask: When do you feel like a nobody? What's it feel like? What can you do about it? How can you notice when other people feel inferior? What can you do to help them?

3. Discuss—Have everyone look at the "What to Do" list. Ask the kids to add other suggestions.

WHAT TO DO

- Refuse to compare yourself to others.
- Realize that God formed you before birth.
- Remember that growth is a process.
- Respond to your shortcomings in the right way.
- Use your abilities to the fullest.
- Set some realistic goals.
- Talk with your friends.
- Talk with God.

—*Teresa Cleary*

4. Bible Study—Hand out slips of paper, numbered one through seven and each having a scripture verse written on it. Ask question number one and then let the person with slip number one read the verse. Encourage discussion.

- What does God think of his creation? (One—Genesis 1:27, 31.)
- But what about each individual person? (Two—Jeremiah 1:4-5.)
- Just what does God see that's special in me? (Three—1 Peter 3:3-4.)
- But I'm so young still; I don't really matter. (Four—1 Timothy 4:12.)
- Don't older people know it all, though? (Five—Job 32:9.)
- How can I feel better about myself? (Six—Psalm 111:10.)
- Will it really help me to improve myself? (Seven—Psalm 119:99.)

5. Affirmations—Tell everyone that God made us each special and unique. We shouldn't feel inferior, because everyone is loved equally by God.

Play an affirming activity called "Warm Fuzzies" from **Building Community in Youth Groups** (Group Books). Form a circle and ask one person to go to the center. Go around the circle and have each person share something he or she appreciates about the person on the "hot seat." Continue until everyone has been affirmed.

Close this exercise with a prayer. Ask each individual to express what he or she appreciates about God.

ARE YOU A CHRISTIAN SNOB?

1. Before the Bible Study—Collect enough baby-food jars (or other small containers) to give one to each person. Ask an artistic young person to design a clever prescription label for the jars. It should say something like: ''Prescription: When you suffer from the painful discomforts of judgmentalism . . . For relief, take one or two verses, as necessary. Warning: Keep this medication within your reach and you will see a great change! In case of further discomforts, contact your Great Physician.'' Make enough copies of the label to attach one to each jar.

Make a list of Bible passages for each person: Matthew 5:44-48; 6:1-5; 7:1-5; 23:25-28; John 7:24; 8:1-11; Romans 2:1, 11; Galatians 6:1-2; 2 Timothy 4:8. Cut the list into separate strips with one verse on each strip. Fold the strips and place a complete list in each person's jar. Keep the jars hidden until that part of the meeting.

Gather a pencil, three small squares of paper, Bible and copy of ''Who, Me?'' for each person. You also will need stickpins and a bulletin board, Styrofoam square or large pincushion.

2. Judgmental Jabs—Gather the group members in a circle. Give each person three small squares of paper. Instruct kids to write a ''judgmental jab'' on each square. The jabs should be judgmental comments they or others have made in the past two weeks.

In the center of the group, place a blank bulletin board or Styrofoam square or large pincushion. As members each tell their jabs, have them stick each square into the object with a stickpin. When everyone's finished, ask: How does judgmentalism jab and hurt people? Why is it so painful? Why do people make judgmental remarks? How does it feel to be ''jabbed''?

3. A Look at Yourself—Have each person complete the following ''Who, Me?'' quiz individually:

WHO, ME?

Are you a judgmental person? Take this quick self-test to see.

Mark each statement yes or no:
  Do I ever judge people:

•by how they look?	Yes☐	No☐
•by the color of their skin?	Yes☐	No☐
•by how they talk?	Yes☐	No☐
•by who their friends are?	Yes☐	No☐
•by where they live?	Yes☐	No☐
•by the school they go to?	Yes☐	No☐
•by the church they go to?	Yes☐	No☐
•by their age?	Yes☐	No☐
•by the country they come from?	Yes☐	No☐
•by their past mistakes with no reference to how they're living now?	Yes☐	No☐
•by their interests?	Yes☐	No☐
•by their intelligence?	Yes☐	No☐
•by their clothes?	Yes☐	No☐
•by what their father or mother does for a living?	Yes☐	No☐
•by what classes they attend?	Yes☐	No☐
•by the house they live in?	Yes☐	No☐

Get any ''yes'' answers? If you did, guess what? You're a bona fide judgmentalist! I hope it's not too surprising since everyone's judgmental in some ways at some times. Cheer up; you can do something about it.

—*Bill Stearns*

4. A Cure—Discuss possible cures for judgmentalism such as: Remember, you're not God. Separate the inner person from how he or she looks. Forget the popular status scale of who's inferior and who's superior.

Ask for other ideas, then give each person a ''Judgmentalism Cure'' jar. Have each person take out one slip of paper, look up the verse listed and tell how it will help when someone's tempted to be judgmental.

Have members close by praying silently for forgiveness for times they've been judgmental. Conclude the prayer by saying: Lord, you hear our prayers and forgive us. Help us to be loving and accepting. Be our Cure. Amen.

5. Just for Fun—Instead of only Bible verses in the jars, add colorful jelly beans for a treat.

28 MIRROR, MIRROR

Your young people are "mirror watchers," observing their own physical images and constantly checking out the human "mirrors" of others for reflections of their own self-images.

In this meeting, young people will examine ways others have helped form their self-images. They'll explore how God's Word reflects his grace and love for them. Finally, they'll practice seeing positive qualities in themselves and each other.

1. Objectives—Participants will:
● discuss things they like and dislike about their mirror images;
● explore and evaluate how reflections from others influence their self-images; and
● experience positive reflections from themselves and each other.

2. Before the Meeting—You'll need a full-length mirror; newsprint; tape; markers; scissors; for each person, a reflective symbol made from construction paper, a "Reflections of Myself" handout and two medium-sized (11×14) sheets of newsprint; and, for every two people, a Bible and a scripture reflections card made from a 3×5 card. Optional: carnival or other kinds of mirrors.

Read the entire meeting.

Type and make copies of the "Reflections of Myself" handout for each person.

Hang or lean the full-length mirror against the wall in the meeting room. On the wall next to it, tape a piece of newsprint with a mirror frame drawn on it, so it looks like a mirror. Place markers on a table nearby.

Prepare "reflective symbols" from construction paper by drawing and cutting out a symbol for every person. Cut out the symbols in pairs and draw on them so they'll be mirror images of each other. Use symbols that fit the theme, such as different kinds of mirrors (hand, round, rear-view, silvered sunglasses) or different things that reflect or shine (stars, moon, diamonds).

Prepare scripture reflections cards—enough so every two kids can have one. Write on 3×5 cards the following scripture references. Use one reference per card. Include Genesis 1:26; Psalm 8:4-9; Psalm 23; Psalm 139:1-6; Psalm 139:13-16; John 3:16; 1 John 3:1-2.

For fun, decorate the room by hanging extra mirrors of different sizes at different levels. Another option: Borrow carnival mirrors that distort images; the kids could have fun with these as they arrive for the meeting. Have everything ready so you'll be able to greet kids as they come in.

3. Mirror Images—As people arrive, ask each one to stand in front of the full-length mirror for a few seconds and write a one- or two-word reaction on the newsprint mirror.

4. Reflective Symbols—Hand out reflective symbols and markers. (Hand out both symbols from each reflective pair.)

Ask the kids to think about the time they stood before the full-length mirror. On the back of the reflective symbols they're now holding, have them write their names, two things they *liked* about their individual mirror image, and one thing they *didn't* like about it. Have them find their "mirror partners" by finding the person whose symbol is the mirror image of their own.

When they find their mirror partners, have them stand facing each other. Ask one member of each pair to be the leader and the other to be a "mirror." The leader, without moving away from where he or she is standing, moves his or her hands, arms or entire body and makes faces while the person being the mirror acts as the reflection of those movements. Allow partners to play for 60 seconds and then have them switch roles. After they play for another 60 seconds, ask them to sit facing each other and discuss what they wrote on the back of their reflective symbols.

5. Reflections of Myself—Explain to the group: Just as mirrors affect how we feel about our physical images, other people act as mirrors to affect how we feel about our whole selves or our self-images. Both what people say to us and how they act toward us reflect how they feel about us, and they help us form images of who we are. People can be mirrors that are just as important to us as mirrors hanging on a wall.

Hand out "Reflections of Myself." Ask the group members to read it and mark their answers.

Allow a brief discussion for each situation. Ask: Does someone else's put-down really make someone a less important person? Why or why not?

6. Three-Way Mirrors—Give newsprint to each person. Ask each to draw a mirror with three sections. Encourage them to be creative, but to leave plenty of room to write in each section. Have kids label each section with one of the following: "Family," "Friends" and "Teachers." They should then write words in each category that they think their families, friends, or teachers would use to describe them. Encourage them to write a minimum of three positive things in each category. Next ask them to circle all the words they agree with.

After they've finished, ask group members to sit facing their mirror partners. Have partners tell each other one item they circled from each category and why. When everyone's finished, tape the mirrors on the wall.

7. God's Image—Give each pair a Bible and a scripture reflections card. Ask each pair to read the verse and determine the most important thing God is saying about them in that verse. Have them decide

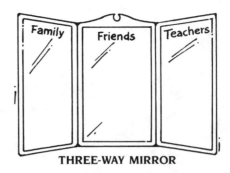

THREE-WAY MIRROR

how that affects how they feel about themselves, and then have each pair develop a short mime or charade to communicate these two things to the group.

When they've had sufficient time to create their mimes, bring the group members together and have all the pairs, one by one, present their mimes. Have the group members guess what they mean, and then have the pairs read their scripture reflection and explain their mimes. Encourage the group to guess each mime's meaning and applaud after each presentation.

REFLECTIONS OF MYSELF

Mark an "X" on the space on each line that best represents your answer.

This is how I feel about myself when . . .

● a friend says: "Thanks for listening to me. I know I can talk to you when I feel bad."

"I'm worthless." _____ **"I'm the best!"**

● my parents say: "Hey, you really did a nice job on the car. You really helped me out!"

"I'm worthless." _____ **"I'm the best!"**

● a teacher says: "So you have the lowest grade in the class. What else is new?"

"I'm worthless." _____ **"I'm the best!"**

● my mom says: "I'm tired of picking up after you. When are you going to stop being such a slob?"

"I'm worthless." _____ **"I'm the best!"**

● my friend says: "That dress looks pretty good on you, even if it is way out of style."

"I'm worthless." _____ **"I'm the best!"**

● my little sister says: "Thanks for fixing my doll. I love you!"

"I'm worthless." _____ **"I'm the best!"**

● a neighbor says: "Will you take care of our cats while we're out of town? We need someone like you we can depend on."

"I'm worthless." _____ **"I'm the best!"**

● a friend ignores me in the hall at school.

"I'm worthless." _____ **"I'm the best!"**

● my teacher writes "good job" at the top of my paper.

"I'm worthless." _____ **"I'm the best!"**

● my dad says: "You never do anything right! That was really dumb!"

"I'm worthless." _____ **"I'm the best!"**

8. Reflective Prayers—Have mirror partners sit on the floor facing each other again. Explain: I'll say a short introductory prayer. When I finish, I'd like you to pray for your mirror partner in your pairs. One of you should start by thanking God for three things about your mirror partner. Then the other member of your pair should do the same. All the pairs can pray at the same time and you may say more than just the three things if you wish. When all of you have finished, we'll say the Lord's Prayer *reflectively*; I'll say a line and you'll repeat it.

Begin the reflective prayers like this: Heavenly Father, you created us in your image, so we can reflect your love and grace to your world. Thank you for the gift of many mirrors you've given us in our parents, friends and your Word. Help us remember we're your people and that even though we're imperfect, your love shines on us. Enable us to shine and help others to shine.

Allow time for mirror partner prayers. Then lead the group in the Lord's Prayer, in which you say each line and have them repeat it in unison.

Close the meeting with group hugs and individual hugs.

—Katie Abercrombie

29 HANDLING FRUSTRATIONS

1. Before the Meeting—Have two or three young people blow up balloons and fill each balloon with one slip of paper. Each slip of paper should have written on it one of these eight words and explanations:

● *Compassion.* As a leader, understand where each person is coming from.

● *Kindness.* Build up the group—even when you're feeling frazzled.

● *Humility.* Humility requires honesty. Admit your mistakes. Then move on.

● *Gentleness.* Gentleness involves speaking with authority and firmness without losing control.

● *Patience.* Patience is the glue that holds a crumbling group together; patience hangs on even when improvement looks impossible.

● *Tolerance.* Some group behavior is acceptable; some violates the limits. The key is balance.

● *Forgiveness.* Take time to reconcile differences and misunderstandings.

● *Love.* As a leader, show love and sincerity. Keep Christ as the center of your love.

If there are more than eight kids in your group, begin the list again. Make as many slips as the number of members in your group. These slips will be used later to break into smaller groups. You'll also need newsprint, markers and sticker labels.

2. Ready to Burst!—Gather group members in a circle.

Toss the balloons in the center and have kids scramble for their favorites. Then have everyone sit down to begin sharing. Ask members to think of a time when they were ready to burst with frustration. Have them each share that time, then pop the balloon. When the slip of paper drops out, have that person read it and tell how putting that word into action could have helped the situation. Continue around the circle until everyone's shared and "popped!"

3. Talk Teams—Have kids create teams by matching with the others in the group who had the same word in their balloons.

Their assignment: Reread your slip of paper and write lists on two separate sheets of newsprint. On one sheet write what happens when you don't practice this word; on the other, what happens when you do practice it.

4. All Together—When everyone's had sufficient time, bring the whole group together. Have the teams tape the "don't practice" sheets on one side of the room, and the "do practice" sheets on the other. As a group, read through the lists. Discuss: What's the difference in the two sets of lists? What do you associate with each set of lists? Which set do you most often act like? How can you improve? How is life easier when the "do practice" lists are in action?

5. Personal Goals—Ask members to each think of which "word" they need to work on the most. Distribute sticker labels. Have kids each write their word on the sticker and stick it on themselves. Then have kids find the others in the group who plan to work on the same thing. Have them form small groups and discuss specific ways to work on their word. For example, if Beth chose compassion, she might say: "I'll call Sara and get together with her Tuesday after school. I want to find out more about her."

6. Closing—Bring the whole group together in a circle. Have one young person read Colossians 3:12-13. As the person reads have the group members take one step into the circle when their chosen word is read. (The whole group should end up one step closer.) Have another young person read Colossians 3:14-17. When the group members hear the words "add love, which binds all things together," have everyone join hands.

 PHOTOGRAPHY/BOB TAYLOR

30

FEELIN' THE BLUES

1. Before the Bible Study—Gather a pencil, Bible, newsprint, marker and copies of the handouts for each student.

2. Opening—Play "Highs—Lows" from **Building Community in Youth Groups** (Group Books). Gather the group in a circle. Go around and ask each member to answer this question: What was the highlight of this past week for you? Why?

Encourage other members of the group to ask questions to clarify or expand the individual's response. Repeat the process with this question: What was the low point of this past week for you? Why?

3. The Blues—Use the exercises on the next two pages to help your young people clarify what causes depression in their lives and how they feel when they're depressed.

4. Discussion—Ask your young people to name some things that make them depressed. How do they know they're depressed? What are the symptoms?

Have your young people think of ways to help beat depression. List these on newsprint. Add these suggestions to the list:

BEAT THE BLUES

- Determine that you really want to get rid of depression.
- Try to identify the basic problem.
- Focus on changing circumstances and changing feelings.
- Look for ways to reward yourself. Do anything to give yourself a positive feeling.
- Do something positive each day. Read the Bible or devotional book, clean something, smile at a friend.
- Set both short-term and long-term goals that you truly believe you can accomplish.
- Work to build open and constructive relationships with friends and family members.

—*John Shaw*

(A copyrighted resource from **GROUP Magazine's Best Youth Group Programs**. Permission granted to copy this list for local church use only.)

5. Bible Study—The following passages are instances or situations when Bible people got depressed. Read the following passages and describe the situations that caused the depression and how the person handled it, if appropriate: Numbers 11:10-15; 1 Kings 19; Psalms 69; 88; 102; Matthew 26:37-40, 75; John 4:1-2.

6. Closing—Have volunteers read through their strategies in "How to Bust Depression." Close by reading 2 Corinthians 12:9.

WHO'S DEPRESSED?

GEORGE
"Stuff It"
Meeks

SYLVIA
"Giggles"
Tupps

JOSH
"Leave Me Alone"
Joshua

SARA
"I Love Everyone"
Lancer

Rank each of these people from 1-10 on how depressed you think they are. "1" is the most depressed, "10" is the least. Place your numbers in the "Depression Quotient" box below each person's name.

Once you've finished, compare your answers with those of your friends. Be sure to tell why you ranked the people the way you did.

Write the name of a person (George, Sylvia, Josh or Sara) on the line beside each of the following questions.

Which person is likely to become depressed the easiest? Why?_____

_____

Which person is least likely to become depressed? Why? _____

_____

Which person has the toughest time with depression? Why? _____

_____

What things cause each person to get depressed?

GEORGE: _____

SYLVIA: _____

JOSH: _____

SARA: _____

How do you suppose each person deals with his or her depression? _____

_____

Do you sometimes have trouble with being depressed? Or do you get those not-so-nice feelings, but don't know where they come from or why you feel that way? If so, work through the following simple exercises. Get ready to deal with those feelings.

ILLUSTRATION/RAND KRUBACK

WHAT'S YOUR DQ?

(Depression Quotient)

Rank each of the following by shading the appropriate amount of each graph.

For example:

When I have to eat in the cafeteria at school.

NEVER DEPRESSES ME		ALWAYS DEPRESSES ME

Try the rest of these for yourself.

When I don't feel well.

Not being included in activities with my friends.

Being overworked.

World problems in general.

My boyfriend/girlfriend.

The opposite sex in general.

My parents.

Stress.

My goals are too high.

Personal problems.

Money.

Thinking about the future.

Other:

CATHY

Cathy couldn't describe the feeling. She felt tired, angry, upset and self-conscious— everything smashed together into one lousy feeling.

And it really bothered her. Christmas wasn't far off. And, knowing that everyone was supposed to be happy and joyful on Christmas made her feel even worse. Why was she feeling this way? What could she do about it?

Can you help her out?

HOW TO BUST DEPRESSION

List things under each of the following steps you can do when you're showing signs of being depressed.

I can reward myself by: (for example, listen to favorite music, watch a funny TV show)

_____

_____

One positive thing I can do each day is: (for example, read the Bible, smile at a friend)

_____

_____

One short-term thing I can accomplish: (for example, finish homework by 8 p.m., call a friend)

_____

_____

One long-term thing I can start working on: (for example, go to college, take more responsibility at church)

_____

_____

One way I can start building open and constructive relationships: (for example, listen better, encourage others)

_____

_____

31

WHAT'S REALLY IMPORTANT?

1. Before the Meeting—Gather a pencil, piece of paper, copies of the handouts on pages 90-92, piece of newsprint and crayon for each person. You also will need masking tape.

2. Setting Priorities—Tell the kids that trying to juggle work, church, school and home is hard to do. It's difficult to determine the importance of one activity over another.

Read Matthew 6:19-21. Ask: What do these verses tell us about setting priorities? For example, since people go to heaven, we could invest our time in building relationships. Or, since we go to heaven, we could invest our time in building personal character. Or, since Jesus is in heaven, we could invest our time time in building our relationship with him.

Distribute pencils and copies of the handouts. Allow time for the kids to complete the exercises.

WHAT I DID THIS SUMMER

Picture this: You've just started to get settled at school when it hits you like a chocolate shake in the face: Your teacher asks what you've done over the summer.

GROUP Magazine editor and mosquito bite specialist Lowell "Bugsy" Schelminsky has prepared a list of topics you can use to impress your teachers and bring instant popularity.

Bugsy's sure-fire topics for "What I Did This Summer":

The week I discovered 16 different ways to floss my teeth

An in-depth soap opera report

How I gained 37 pounds at Maxies Chocolate Parfait Shoppe

My world record sunburn

How I spent $400 at Video-Man and didn't win a free game

My struggle with the heartbreak of psoriasis

How I built an earthworm village this summer

ILLUSTRATION/LAUREL WATSON

PRIORITIZE YOURSELF

Whether or not your summer brought fantastic times, the new school year brings new opportunities and new experiences. It also brings tensions and hassles as you work on setting priorities for your life.

When it comes to setting priorities for my life, I am most like:

prim & proper

putting job first

a terrible mess

cool, calm & collected

a bit confused

a blob

PRIORITIES AND ME

What priority pressures do you face? Take a look at the following priority wheel. Draw a heavy line around three areas where you feel the greatest pressure. Shade in areas where you feel some pressure to set priorities. Use the blank spaces to add other areas where you need to set priorities.

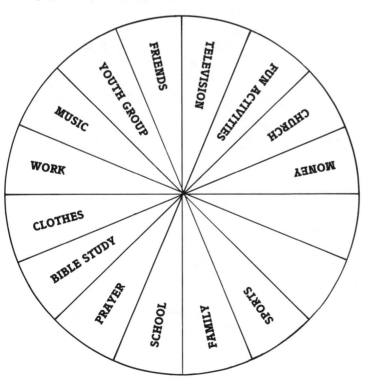

FRIENDS
YOUTH GROUP
TELEVISION
FUN ACTIVITIES
MUSIC
CHURCH
WORK
MONEY
CLOTHES
BIBLE STUDY
PRAYER
SCHOOL
FAMILY
SPORTS

THE BIG QUESTION

Choose a situation or an area where you need to work on setting priorities.

Write the question here:

Should I _____
_____

or should I _____
_____

For instance, your question could read, "Should I stay home and study or should I go with my friends on a youth group retreat next weekend?"

Or, your situation could be, "Should I go to a movie with my friends or should I stay home and give money to a world hunger or missions organization?"

MY PRIORITIZER

Write your "Big Question" one more time in the space below, then check the appropriate box for each question.

Should I _____ or should I _____ ?

	Yes	No	Yes	No
Can I encourage others in this?	☐	☐	☐	☐
Can I build up others in this?	☐	☐	☐	☐
Can I show Christian love to others in this?	☐	☐	☐	☐
Does this choice give me time to think and meditate about my life?	☐	☐	☐	☐
Will this activity contribute toward burnout?	☐	☐	☐	☐
Will this activity leave me feeling refreshed and renewed?	☐	☐	☐	☐
Does this activity keep me from doing God's work?	☐	☐	☐	☐
Does this activity help me exercise my faith?	☐	☐	☐	☐
Will this activity hurt my prayer life?	☐	☐	☐	☐

Based on "My Prioritizer," which activity is better for you at this time?

THE CHOICE

JILL

Jill was active in organizing and leading youth group activities this past summer. In fact, her sponsors would like to see Jill increase her responsibilities as a teenage leader. But she has looked forward to making her school's tennis team. She also wants to spend more time studying and being with her friends.

When she thinks about it much, Jill gets a queasy feeling. If you were Jill what would you do?

What made you decide on that course of action?

BOB

Bob's money situation is tight. He has a part-time job at Burger Freddies, so he has some money to spend. His real problem is deciding what to do with it once he gets paid.

He needs some new clothes. Most of his friends go to movies on weekends. He knows he needs to give 10 percent to the church.

Bob also feels he should give money to a world hunger or missions organization.

He'd planned to save some money for a car and college expenses. But he never seems to have any money left.

If you were Bob, how would you spend your money?

What made you decide on that course of action?

3. Compare Priorities—Divide into groups of three or four and let the small-group members explain how they completed "My Prioritizer."

Give each person a sheet of newsprint or butcher paper and a crayon. Instruct your young people to write their priorities they listed under "Priorities and Me" on their sheet of paper. Tape the priority lists to the wall. Compare the different priorities. Discuss how the priorities differ. Discuss: Is it possible for Christians to have different priorities? Why or why not?

4. Case Studies—Discuss the case studies "Jill" and "Bob." Have your young people meet in groups of three or four and make their own case studies, based on situations they think need to be prioritized.

5. Closing—Give each person a sheet of notebook paper and a pencil. Everyone is to write the statement he or she wrote under "The Big Question." Give your young people 73 seconds to make a paper airplane. Fly the paper airplanes around the room for another 73 seconds. Then, instruct everyone to grab an airplane and pray for the person who wrote the question.

32
SURVIVING THOSE TERRIBLE, ROTTEN, AWFUL PUT-DOWNS

1. Before the Meeting—Gather a pencil and copy of "Put-Downs" for each person. On newsprint, make a "Do" list and a "Don't" list (see step 3). Post these lists.

2. Put-Down Charades—Have everyone sit in a circle. Tell people that you are going to whisper a word in their ears. No one should tell the others what the word is. Give the impression that there is more than one word. Whisper the word "put-down" in each person's ear. When you are finished whispering the word, go around the circle and have your young people act out the word they heard. To portray what they heard, they may only use actions—not words. Don't reveal the word until all have shared their actions. Talk about what was discovered about put-downs by doing this activity. Did everyone do the same thing? What feelings were unearthed? Come up with a group definition of a "put-down."

3. Put-Downs and Me—Ask each member to complete the following exercise. Form groups of three and discuss responses.

Surviving Those Terrible, Rotten, Awful Put-Downs

PUT-DOWNS

How do you handle put-downs? Think of several different situations when you've felt put-down. Look at the things that make up a put-down. Write them in the spaces provided. See if you can make a discovery about yourself and how you deal with the "put-down cycle."

1. Who delivers the blow?
a. _____
b. _____

2. What do they say or do that puts me down?
a. _____
b. _____

5. What can be my Christlike response?
a. _____
b. _____

3. Why does it hurt?
a. _____
b. _____

4. What is my initial reaction?
a. _____
b. _____

Discovery Checklist

	Yes	No
Am I close to the people who put me down?	____	____
Do those people know me well?	____	____
Are most put-downs at home?	____	____
Are most put-downs at school?	____	____
Are most put-downs at church?	____	____
Are most put-downs with friends?	____	____
Am I satisfied with my initial reactions?	____	____
Do I find the Christlike response difficult?	____	____

We don't have much control over other people's actions or words. But we do have a choice about our own. Think about these personal possibilities in handling put-downs:

One thing I'd like to change about myself . . .
Jesus gives me strength in handling put-downs because . . .
Someone I need to forgive is . . .

4. Handling Put-Downs—Say to the kids that too often our response to people who've hurt us is to hurt them back. The Bible gives no magical formula to take away the pain of put-downs, but it does give words of support and strength (1 Corinthians 10:13).

Point out the helpful lists of "dos" and "don'ts" in handling put-downs. Do the young people agree or disagree with the points? Are there any other suggestions the young people could add?

DO
● Pray for patience and God's help. He won't let you down.
● Talk with your offender. The person may not have meant what he or she said to come across as a put-down.
● Be honest. Share your personal feelings by starting sentences with the words "I feel" or "I felt." Be careful not to return a put-down for a put-down.
● Forgive.
● See things in perspective. Think through before reacting.
● Take an honest look at yourself and the person who put you down. Ask if there may be a granule of truth to what he or she said.
● No matter what people say or do, you're still valuable and precious to God.

DON'T
● Think of ways to get even.
● Gossip about the other person.
● Accuse.
● Allow negative statements to control you.
● Let pain and struggle keep you from growing.
The times we mature and grow as persons are probably the times we've hurt the most. So watch for personal growth!

---

5. Role Play—Have group members role play the "Do" and "Don't" lists. Act out the statements one at a time. After each role play talk about the attitudes, feelings and actions they cause.

6. Closing Prayer—Use "Someone I need to forgive is . . ." to spark prayer requests. Join in a prayer huddle. Have each person pray for courage and strength in handling put-downs.

—Joani Schultz

33 FEELING LONELY

1. Before the Meeting—Gather a pencil, 3×5 card and copy of "Rotten Feelings" for each person.

2. Opener—Divide into teams of four or five and role play as many of the following situations as you can. Emphasize that the role plays don't have to be serious. The goal is to portray potentially lonely situations. Allow the different teams five to 10 minutes to prepare. The situations are:

● You dropped the winning pass in the intra-city championship game (or you tripped in a track meet or missed the winning free throw).

● Your friends are taking in a movie and don't ask you. You're sitting at home. The stereo, TV, refrigerator and couch are portrayed by kids and they talk to you as you talk to yourself.

● You've just broken up with a friend and your parents and kid brother/sister don't understand.

3. Loneliness—Get your young people to think about times when they were lonely or how they react to loneliness. Distribute a pencil and a copy of "Rotten Feelings" (pages 96-97) to each person. Let the kids complete all of the activities.

4. A Lonely Group—Give one 3×5 card to each group member. Emphasize that this is an anonymous survey. On one side of the card, have people write how lonely they are right now: use a scale of 1 to 10 ("1" is the least lonely; "10" is the most lonely). On the other side of the card have them list how often they feel lonely: every day, twice a week, once a week, once a month, and so on.

Discuss the results of the survey with the group. Was anyone surprised at the results? Work with the group to set goals and strategies on meeting those needs.

5. Questions—When do you usually feel lonely? How does loneliness make you feel? When and why do lonely feelings usually go away? What do you do to keep from feeling lonely? Why is it that we can be in a crowd and still feel lonely? Should a Christian ever feel lonely? What part should your faith play in helping you deal with loneliness?

6. A Care Outing—Divide into teams of two or three. Go to a mall, park, busy street, bus terminal. The goal is to observe people. As the teams observe different people, have them silently imagine what the person is feeling, why that person might be lonely, and how they could relate to the person.

PHOTOGRAPHY/MICHAEL GOLDBERG

ROTTEN FEE

Check three of the following situations that make you feel most lonely:

- ☐ Your best friend has just moved away.
- ☐ There's no one else around to share your life.
- ☐ You miss three days of school and no one notices.
- ☐ You realize that no one cares how you feel.
- ☐ Your youth group goes on an exciting trip and forgets to tell you about it. You spend the weekend watching TV.
- ☐ You find out that your friends make fun of you behind your back.
- ☐ Eating in the cafeteria alone.
- ☐ You're not sure you'll ever find just the right person for you.
- ☐ No one really understands you.
- ☐ No one listens when you talk.
- ☐ You find out your friends are using you.
- ☐ Your parents separate or divorce.
- ☐ You've just moved to a new school.
- ☐ You go a little too far on a date—and you feel used.

WELL DONE!

- ☐ get wild and crazy
- ☐ tear things up
- ☐ watch 10 straight hours of TV reruns
- ☐ feel sorry for myself
- ☐ become independent—start being my own best friend
- ☐ decide no one gives a rip about me
- ☐ get drunk

When I'm Lonely . . .

Check four ways you react when you feel lonely:

TRY A McLONELY MEAL

The McLonely Cure for Loneliness

One bite and you'll never have to worry about being lonely again—the burger will stay with you forever.

Do a little crazy thinking as you munch on your McLonely Burger—nothing is too stupid.

Ways you can focus on others:

How to let other people know they are important to you:

L I N G S

- [ ] put down people around me with my monumental sarcastic wit
- [ ] join a weird group of people
- [ ] daydream a lot
- [ ] play it safe and don't try anything new
- [ ] decide I'm worth 17 cents
- [ ] eat all the time
- [ ] kick my dog
- [ ] drink a gallon of Scope

DIRECTIONS: Carry this card with you at all times. When you feel lonely, tape or glue this card to your forehead. It is guarantted to work!

Lonely Hearts Fan Club

This card certifies that
. . . .
feels lonely from time to time,
especially when . . . .
. . . .
The bearer of this card can best
be brought out of that rotten state
of loneliness by
. . . .
. . . .

People to risk developing a relationship with:

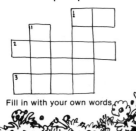

Ways to get to know other people:

Fill in with your own words.

I'm a fake . . . a phony, like a 19-cent plastic figure in the toy section of a cheap discount store. I pretend with award-winning style that I'm carefree and independent . . . like a superstar who needs no one.

But I need you more than you'll ever know. I need you to say hi—to laugh with me—to let me know you care. I'm secretly searching for that smile, laugh or word that lets me know I mean something to you.

Please . . . no matter how independent and uncaring I seem, I need you to tell me by your actions that I'm okay.

You say you're the only lonely person in the world?

Look at me.
I need you.

"Don't be selfish; don't live to make a good impression on others. Be humble, thinking of others as better than yourself. Don't just think about your own affairs, but be interested in others, too, and in what they are doing." —Philippians 2:3-4

34 WHO MAKES UP YOUR MIND FOR YOU?

1. Before the Meeting—Gather a pencil and copies of the article and handouts for each person. You also will need two long ropes.

2. Amoeba Race—Play this game from **More . . . Try This One** (Group Books). Divide your group into two teams and have them remove their shoes. Tie a long rope around each team, bunching everybody to-gether tightly. Set up a course for the two teams to run, perhaps out 50 feet, around a box, over an obstacle, and back again. The teams won't move very fast, but it's great fun.

3. Peer Pressure—Use the following exercises and activities to help your group members think about how peer pressure affects their lives.

A DAY WITH "TEX"

These activities spotlight Morris Schmidt of Herd City High School. (His friends call him "Tex.") One GROUP Magazine staff member and part-time artist Sara "Scratches" Wurtz spent a day with Tex, outlining his activities. Here's her account of Tex's day:

WHAT GETS TO YOU?

For Tex, the hallway is a great place to meet people, tell jokes, see what's going on with other people and a bunch of other stuff. The hall-way also gives him headaches, for it's where he finds out where he fits in with his friends.

When it comes to you fitting in, which of the following situations bothers you most? Use your pen or pencil to shade the bars that follow each situation. For example, if "being a failure" bothers you a lot, you'd shade in the whole bar. If it doesn't bother you much, you'd shade in only a little.

	NO FEAR	SOME FEAR	A LOT OF FEAR	I'M TERRIFIED
being a failure				
being rejected by friends				
looking stupid to people				
looking like a religious fanatic				
not getting invited to a party				
being made fun of				
not being asked out on a date				
asking a person out and getting turned down				

Compare your bars with those of your friends. Why do you and your friends fear the things you do? What are some things that happen as a result of those fears?

ILLUSTRATION/DAVE CARLSON

YOU AND YOUR FAITH

When it comes to living out your faith, which of the following are you more like? Explain.

goes wherever the group goes and does whatever the group does

knows what she wants and believes, takes responsibility for her life and talks with her friends about the pressures she feels

knows the Bible and spouts off all sorts of rules, but life doesn't match talk

fits in well with any group

PRESSURE TO CONFORM

Think for a minute about how you make up your mind. Listed below are several values. In the box above each value, sketch one of the following symbols (found on the right) that best describes which you follow most in making up your mind.

☐ hair style

☐ what you like and dislike

☐ moral beliefs

☐ taste in music

SCHOOL

FRIENDS

☐ which movies to watch

☐ what you do in your free time

☐ religious beliefs

☐ shoe styles

PARENTS

TV

BIBLE

MY OWN IDEAS

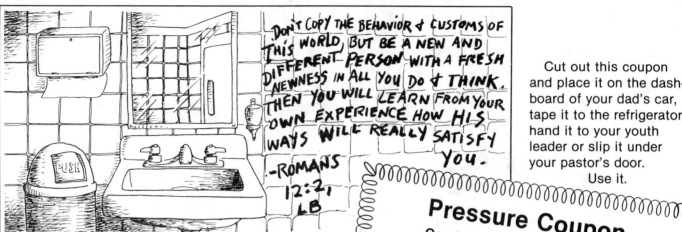

Cut out this coupon and place it on the dashboard of your dad's car, tape it to the refrigerator, hand it to your youth leader or slip it under your pastor's door. Use it.

4. Read—Have the young people read the following information on peer pressure. Then discuss if peer pressure is shaping them into someone they don't want to be.

Pressure Coupon
Good for at least one free talk.
I'm feeling pressure in an area of my life. I'd like to talk about it with you.

_____
SIGNED

WHO MAKES UP YOUR MIND FOR YOU?

Peer pressure is that hungry urge to conform to the standards of others without any conscious or reasonable personal decision to do so. But what can you do if you want to escape the pressures you feel? Here are some suggestions.

● **Set goals.** Do you know where you're going? Do you know what kind of person you want to be or the kinds of things you want to do in your life?

● **Choose a model.** Look past your immediate friends. Whom do you admire? a teacher? a coach? a neighbor? a relative? someone at church? Talk to them. Ask for hints and direction.

● **Talk to others your age.** You'll find they have the same feelings about daily pressures.

● **Decide to take responsibility for your life.** God placed within your hands the responsibility of self development and self control.

Peer pressure has been around a long time. Control it or it will control you. It is God's will that you have the joy of shaping your own life as an offering to him.

—*Charles S. Mueller*

5. Evaluate—Ask your young people to evaluate themselves on how much they think their dress and actions are the result of conformity. Using "Who Makes Up Your Mind for You?" as a starting point, list ways young people can deal with the pressure to conform.

6. Questions—Discuss these questions: What is conformity? Why are most young people so afraid of being rejected by the group? What are good sides to peer pressure? bad sides? Tell about a good or bad time when you felt pressured to go along with the crowd. What are things you do differently when you're with different groups of people? Does being a Christian help you handle peer pressure? If so, how? If not, why not?

7. Closing—Discuss who the students talk to when they feel pressure to go along with the crowd. Do their parents listen? friends? pastors? teachers? Tell the kids that God always is there to listen. Encourage everyone to cut out the "Pressure Coupon" and use it as a helpful conversation starter.

Close with a silent prayer letting the young people pray for any concerns and problems. End the prayer with thanksgiving that God is with us through all of life's ups and downs. We are never alone.

35

DO YOU BELIEVE EVERYTHING YOU HEAR?

1. Before the Bible Study—Gather a pencil, Bible and copies of the handout and test for each person. For snacks, prepare baloney sandwiches.

2. Play "Gossip"—This is an old favorite: Have the group sit in a circle. Begin with the person who enjoys talking the most; have that person whisper a message to the person on his or her right. The person who hears the message whispers it to the next person. Continue around the circle until everyone's heard the whispered message. The last person to hear the message should say it aloud to the group. Play the game a few times. After each round, discuss if the sentence matched the original. If not, talk about why. Then discuss how the game reflects rumors and misconstrued information in real life.

3. Truth-or-Baloney Time—Distribute the following "True-or-Baloney Test." Have each person complete the test individually.

TRUE-OR-BALONEY TEST

_____ 1. When true love hits, you'll know it.

_____ 2. Life is better to a good person than to a mean and nasty person.

_____ 3. God is masculine.

_____ 4. There is no life on other planets.

_____ 5. Life is short, so it's smart to pack in as many experiences as possible.

_____ 6. After Adam and Eve's creation, the different human races developed through evolution.

_____ 7. Money is the root of all evil.

_____ 8. It may be possible to die and be reborn as another person.

_____ 9. The goal in life is to be as happy as possible.

_____10. It's okay to idolize a rock star.

_____11. Your mother had at least one wonderful kid.

Millions of people spend their entire lives believing baloney. Why?

Do You Believe Everything You Hear? continued

Set the test aside. Ask each person to choose one of the following times to share with the group:

● Share a time you trusted your feelings but were wrong.

● Tell a time you ignored the counsel of others and later found their advice was right.

● Talk about a time you did something because of peer pressure.

● Share a time you believed a false rumor and then wished you hadn't.

4. Truth Principles and Quiz Check—Have the young people read the following article and discuss each truth principle separately. Talk about the difficulties in living according to each principle. Then discuss why they're so helpful to follow.

The conclusion of the article gives Bible references and hints about each of the "True-or-Baloney Test" questions. Form groups of four and have each group discuss answers after checking in the Bible.

BALONEY BELIEVERS

Why do humans believe untruths? Perhaps one reason is that we are "not logical." When a couple is experimenting sexually, it's easy to rationalize, "It can't be wrong if it *feels* so right."

So commit this to memory: Depending solely on your senses and feelings can leave you believing in baloney.

Another reason people believe untruths is that they trust "everyone else." They're following the crowd. Throughout history there have been times when people believed:

—the Earth was at the center of the universe.

—traveling faster than 65 mph would kill a human.

So here's another one to remember: Don't believe in what "everyone" says, but think things through and try to decide for yourself.

Finally, sometimes people believe in untruths because they blindly trust authority figures. Your favorite teacher tells you that you have limited career opportunities.

You can respectfully obey the authorities in your life without believing everything they tell you.

How to Know What to Believe

Truth Principle 1: Check with the "source" when you hear a rumor.

Truth Principle 2: Get the facts to get the truth.

● You hear that living on a strict liquid diet will enable you to drop 20 pounds in two weeks. Check the facts in a good nutrition book in the library.

● You hear a girl won't get pregnant the first time she has sex. Check the statistics at any family planning clinic.

Truth Principle 3: Read what God says in the Bible. Going by The Book will take effort and study because

God doesn't always give easy answers. Work through the following study of God's answers to the quiz questions:

1. Read John 15:12. Real love doesn't just hit you; even guy-girl love is something you *decide* to do.

2. See Psalm 73:2-14; Job 21:7-13; 2 Timothy 3:12; and 1 John 3:13. Would the statement be true if it were "The *after*life is better to a good person . . ."? Read Psalm 9:16-18; 73:17-20; and Proverbs 11:18-21.

3. Refer to Genesis 1:27.

4. God knows his universe (see Job 38 and 39), and yet he doesn't mention outer-space life in the Bible. However, nowhere does God state that there are *no* other life forms. Read Ezekiel 1:4-14 to get an idea of how strange some of God's creatures can be, and consider it presumptuous to state conclusively that there is no life anywhere else in the universe.

5. See Psalm 90:10; this statement is true about life on Earth. But think through John 6:51 and Matthew 25:46 to see how long each of us really has to exist.

6. Reread Genesis 1:27.

7. Read it correctly: 1 Timothy 6:10.

8. Read Hebrews 9:27.

9. What is the goal in life? Read Romans 8:29.

10. See Exodus 20:2-17 and Deuteronomy 5:6-22.

11. It's you! No baloney. Read Psalm 139:13-14.

And that's Principle 3: Go by The Book. When you discover God's idea about what you've heard, believe it. He doesn't deal in half-truths or lies.

—Bill Stearns

5. Closing Thoughts—Read John 8:31-32. Join hands for silent prayer. Ask one person to close the prayer aloud, asking for God's guidance with this issue.

6. Baloney!—For fun, serve baloney sandwiches as a snack.

36

FAILURE

1. Objectives—The objectives of this study are:
● to explore failure and the impact it has on our lives.
● to recognize God's promise to be with us through all circumstances.

2. Before the Bible Study—Gather a pencil and Bible for each person. You also will need a skein of yarn and scissors.

3. For Starters—Create a line on the floor using the yarn. Stretch it from one end of the room to the other. Designate each end of the yarn with the answer choices provided. Read the following statements and ask kids to stand beside the place on the yarn that best expresses their answers. Discuss reasons for their choices. Here are the statements:

● I'd describe failure as . . .
birth _____ death
● It's best to . . .
forget failures _____ remember failures
● Failures are . . .
destructive _____ constructive
● Failures . . .
strengthen faith _____ weaken faith

Next have group members line up alphabetically according to first names; one end of the yarn is "A" and the other is "Z." When they are in place, ask them to pick up the yarn and hold it. With scissors, cut the yarn into approximately two-foot pieces, one piece for each person. Beginning with the letter "A," have every four people form small teams.

4. Between the Sprockets—Ask people to keep their pieces of yarn while they lie or sit on the floor with their eyes closed. Allow a minute or two for everyone to relax. Then read the story on the following page. (Make sure you've read through it beforehand so you can add appropriate pauses and expression.)

5. About the Story—Have group members get in their teams of four and complete these sentences:

● The part of the story I identified most with . . .
● If I were the guy in the story, I'd feel . . .
● If I were one of the guy's good friends, I'd tell him . . .
● If I were the teacher who asked him to resign, I'd feel . . .
● If I were the guy, I'd tell the teacher who asked me to resign . . .
● The saddest part of the story was . . .

6. About You—Have each team of four sit close together in a circle. Tell participants to drop their pieces of yarn in front of them; the crumpled piles of yarn will illustrate failure. Have them leave the yarn on the floor during their discussions.

Have group members complete these sentences:
● This pile of yarn is like failure because . . .
● A time I felt like a failure . . .
● When I fail it's comforting to know . . .
● (Read Romans 5:3.) These words can be comforting because . . .
● Failure can be seen as potential for new life when . . .
● (Read Romans 8:31-39.) The good news in these words is . . .
● (Read Job 1:13—2:10.) I'd describe Job's attitude as . . .
● God's attitude toward Job was . . .
● God's attitude toward me is . . .
● (Read Job 1:21 and 2:10.) A time I've felt like that was when . . .

7. Closing—Ask group members to pick up their yarn pieces. Talk about how picking up the yarn and starting over is like failures and fresh starts. Have everyone complete these sentences:
● Picking up the yarn and starting over is like the time I . . .
● (Read Romans 8:28.) God helps me start over by . . .

Have each team create a yarn symbol of hope.

Get all group members together in a big circle. Ask each team to show and share the meaning of its symbol.

Failure continued

Read Romans 8:37 aloud. Have each person in the circle say to the person on his or her right, "(Name), you have complete victory through him who loves us."

Pray: Lord, we thank you that you haven't abandoned us. You promise to work things out for good with those who love you. That means you take our failures and bring new life and hope to us. Forgive us, renew us and help us to trust in your victory promises. Amen.

—Joani Schultz

BETWEEN THE SPROCKETS

The jocks were at the top of the social heap in our school. It was hard to find a rung on the ladder if you didn't hang out in locker rooms.

I thought that I had found my place when I heard a public announcement one morning. I went to the organizing meeting of the Projection Club. We were the people who ran the movie projectors. The 15 people in the room looked like losers to me. They were the funny kids who were shorter and had more zits than did the more popular students. It seemed that most of them wore glasses. Looking back at the scene from my perspective as an adult, I know that they were also the more intelligent kids. They were the ones who would go on to do some significant things in the technical field.

The teacher who sponsored the club took several sessions to train us. At that time in American educational history, the audio-visual field was considered the salvation of the public school. Just aim the 16mm projector at a screen and the students will learn what they need to learn. This meant that we were cautioned about the use of the equipment. "You must be very careful never to damage the equipment. More importantly, *never* damage the film!"

Unfortunately, I really didn't fit into this group. I wasn't into science fiction and didn't have superior technical interest. It is true that I had more zits than normal and was short, though.

My first test as a member of the Projection Club came with the showing of a government film. About 300 kids filed into the auditorium with its nailed-down desk chairs. I had the machine threaded and ready to roll. A sense of power swelled in me. You would have thought that I was the projectionist at Radio City Music Hall or something. I kept my feet in the aisle as the kids filed past me. I wanted them to see and know who was at the helm. On my shirt everyone could see the bold yellow badge, Projection Club. An automatic hall pass!

I signaled for the lights to be lowered. I switched on the Bell and Howell and let the 45-minute film roll. The picture was fine. However, the sound was strange. The music and words growled out at us. No one complained. The teachers didn't even seem to be listening to the sound track. I kept checking and twisting knobs. The machine seemed to be working fine.

About 10 minutes into the movie, I noticed that the take-up reel was completely filled. How could this be? As I looked closely at the film coming out of the projector, I realized in horror what was happening. I had misthreaded the film. The projector was systematically punching new sprocket holes between each set of existing holes! The color film was being completely ruined.

That afternoon I was asked to resign from the Projection Club. One teacher even hinted that the FBI would probably be checking up on me for having destroyed government property.

PART THREE:
RELATIONSHIPS

37 HOW TO LIGHT UP SOMEONE'S LIFE

1. Before the Meeting—Purchase enough small candles to be able to give one to each person in the group. You also will need matches, paper, pencils, ribbon, scissors, thin cardboard, glue, gold seals, crayons, markers, etc.

2. In the Dark—Begin the meeting in the dark. Have group members sit in a circle.

Distribute unlighted candles to everyone. Have group members, one by one, tell about one person who's been a light in their life. As each person shares, he or she should light the candle. At the end of this exercise, all the candles should be lighted.

When everyone's finished, ask: How is receiving encouragement and compliments like light in the darkness? How do you receive compliments? Are you more a receiver or giver of encouragement? Explain. What feelings does encouragement bring? (Blow out the candles.)

3. Applauding Others—Tell the group that one way to light up people's lives is to express your appreciation and "applaud" them.

Have members form groups no larger than 10 people. Give each group only one lighted candle. The person with the candle starts by saying something positive about someone in the group *without mentioning that person's name*. After the words of encouragement have been spoken, the person with the candle hands it to the one he or she was talking about.

PHOTOGRAPHY/JOE COCA

The process continues until everyone's received the candle *at least* once. (Blow out the candle.)

4. Expressing Love—Tell the youth that another way to light up people's lives is to openly express your love to them.

Give each person a sheet of paper and a pencil. For the next five minutes (depending on the size of the whole group) have kids hug as many people as possible and get their autographs.

5. People Who've Triumphed—Point out to the kids that a method of encouragement is to remind one another of people who nearly failed, but triumphed in the end; for example, David, Elijah, Moses and Peter.

Bring the group together and have everyone join hands. As a circle prayer, have each person give a prayer of thanks for someone they know who's nearly failed but triumphed. For example, it could be a Bible person such as Paul or Abraham, or it could be Aunt Susan who's bravely recovering from cancer treatment.

6. Affirmation—Play an affirming activity from **Building Community in Youth Groups** (Group Books). Divide the class in half and appoint a leader for each group. Tell the students that they will be creating awards for each individual in the other group. The awards must focus on positive qualities and refrain from offensive humor and put-downs.

Distribute the ribbon, scissors, cardboard, glue, etc. Instruct each group to go to a separate room and brainstorm for ideas for an award for each individual in the other group. Have them use the art supplies to create the awards.

Reunite and hand out the awards one at a time. Explain how each award was selected.

7. A Hopeful Reminder—Once again gather the group members in a circle. Give each an unlighted candle. Have one young person begin by lighting someone's candle and saying, "(Name), keep this candle as a reminder of the light and love we have as Christians." Then the next person passes on the light and repeats the same words.

In the glow of lighted candles, sing songs of hope and light. How about "This Little (Gospel) Light of Mine" or "You Light Up My Life"?

BUNDLES OF BLESSINGS

Sometimes it's easier to see someone else's blessings rather than our own. Here's a way to help your young people look closely at one another's blessings. It also provides each group member a special over-a-long-period-of-time way to rejoice in what he or she *does* have.

Begin by explaining how to create a "bundle of blessings" for each person. Give each person *at least* one sheet of paper for each group member.

Ask young people to write at least one thing about each person in the group that they feel that particular person can be thankful for and tell why. Have them complete the sentence: "You, (name), can be thankful for . . ." Encourage group members to complete the sentence more than once for each person. Make sure they write something positive, something they admire about the other person's life. Remember to include tangible and intangible blessings. (Some examples include: You can be thankful for your sparkling smile because it always brightens my day; you can be thankful for your ability to run on the track team—it demonstrates your determination; you can be thankful that you have two parents who love you—that's something to treasure!) Group members have the option to sign their blessing reminders.

Have them write one answer per piece of paper, then roll the paper into a scroll and tape it closed with transparent tape or a brightly colored sticker. Gather the scrolls together for each person. (Make sure you don't confuse whose bundle is whose!) Provide brightly colored ribbon to tie "bundles of blessings" together. For an added touch, attach a gift tag that says, "(Name), you've got a lot to be thankful for!"

Tie the bundles, attach the tags and have everyone take his or her "bundle of blessings" home. Invite group members to open scrolls one at a time—and only when they feel down or think there's nothing to be thankful for.

38 THE PORTRAIT OF TRUE FRIENDSHIP

1. Before the Bible Study—Collect a pencil, Bible, piece of paper and copy of "True Friendship" for each person. You also will need masking tape.

2. Comparisons—Have your kids read the following information and compare their best friends with the friendship traits. Then have them compare themselves with the traits.

3. Stick Together Friendship—Divide your group into pairs. Have each pair stand back to back as you tape them together around their waists with masking tape. Then have the pairs run an "obstacle" course: forward, backward, sideways, pick objects off the floor, etc. The funniest pair wins a roll of masking tape.

4. Friendly Sculptures—Divide into teams of four to six. At least two members of each team will be the sculpture. The goal is to mold the sculpture people into some form that says something about friends or friendship. If you wish, use old sheets to cover the "sculptures." Then uncover each masterpiece as the non-sculpture team members explain the sculpture.

5. Bible Study—Ask everyone to list the qualities or principles of friendship found in the following passages: Proverbs 17:17; 27:6; Mark 11:25; 12:30-31; John 4:7-15; 21:15-22; Romans 12:10; Ephesians 5:21; 1 Thessalonians 5:11.

6. Best Friends/Worst Friends—As a group, list the qualities that make someone a best friend. Make another list of things that make people "worst" friends.

Choose the top five best and worst qualities. Have each person evaluate himself or herself on each of the best and worst qualities.

Discuss ways people can become stronger friends.

7. Closing—Ask each of the kids to think of one good friend. Commission each of the students to call the friend during the next week and say why they appreciate him or her.

TRUE FRIENDSHIP

Many have heard the name of David; far fewer have heard the name of Jonathan. Jonathan was one of the single greatest strengths in David's memorable life—Jonathan was his best friend.

They were from opposite backgrounds: David was a shepherd boy; Jonathan was the son of a king. Yet God gave them a rich friendship that stands out among others in the Bible.

What are some characteristics of friendship we can learn from Jonathan?

● **Love deeply.** The Bible says Jonathan loved David as much as he loved himself—and he loved him like this from the start. See 1 Samuel 18:1.

● **Be willing to sacrifice.** Jonathan at first gave his personal garments to David, then later nearly gave his life because of his loyalty to David. Friendship takes guts. See 1 Samuel 18:4 and 20:30-34.

● **Always speak well of your friend.** More than once, Jonathan delayed his father's attempts to kill David, by pointing out the good David had accomplished for Saul's kingdom. What good things have your friends done lately? See 1 Samuel 19:4-7.

● **Keep your promises.** Jonathan made many promises to David—promises that required risks and danger—and he kept each one. Talk about building trust! See 1 Samuel 20:12-42.

● **Help your friend realize God's purpose for his life.** Jonathan went out of his way to encourage David in the purpose God had for him. Ever genuinely considered what God's will is for your friends—and then helped them think about it? See 1 Samuel 23:15-18.

For more insight into true friendship, read about David and Jonathan in 1 Samuel chapters 18—20, 23 and 2 Samuel chapter 1.

—*Cindy Parolini*

39

A LOVE BIBLE STUDY

The passage, "When I was hungry you fed me, thirsty and you gave me a drink . . ." is central to Jesus' story of the final judgment. Most of us have heard those words more than once. But they just don't sink in.

We complain, "If we'd known it was Jesus—*that* would have been different!" And that's the point! Anybody can "put on" love for a little while. But it's the day-in-and-day-out love that matters most.

Let this relational "love" study motivate your group to action.

1. Objective—To re-evaluate love in terms of Jesus' words, "Whenever you did this for one of the least important of these brothers of mine, you did it for me" (Matthew 25:40).

2. Before the Bible Study—Read the following imaginative "love" journey ahead of time; become acquainted with the exercise and appropriate pauses to effectively lead the group.

Get Bibles, pencils, paper, newsprint, markers and background music.

3. Take an Imaginative "Love" Journey—Begin with group members finding a comfortable spot to lie down or relax. Make sure each person has enough space so nobody's touching. Play soft background music. (Neil Diamond's **Jonathan Livingston Seagull**, Columbia Records, is good.)

Explain that you're taking the group members on an imaginary "love" journey; you need their attention and cooperation.

Say: Close your eyes . . . Take a few deep breaths . . . And relax . . . Ease the tension out of your muscles . . . Begin with your toes . . . Relax your toes . . . Your feet . . . Your legs . . . Your hips . . . The trunk of your body . . . Your arms . . . Your hands . . . Your shoulders . . . Your neck . . . Relax your head . . . Breathe slowly and concentrate on easing all the ten-

sion out of your body . . . (pause) . . . Now think of everybody who's here in this room right now . . . How do you feel about being with these people? . . . Are you comfortable? . . . Do you wish you were somewhere else? . . . Get in touch with those feelings . . . Now think of one specific person in the group who you feel needs a special dose of love right now . . . Maybe it's someone you know well . . . Maybe it's someone you hardly know at all . . . Focus in on that one person in your mind . . . Picture that person . . . How that person looks and acts . . . How that person feels to be around you . . . What does that person need most right now . . . What is something that you can say or do that would help that person realize how much you care? . . . Think of some ways you can make that happen . . . Now imagine someone has just given you a special message about that person . . . And the message is this: The person you've chosen to love is actually Jesus Christ . . . What feelings do you have about that message? . . . Does it make you feel guilty? . . . Self-conscious? . . . Excited? . . . Get in touch with those feelings . . . In Matthew 25:40, Jesus says, "I tell you, whenever you did this for one of the least important of these brothers of mine, you did it for me!" . . . Just imagine! . . . The way you love other people is really another way of loving God . . . Think about that . . . Then when you're ready, slowly open your eyes.

4. Talk About Your Journey—Now talk about the imaginary "love" journeys. Use this guideline: Don't tell the person's name thought of in the journey. The reasons: The discussion won't put anyone on the spot and the anonymity will create an interesting dynamic for sharing. Encourage members to follow up on their "love" thoughts later.

Ask: What feelings did you have about the group? What process did you use in choosing one person? How was it difficult? How did you feel about the person really being Jesus Christ? What did you learn about yourself during the journey?

Find two volunteers to read Matthew 25:31-45, alternating verses.

Ask: Would you treat someone differently if you discovered that the person really is Jesus? Why or why not? What is our motivation for love? Read 1 John 4:19. Is this verse always true? Why or why not?

5. Create "Love" Questions—Form teams of three. Have each team read 1 John 4:20-21 and discuss: How can you separate the love of God and the love of people? If we hate a person, do we hate God too? Explain.

Ask teams to create questions to "stump" the other teams. The questions must come from 1 John 4:20-21.

Bring the teams together to ask the other teams their questions.

Say: One problem in loving is an inability to recognize Jesus among us. Have one young person read Luke 24:13-16. Ask: What are the barriers on the road to Emmaus? How can we remember Jesus is with us?

6. Pray Together—Have group members sum up one thing they've learned from this study. Instruct members to write their learnings on a piece of paper and place it in the middle of the group.

Stand in a circle. Have everyone grab a different piece of paper from the center and read the learnings as a prayer of thanks.

Close the circle prayer with an amoeba hug: Two people hug; then three; then four; until the entire group becomes the amoeba.

PROGRESSIVE POST CARDS

Ask each person to think of someone who needs special love right now. Distribute three post cards, construction paper or 3×5 cards to make "original" post cards. Have each person think of a three-word message. For example: "I love you," "You are loved," "You are special," or "Thanks so much!" Instruct group members to design the post cards with one word per card, and then mail the post cards, one day at a time, so the recipient gradually gets all the cards and adds the message together. The more economically minded can send "Thanks" or "Love"; the more extravagant can send "I'm so glad you're in my life!"

40
A LOVE PRAYER IN ACTION

1. Before the Prayer Experience—Let your group members discover a personal message through the prayer of St. Francis.

In preparation, ask an artistic young person to copy the prayer of St. Francis in nice print or calligraphy. (The prayer is printed below.) Make a copy of the prayer for everyone in the group.

Gather the following supplies: upbeat music—records or tapes if no one plays guitar; rhythm instruments (wood blocks, tambourines, rhythm sticks, whatever); marigold or zinnia seeds; potting soil;

PRAYER OF ST. FRANCIS

LORD make me an instrument of your peace.
Where there is hatred, let me sow love;
where there is injury, pardon;
where there is doubt, faith;
where there is despair, hope;
where there is darkness, light;
and where there is sadness, joy.

O DIVINE MASTER, grant that I may
not so much seek to be consoled as to console;
to be understood as to understand;
to be loved as to love;
for it is in the giving that we receive,
it is in the pardoning that we are pardoned,
and it is in the dying that we are
born to eternal life.

---

planting containers (cups, milk carton halves, tiny clay pots, etc.); newsprint; marker; paper; and pencils.

2. Instrument of Peace—Provide rhythm instruments for everyone. Begin with a grand musical celebration. If some young people play guitar, encourage them to accompany your group's favorite songs. If no one in the group is musically inclined, play upbeat records or tapes for the group to accompany with their rhythm instruments. Have fun!

After a sufficient musical celebration, have a young person read the first line of the prayer: "Lord, make me an instrument of your peace."

Invite each group member to choose an instrument (not necessarily the ones in your midst) that best describes him or her and tell why. Ask the group: Why is an instrument a good illustration for God's people? How does God use you, as an instrument, to bring peace?

3. Sow Love—Have another young person read: "Where there is hatred, let me sow love; where there is injury, pardon; where there is doubt, faith; where there is despair, hope; where there is darkness, light; and where there is sadness, joy."

Write the following words on newsprint: hatred—love; injury—pardon; despair—hope; darkness—light; sadness—joy.

Tell group members to each think of five different people they know who are struggling with those five different issues. Say: On paper, write the category and a struggling person you know for each. For example: despair—hope: "My aging grandmother feels like there's nothing left to live for." Then beside it, write a practical, measurable, helping action you can accomplish. For example: "I will call my grandmother tonight just to say I care." Do that for each category.

write a practical, measurable, helping action you can accomplish. For example: "I will call my grand-mother tonight just to say I care." Do that for each category.

When everyone's completed the written task, get out the potting soil, containers and seeds. Have group members each take five seeds, one for each person they plan to help, and plant the seeds in the container. Use individual take-home containers or one large youth group "prayer pot" to remind the group of its ministry efforts.

Invite group members to tell about one of the five people they chose and explain what they plan to do.

4. Seek to Console—Have another young person read the next portion of the prayer: "O divine master, grant that I may not so much seek to be con-soled as to console; to be understood as to under-stand; to be loved as to love."

Give these instructions: Everybody find a partner. After I finish these instructions, the two of you find a nearby, quiet place to talk together. Each person will have about two minutes to tell the other person one problem he or she is struggling with right now. It can be a problem at church, school, home, work, what-ever. While one talks, the other person listens atten-tively. This is how we'll put this prayer into practice. After two minutes, it's the other person's turn to talk while the other listens. I'll call "time" after each two-minute segment.

After four minutes, call the whole group together. (Depending on the relationships in the group, this portion may take longer. That's okay, because it's a great opportunity for ministry within the group.)

5. Give—Ask another young person to read: "For it is in the giving that we receive; it is in pardoning that we are pardoned; and it is in dying that we are born to eternal life."

List these three prayer portions on newsprint:
- In giving we receive.
- In pardoning we are pardoned.
- In dying we are born to eternal life.

Ask: Why are those sentences sometimes difficult to understand? How do the words contradict the world's point of view? Give examples. Which of the three lines holds the most meaning for you person-ally? Why?

6. Closing—Give each group member a copy of the prayer prepared beforehand. Close your "prayer in action" by joining hands and praying together the prayer of St. Francis.

PARENTS' TREASURE HUNT

Give at least 10 note cards or slips of paper to each group member. Instruct kids to write on each a special word of care for their par-ents. Words could include, "I love you, Mom"; "Thanks for helping me with my homework, Dad"; "You're a great cook." Then have each young person go home and place the notes throughout the house to surprise parents. Suggest that they put them on the bathroom mirror, in a cupboard door, in the refrigerator, on the car's steering wheel, in a favorite cof-fee cup.

Planting these notes throughout the house brings hours of fun and care—something par-ents will treasure.

41

DEALING WITH FAMILY PROBLEMS

Families come in various shapes and sizes. Some are two parent families; others are single-parent families. Still others are no-parent families. Some families are large, some small. Traditional family members were related by birth. But that's not always the case with contemporary families. Some families exist because of circumstance. Others exist because of convenience.

For this Bible study, "family" is defined as the group of people God intends us to relate to most intimately.

Along with family intimacy comes family problems. That's because people are different; God made us that way. In the beginning those differences were good. But sin got in the way. Today those differences mean conflict.

This Bible study will help your group members face their family struggles. It will also give hope for healing.

Dealing With Family Problems continued

1. Objectives—Use this Bible study to:
- discover basic biblical principles for parent/teenager relationships;
- consider positive and negative aspects of family relationships; and
- realize the responsibility of ministry to family members.

2. Before the Bible Study—For this Bible study you'll need: a Bible for each person, pencils, paper, large sheets of newsprint, colored marking pens, masking tape and a box of large or medium-sized Band-Aids.

Skim the entire Bible study for an idea of its content. Carefully read each section you plan to use. Make notes for yourself and anticipate the time needed to do each section.

During the study, be sensitive to group members who come from less traditional homes such as single-parent and blended families. Know what kind of home environment the participants come from. Remember: Talking about families is a delicate and difficult issue with some young people. As much as possible, anticipate the needs of the group. Don't be afraid to confront painful issues, but be ready to deal with the potential emotions expressed.

Have additional adults present who have good counseling and relational skills. Use them to provide "one-on-one" counseling if needed.

3. For Openers—Bring the group together in a circle. Ask each person to complete this sentence: "One word that describes family is . . ." Encourage kids to give reasons for their responses. Ask one young person to record all the words on newsprint for display during the Bible study.

State the purpose of the Bible study. Say: During our time together we'll seek what the Bible says regarding family relationships. We'll also discover new ways to minister within our family structures.

Encourage openness and honesty. Remind participants to establish a Christian community that supports and encourages each other. (Offer the possibility of an ongoing family support group as a result of this study.)

4. Into the Word—Make sure everyone has a Bible. Have someone read aloud Ephesians 6:1-4.

Distribute paper and pencil to each person. Ask participants to read Ephesians 6:1-4 again, this time silently to themselves.

This portion of Ephesians deals with the responsibility to both parents or guardians and children. Have each young person write two paragraphs: One paragraph on the passage's implications for parents; the other on its implications for children. Allow five to seven minutes for everyone to finish writing.

When all have completed the task, divide kids into groups of four to six people each. Give each small group a large sheet of newsprint and a marking pen. Ask small group members to divide the paper into two columns. On one side they should write "Parent Responsibilities" and on the other, "Youth Responsibilities."

Ask small group members to each share their two paragraphs with their small group. After all have shared, have small groups discuss the various parent or youth responsibilities and record all their ideas on newsprint in the appropriate columns.

As small groups finish, have kids tape their newsprint sheets on the wall.

Refer the entire group to Exodus 20:12. Write the following questions on newsprint. Allow the whole group to react to them.
- How does Ephesians 6:1-4 compare with God's plan as stated in the commandments (Exodus 20:12)?
- Is it realistic to think in these terms today? Why or why not?
- How has our modern society distorted God's concept of the family?

5. The Reality—Say: Conflicts are a reality within the family. Sin shows its effect—even within the homes of God's people. Next let's look at potential problems which can develop between parents and teenagers.

Break the larger group into small groups of four to six people again. Direct group members to look at two Old Testament family relationships:
- Isaac, Rebekah, Jacob and Esau (Genesis 27:1-29); and
- Saul and Jonathan (1 Samuel 19:1-3; 20:1-16).

Ask each group to develop a role play based on a specific area of concern between parents and teenagers. The role play could be sparked from the Bible reading or modern-day issues. For example, a parent confronting a teenager who comes home after curfew, or a teenager who receives a failing grade and won't be able to graduate on time. Allow about fifteen minutes for each group to plan and share its role plays with the large group.

List on newsprint the problem areas shared from the role plays. Have participants add additional concerns to the list based on personal experience. Raise these concerns to help participants see that most families share the same problems. Keep the discussion open and honest. The adult leaders working in the small groups should be reminded not to criticize or belittle any concern raised.

6. Healing—Direct the group's attention to Ephesians 3:14-21. If all participants share the same Bible translation have them read the passage together. If they don't have similar translations, ask for a volunteer to read the passage aloud.

Encourage young people to share how love affects family relationships. Emphasize the overriding theme of love which needs to influence all our relationships.

In the large group discuss the following questions. Keep in mind Ephesians 6:1-4.
- Where does the power to love come from?
- What is the best example of love?
- How is it possible to accomplish even the most difficult task?
- What are ways to ensure a loving atmosphere within a home? (Examples: family devotions, prayer)
- What should be our response when someone treats us unfairly? Should our reaction be different if that someone happens to be our parent or a member of our family? Why or why not?

7. Closing—End this study with one of these prayer experiences:
- Distribute Band-Aids so each person, including counselors, has one. Ask participants to each think of at least one hurt their family has at the present time. Then have them each stick the Band-Aid on the back of their hands. Have group members say a silent prayer for healing of the hurt as they apply the Band-Aids.
- Distribute Band-Aids. Write Ephesians 6:1-4 on a sheet of newsprint. Have everyone read the verse in unison. Then have group members apply their Band-Aids representing family hurts to the newsprint. Close with group members praying for one another.

8. Follow-Up—This Bible study could require some special follow-up since it emphasizes uncovering family problems. The following suggestions offer potential for continued discussion which could involve both youth and their parents. Close the Bible study by discussing different options with the group. Be open to additional suggestions the group might generate.

- *Monthly youth/parent nights*—Consider monthly or short-term events to which both youth and parents are invited.

Allow time for small group discussion at these events. Both teenagers and parents can benefit from hearing others in similar situations who share the same problems and concerns.

Helpful discussion materials are available from Serendipity House, Box 1012, Littleton, CO 80160.

- *Troubled families support group*—Provide support and insight for families with serious problems. Privately invite teenagers from hurting families to meet regularly. If you don't feel qualified to handle a support group such as this, seek outside professional help in carrying out this vital ministry.

Consider a similar support group for parents. This could be more difficult to begin since your initial contact is with the young people.

- *Film or speaker series*—Sponsor a film series dealing with parent and teenager relationships. One series by Family Films (14622 Lanark Street, Panorama City, CA 91402) features comedian Pat Hurley. One film, **Moms, Dads and Other Endangered Species** would be particularly appropriate. Another excellent series is the **Lutheran Family Challenge Series** (Lutheran Family Challenge, 405 S. Rush, Roselle, IL 60172). The youth could take a freewill offering to help cover expenses, serve refreshments, and offer a babysitting service for parents with younger children.

- *Parent-teenager dinner*—Host a meal at the church for parents and teenagers in your congregation. Create a cozy, warm atmosphere for sharing. How about small tables for four, candlelight and soft background music? Give each parent-teenager team a copy of the "Table Talk" menus (see pages 116-117).

Close by bringing the whole group together to share insights. A special devotion and prayer would be appropriate.

- *Communication skills*—Teach a class on listening and communication skills. Invite parents of teenagers, teenagers or a combination of both. Send copies of "Table Talk" menus (see pages 116-117) home with participants to encourage further conversation.

- *Retreat*—Plan a retreat, camp out or lock-in for parents and teenagers. Often the move to a different environment and more relaxed atmosphere allows for more open communication.

—Tom Couser

42

TABLE TALK

Parent's Menu

A Fine Assortment of Questions to Ask Your Teenager

HOW TO USE "TABLE TALK"

These "Table Talk" menus happen to be "conversation menus"; they're meant to help you make new discoveries about each other. You're free to select and ask questions from any section. You can use the menus again and again for listening and finding out more about your family members. "Table Talk" promises to bring a new and exciting perspective to your relationship.

But before beginning, there's one important rule: The person who asks the questions must *listen*. No arguments, defensiveness, put-downs or shouting allowed. Just listening and understanding. (Remember, this is "Table Talk," not "Family Fight"!)

So go ahead. Ask the questions and see what course your conversation takes!

Appetizers
Ask: What's your favorite and tell me why.
- your favorite time of the day
- your favorite room in the house
- your favorite subject in school
- your favorite food
- your favorite kind of music

Soups 'n' Salads
Ask: When was the last time you felt . . .
- glad?
- mad?
- confused?
- embarrassed?
- thankful?
- pressured?
- content?
- hurt?

A La Carte
Read Ephesians 4:2: "Be always humble, gentle, and patient. Show your love by being tolerant with one another."

What quality is most important to our relationship—humbleness, gentleness, patience or tolerance? Why?

Together decide practical ways to show these qualities of love to one another.

The Main Course
Ask: What item on the table best describes your feelings about . . .
- your friends?
- your family?
- your grades?
- your church?
- dating?
- your parents?
- work?
- your home?
- your choice of clothes and hairstyle?
- yourself?
- your faith?
- your choice of music?

(Don't forget to have your teenager explain why!)

Dessert
Complete one or more of these sentences:
- Our most memorable family meal together was . . .
- Three things I really appreciate about my parent(s) are . . .
- What I enjoy most about my family is . . .
- What I need most from my parent(s) right now is . . .
- One thing I'd really like to say is . . .

A MESSAGE TO THE LEADER

Looking for ways to improve the quality and quantity of communication between parents and teenagers? Use "Table Talk"!

Some researchers say parents and kids *want* to talk with each other—but they don't know where to begin. Here's a fun tool to encourage conversation between moms, dads and teenagers. It can break old patterns of communication and help start new ones. "Table Talk" is designed for use at the table during family mealtimes. Parents and young people ask questions from their "menu" selections and make special discoveries about one another.

Give copies of "Table Talk" to both parents and teenagers. Challenge them to communicate with one another. Remind them they can have fun doing it too!

Use "Table Talk" as part of class for improving listening and communication skills of parents and teenagers.

Table Talk — *Teenager's Menu*

A Fine Assortment of Questions to Ask Your Parent(s)

HOW TO USE "TABLE TALK"

These "Table Talk" menus happen to be "conversation menus"; they're meant to help you make new discoveries about each other. You're free to select and ask questions from any section. You can use the menus again and again for listening and finding out more about your family members. "Table Talk" promises to bring a new and exciting perspective to your relationship.

But before beginning, there's one important rule: The person who asks the questions must *listen*. No arguments, defensiveness, put-downs or shouting allowed. Just listening and understanding. (Remember, this is "Table Talk," not "Family Fight"!)

So go ahead. Ask the questions and see what course your conversation takes!

Appetizers

Ask: What's your favorite and tell me why.
- your favorite day of the week
- your favorite time of the year
- your favorite way to relax
- your favorite place to visit
- your favorite sport

Soups 'n' Salads

Ask: When was the last time you felt . . .
- happy?
- discouraged?
- satisfied?
- zany?
- angry?
- put down?
- pressured?
- carefree?

A La Carte

Read James 1:19: ". . . Everyone must be quick to listen, but slow to speak and slow to become angry."

What makes this verse difficult to follow? What could we do to make it easier?

Together devise a specific plan to put this verse into action in your communication.

The Main Course

Ask: What item on the table best describes your feelings about . . .
- right now?
- your work?
- your friends?
- your child(ren)?
- your expectations of me?
- church involvement?
- family relationships?
- God?
- the future?
- the past?
- the present?
- being a parent?

(Make sure your mom or dad gives reasons for answers.)

Dessert

Complete one or more of these sentences:
- I wish we'd be able to . . .
- Three qualities I really admire in my teenager are . . .
- I'm really proud of my teenager when . . .
- If I could be alone with my teenager for one whole day, I'd like to . . .
- One thing I need from my teenager right now is . . .

43
WHY IS IT SO HARD TO SAY "I LOVE YOU"?

1. Before the Bible Study—Gather a pencil, Bible and copy of "I Love You" for each student. You also will need newspapers, magazines, tape, staples and markers.

2. Opener—Divide into teams. (Adapt the size of the teams to the number of young people at this session.) Give each team one of the following roles: Dad, Mom, Brother, Sister, Dog, Cat. Bring newspapers, magazines, tape, staplers, markers and other junk to this session. Each team chooses a person to be the Mom, Dad—whatever they've been assigned—and dresses that person up as humorously as possible. Set a time limit of 15 or 20 minutes.

After the time limit has passed, assemble the family members and introduce them as "The (name of your church or youth group) super family!"

3. Crazy Skit—Divide into small groups. Act out crazy ways parents could react when their son or daughter says, "I love you." Incorporate the humorously dressed people from the first activity.

4. Saying "I Love You"—The following exercises are designed to help your young people tell their parents, "I love you." Give each person a pencil and

copy of the exercises. Discuss the answers when the kids finish.

5. Bible Study—After reading the following passages, have your group list biblical principles and rules on the relationship between parents and their children. The passages are Genesis 33:5; Deuteronomy 5:16; 6:4-7; Proverbs 3:12; 13:24; 23:22; 29:17; Ephesians 6:1-4; Colossians 3:12-13, 20-21.

6. Show "I Love You"—List ways your young people can *show* their parents they love them (clean up room, wash dishes, turn down stereo, smile). Encourage your kids to pick one action for the coming week and not tell their parents about it. Debrief at the next meeting. Did the parents notice? How did they react?

7. Parent/Youth Night—Invite parents to attend a special session. At the session, the parents and youth meet in separate groups. The parents list 10 common problems they face with their children. The young people list 10 common problems they face with their parents. Each group shares its list with the entire group.

Have the groups meet separately again. This time, they list 10 positive traits about the other group and share them with the entire group.

I LOVE YOU

We contacted world famous parents and football fanatics Morris and Sylvia Fritch. They're also the writers of the fantastic new TV show "All My Children."

The Fritches, who have raised 24 children of their own, have spent at least 14 minutes writing and designing "I love you" exercises.

Morris and Sylvia really love it when their kids tell them "I love you" each morning. In fact, it takes nearly seven minutes for everyone to get through all the "I love yous."

These simple exercises will help you tell or show your folks that you love them. Join the Fritch family and work through these exercises.

WHY IT'S TOUGH TO SAY IT

What makes it so hard for you to say "I love you" to your parents? Rate each of the following statements on how true it is for you. "10" is unbelievably true, "1" is not true at all. Put the appropriate number in the circle beside each of the following statements.

Saying "I love you" is hard because:

☐ my folks already know I love them.

☐ my parents will think I really need to depend on them.

☐ I'm afraid I'll sound childish.

☐ I might get too emotional.

☐ my folks might get too emotional.

☐ they might laugh at me.

☐ no one says "I love you" anymore.

☐ I won't know what to say next.

A DO-IT-YOURSELF FRIGID LOVE NOTE

Do you feel uneasy about saying "I love you" to your parents? If so, adapt this note to fit your special home situation. Write the note in your own handwriting and leave it in the refrigerator, maybe taped to the milk carton or stuffed into the meatloaf. Then get ready for some positive reactions.

Dear _____ (Mom and Dad) (Mom) (Dad)

I love you. It's hard for me to tell you this to your face because...

(use one of the reasons from "Why It's Tough to Say It")

I'm working on telling you that I love you out loud. So be ready.

Your _____ (son/daughter)

Why Is It So Hard to Say "I Love You"? continued

Do you want to tell your parents that you love them, but aren't quite sure what to say and how to go about it? First, read "Why Is It So Hard to Say 'I Love You'?" Then work through the following activities.

MY "I LOVE YOU" PLAN

Work through the following simple outline to come up with a great strategy for telling your parents "I love you."

Day: *(When's the best day to tell them?)* _____
_____

Time: *(When's the best time to tell them?)* _____
_____

Place: *(Where's the best place? kitchen? car? etc.)*
_____

The words: *(How will you introduce "I love you"? What will you say?) Write the words here:* _____
_____

Complete this caption!

Do not let anyone look down on you because you are young, but be an example for the believers, in your speech, your conduct, your love, faith and purity.

1 Timothy 4:12

44

"It's my room. If I don't want to clean it, what should you care?"

"You're grounded."

"You're old-fashioned."

"When I was a boy . . ."

Sound familiar? It seems everyone experiences some difficult times with parent-teenager relationships. Your group can plan a special evening to deal with some of these difficult times.

"Family Adventure" is designed for your members and their parents to come together for a time of communication, self-examination, idea exchanging and fun. Parents and kids will learn some communication skills that, if used at home, will help defuse potential family problems. "Family Adventure" gives participants the opportunity to feel that they're really being heard and understood.

"Family Adventure" should not be viewed as an attempt to solve the family problems of parent-teenager relationships. Rather, as the name implies, it's an adventure to explore how families tick. It's a "hunt" for the kinds of communication and understanding that will help your family open up and become fully the kind of lov-

ing units God intends for you.

Activities for this special parent night include a quickie course on communication skills, a "how do others see me?" activity, a board game to help see how families handle typical problems, a role play segment based on tough family conflicts, and a debriefing and fellowship time. Feel free to adapt, add to or subtract from any of these activities to fit the needs of your group.

Announce your "Family Adventure" night well in advance. Encourage all members and parents to attend. Send special invitations, put up attractive posters, make announcements. Assure everyone that this will be a night of discovery and fun.

Here are some hints for a successful "Family Adventure."

GETTING READY

Welcome everyone and explain that the purpose of the "Family Adventure" is to provide an opportunity to share enough with each other to grow closer together as persons and as families. Part of the activities will also give you a chance to hear viewpoints from other families in response to common issues involving parents and teenagers.

Offer a prayer for God's help in opening the avenues of communication and understanding in the home. Ask that God's Spirit will be a vital part of the night's interactions.

Start the activities with a brief introduction (or refresher practice for those already familiar) to listening skills. Your statement could

continued on page 127

PHOTOGRAPHY/THOM SCHULTZ
ILLUSTRATION/RAND KRUBACK

What's your personality?

gives feedback

FORTUNE TELLER inquisitive, curious

RINGMASTER outgoing, a leader

TRAPEZE ARTIST energetic, ambitious

COTTON CANDY MAKER cheerful, warm, friendly

KNIFE THROWER'S ASSISTANT self-giving

CLOWN fun, entertaining

LION TAMER serious, deep thinker, intelligent

STRONG MAN strong, supportive

TIGHTROPE WALKER shy, quiet

NET forgiving

PURPOSE:

To open lines of communication within the family; to help identify how family members view one another; to get acquainted with at least one other family; to enjoy time together in a fun learning experience.

DIRECTIONS:

1. Assemble in groups consisting of two or three families. Look over the three sets of choices on this poster.

2. Select a choice from the first category that most closely describes the kind of worker you are. Without revealing the choice to others, write on a slip of paper your name and your choice.

3. On separate slips of paper, repeat this process for the other two categories.

4. Now think about what kind of worker the others in your family (who are present tonight) would most resemble. For each person in your family, write on a slip of paper his or her name and the associated kind of worker.

5. On separate slips of paper, repeat this process for the other two categories.

6. When all families are finished, it's time to see if we see ourselves as others see us. Take one family at a time. Have everyone in that family show his or her "worker" sheets for Mom. If everyone in that family wrote the same tool for Mom, everyone in the group gets a reward from the snack bowl (nuts, hard candy, fruit, cheese, or whatever). If the tools for Mom don't match, everyone must explain his or her reason for assigning Mom the tool he or she chose. Use the feedback process learned earlier.

7. Follow the same procedure for Dad and kids.

8. Now repeat this procedure for the "communicator" and "personality" categories.

9. When the first family completes all three categories, go on to the other family(ies) in your group.

MATERIALS:

For every two or three families: game poster, several slips of paper for each person, pencils, bowl of candy or nuts.

APPROXIMATE TIME REQUIRED:

Twenty minutes.

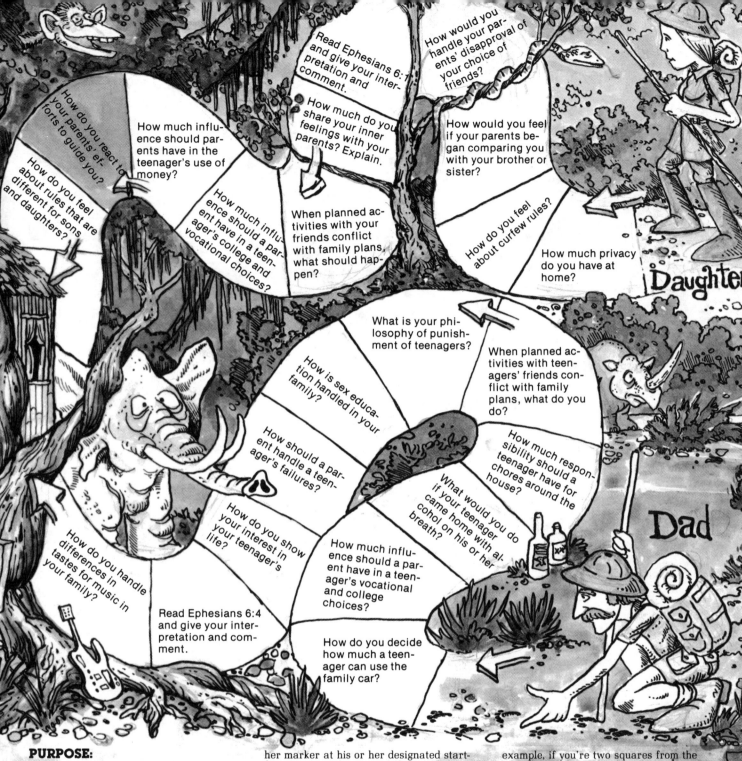

The board game spaces contain the following questions:

- How do you react to your parents' efforts to guide you?
- How do you feel about rules that are different for sons and daughters?
- How much influence should parents have in the teenager's use of money?
- How much influence should a parent have in a teenager's college and vocational choices?
- Read Ephesians 6:1 and give your interpretation and comment.
- How much do you share your inner feelings with your parents? Explain.
- When planned activities with your friends conflict with family plans, what should happen?
- How would you handle your parents' disapproval of your choice of friends?
- How would you feel if your parents began comparing you with your brother or sister?
- How do you feel about curfew rules?
- How much privacy do you have at home?
- What is your philosophy of punishment of teenagers?
- When planned activities with teenagers' friends conflict with family plans, what do you do?
- How is sex education handled in your family?
- How should a parent handle a teenager's failures?
- How much responsibility should a teenager have for chores around the house?
- How do you show your interest in your teenager's life?
- What would you do if your teenager came home with alcohol on his or her breath?
- How much influence should a parent have in a teenager's vocational and college choices?
- How do you handle differences in tastes for music in your family?
- Read Ephesians 6:4 and give your interpretation and comment.
- How do you decide how much a teenager can use the family car?

Daughter

Dad

PURPOSE:

To enable members of families to hear viewpoints from outside their own families on common family issues; to symbolically show that as they share more about themselves, they grow closer together.

DIRECTIONS:

1. Assemble in "family" groupings of three or four people, each person from a different family. For example, a group might consist of Mr. Smith, Mrs. Jones, Todd Baker and Nancy Miller.

2. The object is to arrive in the center.

3. Each person selects a token as a game marker. You might use a ring, button, coin, sugar cube. Each person places his or her marker at his or her designated starting point.

4. Place four pennies in a paper cup. The son or daughter may start by shaking the cup and spilling the pennies onto the game board. The number of pennies that lands heads-up determines the number of squares the player will advance.

5. The first player must now share his or her insights as required by the square upon which he or she landed.

6. After the first player shares, move in a clockwise direction to the next player.

7. The game continues until all players have reached the center.

8. Any way you reach the center, even with extra "heads," you've finished. For example, if you're two squares from the center and you roll four heads on your pennies, that's okay.

9. If you roll four tails, move back one space.

10. When everyone arrives in the center, use any remaining time to discuss how feelings about family relationships may be different now than they were before tonight.

MATERIALS:

For every three or four people: game board, four pennies, paper cup, Bible, game tokens.

APPROXIMATE TIME REQUIRED:

Thirty minutes.

FAMILY ADVENTURE

TRADING PO

RAND KRUBACK

PURPOSE:

To help teenagers and parents understand the viewpoints, feelings, pressures and motives of others during a family conflict situation; to allow teenagers to step inside the role of parents, and vice versa.

DIRECTIONS:

1. Assemble in groups consisting of your own family and one other family.

2. Each family looks over the choices of situations and selects one that seems interesting or one that resembles a situation that has faced that family in the past.

3. Now, the first family acts out the situation. But the roles are reversed. That is, the father would play the son, the son would play the father, the daughter would play the mother, and the mother would play the daughter. If you need an additional character, obtain one from the other family. For instance, if you need another teenager to play Mom, use a teenager from the second family. This stand-in may need a little coaching from the first family as to how Mom might react in this situation.

4. Each character in the role play should read the situation carefully and act out his or her character as realistically as possible. For example, a father should play the part of his son just as he perceives his son would act in this situation. Feel free to rearrange chairs to better simulate the situation.

5. Allow about four minutes to complete the role play. During this time, take the situation from its beginning as outlined below, enlarge upon it and carry it through to some kind of resolution.

6. When the role play is completed, each character should explain how he or she felt during the exchange. Any surprises? Any new insights? Also discuss how realistic you felt the portrayals were. Would the situation be handled like this in real life? The other family is also invited to ask questions and offer insights that were learned while watching the role play.

7. Now it's the other family's turn. Repeat steps 2 through 6.

MATERIALS:

A "Trading Post" page for each family.

APPROXIMATE TIME REQUIRED:

Twenty-five minutes.

1. Curfews. Mom and Dad are sitting in the living room. The son/daughter enters and explains that he/she wants to attend a school Latin Club party Friday night that won't be over until 1:00 a.m. Regular curfew time set by parents is usually 11:30 p.m. The teenager wants to re-evaluate the whole idea of curfews. He/she mentions that "all the other Latin Club members can stay out till 1:00 a.m."

2. Pot. While home alone one morning, Mom finds a baggie of marijuana in her daughter's/son's closet. At the dinner table that night, Mom mentions her find. The teenager responds that the pot belongs to her/his locker partner. And she/he brought the pot home because of an impending locker check by school officials. She/he "only wanted to protect" the locker partner who "was home sick."

3. Grades. In the living room, Mom, Dad and teenager are discussing the kid's school grades, which have dropped slightly during the last grade

ILLUSTRATION/RAND KRUBACK

Family Adventure

continued from page 121

period. The teenager explains that he/she wants to escape the pressure of grades, and has decided that he/she doesn't want to attend college after high school. He/she has decided to seek a job at a resort for a year or so while deciding what career to pursue.

4. Choosing friends. In the living room, Mom and Dad are reading the newspaper. The daughter/son comes in and announces that she/he is going out with Ralph Howker for the evening. The parents are upset because they've heard that Ralph has been arrested previously for shoplifting.

5. Rules. At the dinner table, the son/daughter wants to discuss with the parents reasons for rules that have been set in the family. He/she states that it's hard to accept rules that he/she doesn't understand.

6. Comparisons. While riding in the car, Mom and Dad ask the daughter/son, "Why can't you be more like your older sister? She always cleaned up her room, did all her duties around the house, and got good grades—all without complaining."

go like this: "Complete communication is the backbone of understanding in families. The three parts of a message are: 1) the words; 2) the feelings supporting the words; 3) the general context of the conversation (when and where it happened and who was present). Communication is complete only when the message given has been returned to the sender by the listener, using the listener's own words."

Here's an example. Sender: "I think I'll go outside for some fresh air." Listener (feedback): "You'd like to get out of the house right now, since your dad is opening your report card and you're feeling nervous."

Ask the teenagers to pair up with their own parent or parents (taking turns if there's two parents and one kid, etc.) and practice feedback listening. The message-senders could tell how they feel about the amount of time their family spends together. Have each person practice giving feedback at least one time.

Then have the teenagers get with someone else's parent or parents. Again, each person will practice feedback. Have the message-sender tell what he or she personally would like to accomplish during the coming activities of parents' night.

The total time for "Getting Ready" should be 15 minutes (keep folks moving).

REFLECTING POOL

Before breaking into small groups be sure everyone understands the purpose and directions for the activity (as noted on the "Reflecting Pool" poster). Encourage everyone to be honest during the game, but to emphasize the positive. Be sure families are urged to use the feedback process when discussing differences in

their answers during the game.

As family groups are formed, hand each group a "Reflecting Pool" poster and other necessary materials.

RENDEZVOUS

After you've completed the "Reflecting Pool" game, quickly reassemble and announce the plans for the "Rendezvous" game. Be sure everyone understands the purpose and rules for the game, as outlined on the game board.

Encourage everyone to find two or three others from different families as quickly as possible. Ask them to be seated as soon as they've found a group. As groups sit, give them a game board and other necessary materials.

TRADING POST

By now everyone should be ready to tackle some typical family conflicts—through the method of role reversal.

Explain how role plays work. And be sure everyone understands the directions for the "Trading Post" activity.

You may wish to send the families to separate rooms for this activity, which would provide more privacy and fewer distractions.

Make sure each family has a "Trading Post" page.

DEBRIEFING

After the "Trading Post" activity, all participants should reconvene. A leader should ask volunteers to tell what was learned during the evening. What helped you most? What things did you discover tonight that might help you in your family situation? Keep this session brief. Close with a prayer.

Allow discussion to continue informally as you break to enjoy some refreshments and fellowship.
—*Thom Schultz and John Shaw*

45

SIMPLE WAYS TO HELP KIDS OPEN UP

From time to time, we're a little stale when it comes to finding fresh, crisp ways to help get our young people into youth group discussions.

Here are nine simple, but effective, ideas for you to try with your group. Before using the following ideas, develop your own specific content and discussion questions. For unless you know what you want to discuss, the ideas you choose from this menu may become nothing more than meaningless gimmicks.

Once you've developed your discussion questions, plug them into these ideas. Better yet, overhaul the following ideas to make them fit your group's special tastes.

Sample these . . . they may add spice to your discussions.

1 HANGING QUESTIONS

Write your discussion questions on 3×5 cards; one question for each card. Then hang the cards at various locations around the church or house—wherever you hold your meetings. For the discussion period, your group wanders around, searching out the questions. Once the group finds a question, everyone stops, sits down and discusses it. Then the search begins for other questions.

If you have a large group, plan to break into small teams and color code the questions. Write each small team's questions on a different-colored set of cards.

Divide your large group into small teams; assign each team one of the colors at the beginning of the session. When the time comes for the discussion, each team will search for its color on the hanging questions.

2 PAPER-CUP QUESTIONS

Don't wait till the meeting is over to serve refreshments. Instead, serve snacks in the middle of the session, before the discussion time.

Serve drinks in Styrofoam cups. Before the meeting write the discussion questions on the inside of the cups. Try this ahead of time to make sure you can actually write on the cups you've purchased.

Eat, drink and discuss.

3 BACK-SEAT DISCUSSION

Use sheets of newsprint (available at office-supply shops or at many newspapers) to turn your meeting room into whatever you're discussing. Let your group members use their imaginations to help you. For instance, if the topic of discussion is television, have your group turn your room into a TV studio, complete with newsprint cameras and a setting from a current TV show. Or if you're talking about dating hassles, you could turn your room into a gigantic car back seat. The idea potential to add newsprint realism to your discussion is endless.

4 HEADBAND QUESTIONS AND ANSWERS

Here's a simple technique for getting both questions and answers from your group. Cut an old white sheet into strips 20 inches wide and 28-34 inches long. Then fold the strips to fit group members' foreheads. Use safety pins (or sticky-backed notes available at most office-supply stores) to attach a discussion question to each person's headband. (If you want to experiment, try writing the questions on the sheet with laundry markers.)

Give each person in the group a pencil and small pieces of paper. Before the discussion period, have your group members mill around, read the questions on the foreheads, jot notes and thoughts on their small pieces of paper, sign their names to the papers and attach them to the appropriate headbands.

When everyone has answered each of the headband questions, have one person at a time remove his or her headband, read the question and summarize the answers. Ask various individuals to explain their notes.

5 TONGUE-DEPRESSOR CONTRAPTIONS

Divide your group into teams of three or four. Give each team a handful of tongue depressors, glue and several ink markers.

After introducing the area of discussion and study, have each team write their thoughts, feelings and ideas on the tongue depressors.

Then give the teams 15 minutes or so to make some outlandish contraption, using the written-on tongue depressors. The more responses a team has, the more tongue depressors it has to make the contraption.

Once the construction is completed, ask discussion questions and let the team provide answers, using their contraptions as guides.

6 COOKIE QUESTIONS

Get with a few young people from your group who like to bake, and whip up a batch of cookies. But first, plan your meeting and develop your discussion topic. Then come up with several discussion questions, type them on strips of paper and work them into the dough. One question for each cookie.

Plan to eat cookies and have a great discussion at the same time. By the way, you can incorporate the "paper-cup questions" idea into your snack period too.

7 "ME" SOCKS

Try this variation of the "me" exercise to help your young people talk about themselves. Have group members remove their shoes and socks. (Bring extra socks in case someone doesn't wear socks to the session.)

Encourage your young people to walk barefooted around the church, or wherever your meeting is held and collect in their socks objects they can use to tell something about themselves. For instance, someone might choose grains of salt from the kitchen to symbolize their sometimes "salty" disposition.

Bring magazines, paper and pencils for young people to use to cut out photos or write words or phrases that they can use to describe themselves.

After 10 minutes or so, come together as a group and have each person empty his or her socks, show the objects and explain what each stands for.

If you really want to get gross, play a fast-paced field game (soccer, football, tag, etc.) before starting this activity.

8 OBJECTS, OBJECTS, OBJECTS

Want to add a touch of realism to your discussion? Bring objects that relate to whatever you're talking about.
- alcohol, bring empty beer cans.
- abortion, bring a doll.
- the cross, bring pieces of wood for everyone.
- self-image, bring small mirrors.
- handicaps, bring blindfolds, crutches, etc.
- shyness, have paper bags for group members to put over their heads.

If you're studying a passage of scripture, take a seven-minute break and have everyone collect items mentioned in the text. For instance, objects in Mark 10:32-40 could be:
- rocks (from the road to Jerusalem, verse 32);
- Jesus' footprints in a box of dirt (verse 32);
- spit (verse 34);
- seats for right and left hand of Christ (verse 37);
- cup (verse 38); and
- water (verse 38).

Pass the objects around the group as you discuss the topic or study the scripture.

9 "DEAR ABBY"

How would young people in your group answer this question:

Dear Abby:
I'm feeling really terrible. Last night I got into a nasty fight with my best friend. I called another friend and said a lot of bad things about my best friend. Today at school I saw my best friend and the other friend talking together. They seem to be ignoring me. Now I'm afraid I'll lose both friends. What should I do?

This ageless discussion technique can help your group struggle with contemporary, personal problems. Here are a few ideas for using this approach:
- Introduce the topic for study and have your group write questions and hand them in to you. Invite a panel of other youth and adults to answer the questions.
- Divide into teams of two or three. Have the questions prepared ahead of time. The team members are the experts who answer the questions.
- Have your young people write the questions. Then read the questions aloud and let the entire group offer answers.
- Cut actual questions from the "Dear Abby" column and let your group answer them. Then read Abby's response and compare the answers.

—Gary Richardson

46

HOW TO SUCCEED WITH THE OPPOSITE SEX

1. Before the Bible Study—Gather a pencil, Bible and copy of "Relating to the Opposite Sex" (pages 131-132) for each person. You also will need two or three cans of soda pop.

2. Opener—Begin with a "Carry the Can Dash," a contest where couples compete against each other by racing around a course. The only catch in the race is that each couple has to carry a soft drink can between them without touching it with their hands. At different points along the course, the couple has to carry the can with their elbows, their shoulders, their noses and finally their hips.

3. Relationships—Distribute a pencil and copy of "Relating to the Opposite Sex" to each person. Use "For Guys Only" and "For Girls Only" and have guys and girls compare their answers.

"Easy Eddie's Customized Kars" is designed to help young people clarify what traits they like in the opposite sex. Have them list those traits, then discuss and compare them. Finally, have each person grade himself or herself on the five traits.

4. Scripture Study—As a group, agree on the top 10 qualities your group likes in other people. The following passages are examples of men and women who exhibited attractive inner qualities. Have your young people read the passages and compare those qualities with the ones they listed. The passages are Mark 14:3-9; Luke 1:5-6; John 21:9-19; Acts 9:36; 16:14-15; Romans 16:1-2; 2 Timothy 1:5.

5. Role Switch—Divide into groups of two or three guys and girls each. Then role play different situations where the guys take on the role of girls, and the girls take on the role of guys: a trip to the movies, eating lunch together in the cafeteria, standing in the hall at school, saying goodnight on a date, and so on.

6. Closing—Have volunteers read their answers to "The Personal Touch." Have everyone follow through with what he or she wrote.

RELATING TO THE OPPOSITE SEX

Have some fun discovering how you can best relate to the opposite sex. You can find lots of helpful and humorous ideas in these exercises.

Rate each of the following traits the way you'd like to see them in guys.

	I hate to see this in guys		I'm not sure		I like to see this in guys	
1. Is tough, macho	1	2	3	4	5	6
2. Cuts other people down with his sarcastic wit	1	2	3	4	5	6
3. Swears a lot	1	2	3	4	5	6
4. Spits tobacco	1	2	3	4	5	6
5. Is meek	1	2	3	4	5	6
6. Has a sense of humor	1	2	3	4	5	6
7. Drives a fast car	1	2	3	4	5	6
8. Drinks	1	2	3	4	5	6
9. Wears great clothes	1	2	3	4	5	6
10. Takes life seriously	1	2	3	4	5	6
11. Loving	1	2	3	4	5	6
12. Sensitive	1	2	3	4	5	6

Rate each of the following traits the way you'd like to see them in girls.

	I hate to see this in girls		I'm not sure		I like to see this in girls	
1. Lots of makeup	1	2	3	4	5	6
2. Looks like she stepped from a fashion catalog	1	2	3	4	5	6
3. Gentle spirit	1	2	3	4	5	6
4. Sexy body	1	2	3	4	5	6
5. Loving	1	2	3	4	5	6
6. Makes all the guys drool	1	2	3	4	5	6
7. Takes life seriously	1	2	3	4	5	6
8. Spits tobacco	1	2	3	4	5	6
9. Acts cool and uncaring	1	2	3	4	5	6
10. Sensitive	1	2	3	4	5	6
11. Cuts other people down with her sarcastic wit	1	2	3	4	5	6
12. Swears a lot	1	2	3	4	5	6

Get personal with yourself for three minutes and complete the following statements. Write very small if you don't want anyone to read what you've written.

The strongest trait I have that would attract someone of the opposite sex is

_____

One trait I have that would most likely turn someone of the opposite sex off is

_____

The trait I want most to develop is

_____

Here's how I plan to develop the traits that will make me famous with people of the opposite sex:

_____

EASY EDDIE'S CUSTOMIZED KARS

One day last month, one of our magazine editors withdrew her life savings ($243) to buy a personalized, customized car from Easy Eddie, ace mechanic and part-time fry cook at Burger Junior's. Easy Eddie's new twist in car sales is to rebuild existing cars to fit the personalities of their new owners.

Here are license plates from some of the cars in Easy Eddie's showroom:

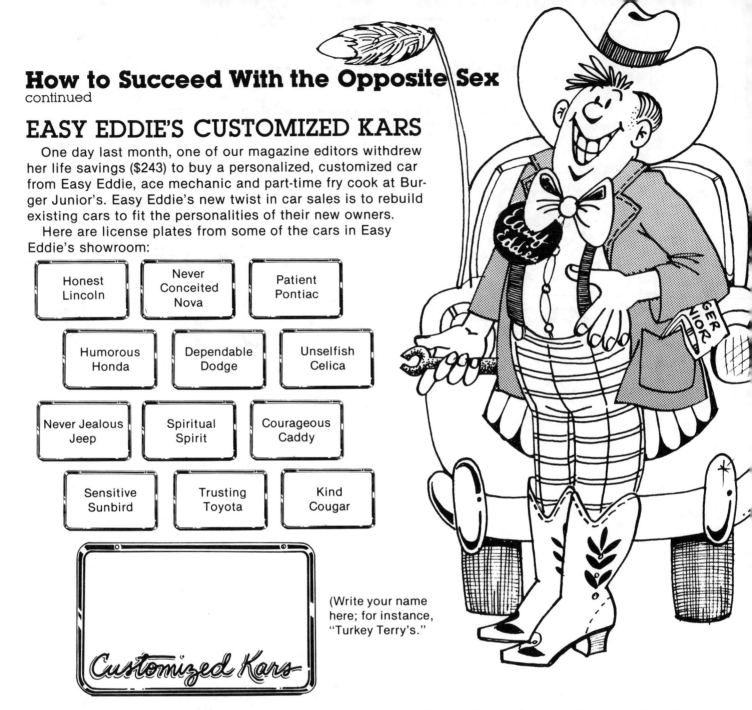

Honest Lincoln

Never Conceited Nova

Patient Pontiac

Humorous Honda

Dependable Dodge

Unselfish Celica

Never Jealous Jeep

Spiritual Spirit

Courageous Caddy

Sensitive Sunbird

Trusting Toyota

Kind Cougar

Customized Kars

(Write your name here; for instance, "Turkey Terry's."

Which of Easy Eddie's personalized cars—and their personality traits—would you choose for the opposite sex? List them here:

Trait #1	Trait #2	Trait #3	Trait #4	Trait #5

Now go back and evaluate yourself on the same five traits you just listed. Grade yourself from A-F. Which ones need the most work?

A question I'd like to ask an expert about people of the opposite sex is:

Love is very patient and kind, never jealous or envious, never boastful or proud, never haughty or selfish or rude. Love does not demand its own way. It is not irritable or touchy. It does not hold grudges and will hardly even notice when others do it wrong. It is never glad about injustice, but rejoices whenever truth wins out. If you love someone you will be loyal to him no matter what the cost. You will always believe in him, always expect the best of him, and always stand your ground in defending him.

1 Corinthians 13:4-7, LB

47
PRIORITIES IN RELATIONSHIPS

Challenge your group to a creative learning adventure. Set up the following four interest center activities designed so participants can reflect on priorities in their relationships. The four topics include each person's relationship with self, God, family and friends.

The interest center concept depends on kids making choices and focusing on areas where they feel the most need. Allow time for participants to choose one center, do the activities there, and move on to another center. Plan for completion of at least three of the four centers.

In preparation, read all the interest center ideas.

Then gather the necessary supplies for each center. Designate a certain corner of the room for each and set up the center with everything needed to complete the assignment there.

Before starting, give the total group instructions that explain the interest center concept. Depending on your group's needs, have kids work individually or with small groups of three or four. Set a time frame (approximately 15 to 20 minutes per center). Let them choose and experience the centers of their choice. At the end of your time together, hold a brief sharing time with everyone to highlight what was learned in this activity.

FRIENDS: "WHAT-YOU-WOULD" SQUARES

Objective:
To explore "friendship" actions and ways to reach out to your own friends.

Supplies:
A large nine-square grid made of newsprint, yellow and red stickers (about ¾ inch in diameter), a small nine-square grid for each person, pencils and instructions.

Preparation:
On newsprint, create a giant nine-square grid. Write one of these words in each square: listening, talking, laughing, accepting, hugging, helping, giving, taking, solving.

Create another nine-square grid on 8½×11 paper. Write these words: name, action, when. Make copies for everyone.

GIANT GRID SMALL GRID

Here's What You Do:
1. Take two red and two yellow stickers. Put your initials on them.

2. Look at the giant grid. Place the two yellow stickers on the two most important actions you and your friends share.

3. Place the two red stickers on the two least important actions you and your friends share.

4. On the small grid, write the names of three special friends on the space labeled "name."

5. Think of one special action you need to work on with that friend and write it in the space labeled "action."

6. Write the time and place you'll put it into action in the space labeled "when."

7. Offer a personal silent prayer that God will be with you as you reach out and take action with your friends.

8. (Optional) As a whole group discuss where people placed the stickers on the giant grid. Ask: Why are some actions more important than others? Do you experience all nine activities with all your friends? Why or why not?

Priorities in Relationships continued

A GREAT GOD MADE ME!

Objective:
To experience a "quiet time" with God.

Supplies:
Bibles, pencils and "Reflections" worksheet for each person.

"REFLECTIONS"

Here's What You Do:

1. Take these questions, your Bible and a pencil to a quiet place. Go alone, so no one will interrupt you. When you've arrived at your place—stop a few moments. And do nothing. Just sit quietly. Get in touch with yourself. Then imagine God is right there beside you.

2. Read Psalm 8:1-3. List three great things God has done:
   1.
   2.
   3.
   List three great things God has done for *you* personally:
   1.
   2.
   3.

3. Read Psalm 8:4. Complete:
   I wonder about my own worth when . . .

   God's created me because . . .

(See Ephesians 1:4-8; 2:8-10 and Colossians 3:12, 17 if you're still wondering.)

4. Read Psalm 8:5-8. When I read this verse, I feel . . .

5. Read Psalm 8:9. My relationship with God right now is . . .

   To make my relationship with God greater, I need to . . .

6. Read Psalm 9:1-2. A prayer from my heart right now is . . .

(A copyrighted resource from **GROUP Magazine's Best Youth Group Programs.** Permission granted to copy this worksheet for local church use only.)

LOVE YOURSELF!

Objective:
To reflect on loving yourself and why that's so important.

Supplies:
Bibles, "I Love Me" worksheets, pencils, and a bowl of popcorn, nuts or other treat.

"I LOVE ME"

Here's What You Do:

1. Read Matthew 22:37-39. What's the greatest commandment?

   What's the second most important?

2. Energy spent on loving others doesn't mean much—unless you *love yourself* first! Grab a handful of goodies and reflect on how much you love *you*. Then answer the next few questions.

3. One thing I don't like about myself is . . .

4. What I could do to love myself more is . . .

5. Look closely at your last answer. Double-check it. Does it meet these requirements:
   - It depends on *me* alone to accomplish.   yes/no
   - I'll know for sure whether I've done it.   yes/no
   - I know exactly when I plan to do this.   yes/no

   If you answered no to any of these statements, change #4 so it does meet these qualifications.
   Write the changes here if needed:

6. This is how I'd feel if I loved myself more . . .

7. Loving myself would affect the people around me by . . .

8. Share some of the treats here with someone else in the group. Tell that person what you plan to do to love yourself more. Ask that person to pray for you.

(A copyrighted resource from **GROUP Magazine's Best Youth Group Programs.** Permission granted to copy this worksheet for local church use only.)

FAMILY: PIECING IT TOGETHER

Objective:
To evaluate family relationships and set goals to improve them.

Supplies:
Bibles, paper plates, scissors, color crayons, masking tape, instructions and a completed sample to illustrate the activity.

Here's What You Do:

1. Cut a paper plate into sections, with each section representing a family member. For example, cut it into thirds if you have a mom, dad and brother.

2. Label each piece with their names.

3. Imagine each piece represents the total amount of time you spend with that person.

4. Choose a color that best describes each relationship.

5. Color each piece with that color to signify the amount of time spent with that person in "constructive conversation" (good, positive, helpful, kind words).

6. Now think of time spent with that person in "destructive conversation" (arguing, complaining, nitpicking, yelling). Rip the piece to signify the amount of time.

7. Ask and answer: What makes each of my family relationships different? Was the portion ripped from each piece larger than the colored portion? If so, what can be done to improve that relationship? Why is time spent in "destructive conversation"? If you have no ripped portions, how can you make the good relationship even better?

8. On small pieces of masking tape, write ideas to help "patch up" relationships in your family. Tape each paper plate section back together.

9. Read Colossians 3:12-15. Use masking tape to repair the whole plate to its original form. Write key words from that Bible passage on the tape.

48

WHEN YOUR BEST FRIEND LOVES A LOSER

1. Before the Meeting—Ask a few kids to think of 25-30 questions someone could ask a potential date (for example, "What do you like in a person?"). Have them write each question separately on 3×5 cards. These will be used in "the dating game."

Copy each of the following roles on a 3×5 card to be distributed to the "dates" in the dating game:

● You've never attended church and have no Christian values.

● You always get your own way.

● You profess to be a Christian, but attend wild parties with drinking and drugs.

● You're rich, popular, athletic—but *very* conceited.

● You're cruel to anyone you consider "unpopular" and you always put others down.

● You have loose sexual morals.

You also will need a pencil and copy of the quiz for each person.

2. The Dating Game—Explain that you're going to play a dating game patterned after the TV game show, but this dating game has a few unique twists. Plan to play it once or twice, whatever your time allows. Have one volunteer be the "questioner" and three volunteers of the opposite sex be potential dates. The three dates must each play one of the six roles on the cards; they *must* answer their questions from that perspective. The questioner should refer to the potential dates as Bachelor (or Bachelorette) number one, two or three—not by name. It's best if the questioner and dates can't see each other, but the other group members can see them all. Have the questioner use prewritten question cards. Allow about eight minutes per round. After each round, the questioner chooses a date while the group votes also. After each round, talk about the choices. Ask: What was difficult? Were any of the responses similar to real-life situations? Why or why not? What makes choosing a date difficult?

3. A Friend's Feelings—Have each person complete the following quiz and share reasons for one feeling from the list. Ask: What kind of person would you object to dating? Would your best friend have the same values as you? Why or why not? Does your faith play a part in your decision? Why or why not? How would you want to be approached if you were dating a "loser"?

4. What to Say—Next ask two volunteers to role play a conversation between two friends—one who's dating a mismatch, the other a concerned best friend. Have the group members sit in a circle with the two role play actors in the center.

After the role play, discuss: Did both people communicate constructively? Explain. Could you tell the conversation was between two best friends? Why or why not?

5. Discussion—Say that by learning to handle sticky relationships, we can become better friends. Discuss ways to help friends such as by communicating constructively, not giving up on your friend, learning unselfish caring, etc.

Ask: What would you change about the previous role play after discussing things to do? Is thinking of someone as a "loser" unchristian? Why or why not? How can Christians "love everybody" yet not compromise their values?

6. Learnings—After discussing the topic, ask: What did you learn about yourself? about your best friends? about dating? What's one thing you plan to do if this problem comes up in your life?

7. Prayer Time—Ask two different young people to read aloud Ephesians 4:15 and Philippians 2:3-4. Close with a time of silent prayer for friends.

LOVES A LOSER QUIZ

You and your best friend have been "buddies" for a long time. But now your friend is dating the one person in the world you're certain is the *wrong* person for him or her!

True, in the past, boyfriends/girlfriends have come and gone, but this is different. You feel: (Check those that apply.)

☐ angry ("Why would my friend do such a stupid thing?")

☐ insulted ("My best friend chose to date this person; is that a bad reflection on *me*?")

☐ concerned ("What if my friend is making a big mistake, with terrible consequences?")

☐ protective ("I want to save my friend from being hurt by this person.")

☐ betrayed ("My friend and I have always shared similar tastes in everything; how could he or she change so quickly?")

☐ sad ("My friend is slipping away from me . . . we don't see eye-to-eye anymore.")

☐ confused ("I just don't understand why this is happening.")

☐ frustrated ("How can I honestly say what I think without turning my friend against me?")

☐ upset ("I can't believe that now I have to compete with *that* person for my best friend's attention!")

☐ (Fill in the blank:) _____

—*Bill Stearns*

49

THE DRINKING GAME

Alcohol and its abuse affect all of us. To help you and your young people understand the problems, uncover some facts, expose some myths, and sort out personal feelings, a special youth group game was created by GROUP. "The Drinking Game" utilizes drinking-related crowdbreakers, quizzes, common situational problems, role plays and laughs.

"The Drinking Game" is fun. It's meant to be—not to laugh away a very serious issue, but to create a desire to learn and grapple with the problems through the adventure of a group experience.

But the game should not be seen as an end in itself. It's merely a colorful introduction to a deeper probe of the drinking issue. Use the game to open a meeting, series of meetings or retreat on the subjects of drinking and alcoholism. "The Drinking Game" will prepare your group members for an open examination of their thoughts and feelings.

MATERIALS

Your game board is printed on the following pages. You'll need one board for every two to six players. In addition, you'll need about 50 3×5 cards for each group. And each group will need a stack of popular magazines, a Bible, a few glasses of water, and a token for each player. Tokens may be coins, bottle caps, squares of colored paper, or any other batch of dissimilar objects. From a 3×5 card, make a spinner. Cut a half-inch piece from the end of the card. Trim this piece to make an arrow. On the rest of the card, draw a circle, divide it into quarters, and number the

sections one through four. Stick a thumb tack up through the center of the circle and through the middle of the arrow. Bend up the ends of the arrow slightly to allow freer spinning.

RULES

The game is designed for two to six players. If your group is larger than this, divide into smaller groups.

The object is for all players to reach the finish, "Natural High."

Begin with all players' tokens at the start position. Each player, in turn, spins and advances the required number of spaces. The player must then make the indicated action printed on that space.

If you land on a QUIZ space, take a QUIZ card (explained later) from the top of the stack, read it aloud and answer. If correct, spin again and take the required action on the new space. If wrong, move back two spaces and wait your turn (do NOT take required action on that space). Return the QUIZ card to the bottom of the stack.

If you land on a SITUATION space, take a SITUATION card (explained later) from the top of the stack, read it aloud and follow the instructions. Then remain on that space until your next turn. Return the SITUATION card to the bottom of the stack.

When a player reaches the "Natural High" block, all other players tell what they most like about that person. These positive statements may or may not relate to the game. Examples: "I really like the way you treat your friends who are really different from you." "I really like the way you listen to people."

The game is not over until each player reaches the "Natural High" block. All players must remain until the last player reaches the finish.

The Drinking Game continued

QUIZ QUESTIONS

Print or type each of the following questions on a 3×5 card. Each corresponding answer, listed below, should be printed on the reverse side of the card. Each group of two to six players will need a complete set of QUIZ cards. Stack the cards, question side up, near the game board.

1. What percentage of fatal auto accidents involving teenagers happen because someone was drunk?
a. 10 percent   c. 50 percent
b. 25 percent   d. 75 percent

2. Which kills more young Americans?
a. war   c. drinking
b. suicide

3. Will a lighter person get drunk quicker than a heavier person if both have had the same amount of alcohol?
a. yes   b. no

4. Will alcohol affect a person more or less if drinking occurs after eating a good meal?
a. more   b. less

5. What is the best test of a person's ability to drive after having a few drinks?
a. ability to walk a straight   b. clear speech
   line   c. blood alcohol content

6. Will the same amount of alcohol affect everyone the same way?
a. yes   b. no

7. Does a person's emotional condition change the effect alcohol has?
a. yes   b. no

8. What is the most abused drug in the United States?
a. marijuana   c. alcohol
b. cocaine   d. heroin

9. What factors can cause alcohol abuse and alcoholism?
a. social   c. cultural
b. psychological d. all of them

10. Can an overdose of alcohol cause death?
a. yes   b. no

11. Is drunkenness regarded as an abuse of alcohol in the Bible?
a. yes   b. no

12. Which of the following contains the most pure alcohol?
a. a 1.5 ounce jigger of hard   c. a 16-ounce can of beer
   liquor   d. all the same
b. a 5-ounce glass of wine

13. Habitual heavy drinking can ruin a person's ability to perform sexually.
a. true   b. false

14. Habitual heavy drinking does not contribute to depression or suicide.
a. true   b. false

15. Physical exercise, black coffee and cold showers help drinkers sober up quicker.
a. true   b. false

16. Which of the following human functions is likely to be affected first by alcohol intake?
a. muscular coordination   d. speech
b. judgment   e. balance
c. breathing

17. Which of the following is LEAST often the reason for teenage drinking of alcohol?
a. to get high   d. taste
b. to be sociable e. for "kicks"
c. to feel good

18. Teenagers consume alcoholic beverages:
a. to escape from problems   d. all of the above
b. to be accepted by peers   e. none of the above
c. to have fun

19. How do teenagers compare with others in rates of alcohol-related driving accidents?
a. less than others, but only   d. more than others, but only
   for females   for males
b. less than others   e. more than others
c. about the same as others

20. Which of the following statements is/are true of those who drive after drinking? Teenagers are more likely than others to:
a. crash   d. crash with less alcohol
b. be killed if they crash   e. all of the above
c. have passengers killed in
   crashes

SITUATIONS

Print or type each of the following situations on a 3×5 card. Each group of two to six players will need a complete set of SITUATION cards. Feel free to create your own situations to add to those supplied below. Stack the cards, blank side up, near the game board.

1. You are at a party and everyone is urging you to have a drink. You've decided not to drink. What do you say?

2. While at a party, the friend who's driving you home has had several drinks during the past hour. You are ready to go home. What do you do?

3. Since you are the oldest-looking one among your friends, they ask you to try to buy beer for a party. What do you say?

4. Pick three people from your group who'll act the part of friends passing a bottle around. They dare you to chug the bottle. React to them.

5. You are with a date you really like, and he or

21. Why are teenagers more likely than adults to have difficulty driving safely after drinking?
   a. driving is a comparatively new skill for them
   b. they have had less experience with alcohol's effects
   c. they often weigh less than adults
   d. all of the above
   e. none of the above

22. Which of the following is/are true concerning teenager use of alcohol in this country?
   a. almost all teenagers have drunk alcohol by their high school graduation
   b. most teenagers are given their first drink by their parents at home
   c. while beer is still the most common choice, the sale of "pop" wines has increased 1,000 percent in the last four years
   d. all of the above
   e. none of the above

23. Which of the following influences the effects of alcohol?
   a. the amount of food in the stomach
   b. the body weight of the individual
   c. the height of the individual
   d. a and b
   e. all of the above

24. The responsible course of action in regard to drinking and driving is to:
   a. acquire accurate information about the effects of alcohol
   b. analyze one's attitude and feelings concerning the matter
   c. develop plans for handling interpersonal situations where drinking and driving are or could be involved
   d. all of the above
   e. a and c

25. Which of the following statements is/are true?
   a. some persons cannot stop drinking once they start
   b. limiting quantity of intake is easier if decided when sober
   c. since judgment is impaired after drinking small amounts of alcohol, plans about driving should be made ahead of time
   d. all of the above
   e. none of the above

QUIZ ANSWERS

18.) d; 19.) e; 20.) e; 21.) d; 22.) d; 23.) d; 24.) d; 25.) d;
10.) a; 11.) a; 12.) d; 13.) b; 14.) b; 15.) b; 16.) b; 17.) d;
1.) c; 2.) c; 3.) a; 4.) b; 5.) c; 6.) b; 7.) a; 8.) c; 9.) d;

she gets drunk at the party. What do you do?

6. Pick two people from your group who'll role play someone trying to convince another person in your group to loosen up with a drink to enjoy the party more. You overhear the conversation and enter in.

7. Pick three people from your group who'll approach you as friends to ask that you open your house for a party, since your parents are gone for the weekend. Your friends promise to buy the beer.

What do you do?

8. Tell the group how you would react to a group of friends who have several false IDs and want you to go to a bar with them. You are the only one with a car.

9. What would you say to a person who says, "I know I look older when I'm drinking."

10. A friend has returned from college and phones to invite you to a party. You know it will be a beer party. Respond over the phone.

11. You are spending the night with a friend (pick a person from your group) whose parents have left for the evening. Your friend wants to sneak a few drinks from the liquor cabinet. Convince your friend it wouldn't be wise.

12. Pick three people to play the part of popular kids who invite you to ride around with them. After you're in the car, the driver pulls out a beer and brags that it's his fourth. He runs a stop sign, but insists he's okay. React to the situation.

13. A popular member of your youth group drinks for the first time at a party and gets drunk. You are concerned about his reputation and Christian witness. What do you do?

14. You have a friend who recently started drinking. Two times before, you helped him get home, and the last time, he barfed in your parents' car. He comes to you drunk again and asks for a ride home. What do you do?

15. One of your parents has shown a sudden strong dependence on alcohol. You have strong feelings about alcoholism, but love your parent. How do you handle the problem?

16. You have a friend who has a church background that is the opposite of yours. (One allows drinking in moderation; the other forbids it.) You notice some bad feelings starting to develop between you. How do you approach your friend?

HELPFUL HINTS

Ask for a volunteer from each game group to keep notes during the game. Conflicts, disagreements, sensitive issues concerning drinking, and noteworthy comments should be remembered for later discussions. This is particularly helpful if you have several game groups that reconvene for a general discussion after the game. The notes will help each game group report its experiences to the total group.

Here are some Bible passages that you may find helpful in your probe of the drinking issue: Proverbs 20:1; 23:20-21; 31:4-7; Isaiah 5:22; 28:7; 56:11-12; Matthew 11:18-19; Luke 21:34-35; John 2:1-11; Romans 13:11-14; 14:20-21; 1 Corinthians 5:11; 6:9-10; 8:8-13; 10:31; Galatians 5:19-21; Ephesians 5:18; 1 Thessalonians 5:6-8; 1 Timothy 3:1-9; 5:23; Titus 1:7; 2:3.

50

YOU CAN

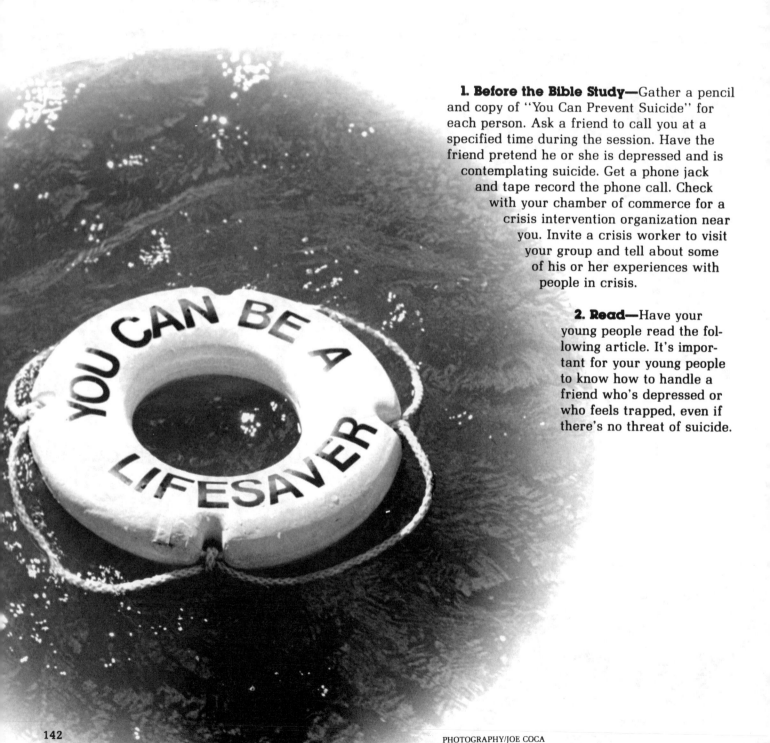

1. Before the Bible Study—Gather a pencil and copy of "You Can Prevent Suicide" for each person. Ask a friend to call you at a specified time during the session. Have the friend pretend he or she is depressed and is contemplating suicide. Get a phone jack and tape record the phone call. Check with your chamber of commerce for a crisis intervention organization near you. Invite a crisis worker to visit your group and tell about some of his or her experiences with people in crisis.

2. Read—Have your young people read the following article. It's important for your young people to know how to handle a friend who's depressed or who feels trapped, even if there's no threat of suicide.

YOU CAN BE A LIFESAVER

PHOTOGRAPHY/JOE COCA

PREVENT SUICIDE

YOU CAN PREVENT SUICIDE

What leads young people to try to take their own lives? What can be done to prevent suicide? What can you and I do when someone we know is struggling with suicidal feelings? What should we do if someone is threatening to commit the act? Are there signs that warn us of the level of danger present in someone who may be suicidal?

Clear and careful answers to those questions could prepare you to prevent tragedy. With more understanding of the factors leading to suicide, you can help defuse some problems before suicidal thoughts become too powerful.

Here are some factors that lead to suicide:

● a sudden upset in life and negative feelings about it

● rejection by a highly valued person

● feeling "down" on oneself and about life in general (depression), cannot sleep or sudden change in mood

● feeling extreme pressure from activities, responsibilities, grades, etc.

● feeling "trapped"—no way out but suicide

● talking about "ending it all,"—and having a workable plan for getting the job done

Other typical contributing factors that can lead to suicidal feelings include:

● severe, long-lasting illness or permanent disability

● history of suicide in the family or among friends

● extended loneliness or loss of supportive friends

Someone who talks about ending life and has a well thought-out plan for suicide is in very big danger of carrying out the plan. Usually, a person feels there are no other choices present. But talking with someone else also means that the suicidal person wants help.

The key to helping a suicidal person is knowing that he or she has two very strong feelings: *1) The only way out of my problems is to kill myself; 2) I want help to keep from killing myself.* These two feelings need to be understood by the helping person. And that understanding then needs to be shared with the person needing help.

The next step would be to work out a practical plan for fixing the problems that face the person.

If the person feels depressed, out of control, can't sleep, is alone, and has worked out a plan for suicide, professional help is needed immediately. Protection from a suicidal act is always the number one priority. Then, a plan can be worked out for handling the problems.

You can find out how to get professional help in your community by asking your pastor or physician. You also can check the yellow pages in your phone book for mental health services, suicide prevention centers or family service agencies. Be sure to find the local phone number for emergency service, so you'll always know exactly who to call if you need immediate assistance.

If the person doesn't have a clear plan for suicide, has some friends or family around all

You Can Prevent Suicide continued

the time, believes he or she is in control of his or her own actions and shows some clear relief from talking about specific alternatives to suicide, the risk is not nearly so great. You can offer to continue helping, particularly if the person chooses not to seek professional help right away.

You can provide effective support by following these guidelines:

- Be calm and help the person stabilize his or her feelings.
- Listen carefully and share your understanding of what the person is feeling.
- Keep considering how much danger of suicide is present.

- Let the person know that you care how he or she feels and that you are willing to help.
- Identify some meaning or value in life that can become important to the person.
- Work together to construct a plan for help.
- Ask the person if you could pray together for God's help.
- Scripture passages should be chosen for reassurance and support; for example: Matthew 7:7; Romans 3:23-24.

Each of us has a beautiful, powerful gift to offer someone who is suicidal—the gift of our love that is a part of God's love. By offering that gift carefully, we can be true helpers.

—*John Shaw*

3. Practice—After reading this article, summarize the points the author makes about suicide—its causes, how to help someone and when to recommend professional counseling. Write the points out so everyone can see them.

Read the following real-life suicide account. Then discuss the questions.

Ken W. was a star athlete. But he had been confined to a wheelchair since breaking his neck in a good-natured wrestling match less than two years ago.

Two of his close friends carried his wheelchair into the woods where he held a shotgun to his stomach and squeezed the trigger.

The dead man's father was surprised when his son's friends where charged with murder for helping carry the wheelchair to the woods. "These men are not criminals," the father said. "They were very compassionate. They tried to help my son along."

What sorts of things would you tell the son if he confided to you that he was planning to kill himself? How do you feel about the father's comment? What would you do if you were Ken's friends? Do you think the friends should have been charged with murder? Why or why not?

4. Phone Conversation—Carry the previous exercise one step further by holding this session near a phone. Have a friend call you at a specified time and pretend that he's depressed and is contemplating suicide. With the whole group working together, determine what to say to the caller.

Tape record the phone conversation and play it back after the phone exercise has ended. What things would the group do differently next time? Have the students experienced a similar situation with a friend or relative? Explain.

5. Case Studies—Divide into pairs. Have one person in each pair create a case study about a person threatening to commit suicide. What is the situation? How does the person feel about life? Why does he or she want to die?

Have the pairs sit back to back. One person in each pair presents the case study in first person; for example: "My parents are getting a divorce. I feel sick about it because I think it's all my fault. If I weren't here, they'd probably get back together . . ."

The other person tries to help by talking the problem through. After a few minutes, switch roles. Discuss as a large group. Was this a difficult exercise to do? Explain.

6. Crisis Intervention—Have a crisis worker visit your group and tell about some of his or her experiences with people in crisis. Have this person show you practical skills in dealing with people who have problems.

7. Closing—End the session by listing concrete ways your group members can be more sensitive and caring for each other.

51
NUCLEAR SIMULATION GAMES

The nuclear issue frightens us all. The issues are so complex that it's difficult to get a personal handle on what it all means. Here are two simple games in disarmament and decision-making. Use the outlines. Adapt them. They're yours.

——— NUCLEAR POKER ———

1. Purpose—To give your young people a feel for the different issues involved in the nuclear disarmament dilemma between the superpowers. In 1 Kings 12, King Rehoboam consulted the elders, who were soft, compassionate leaders, and the young men, who were hard and unfeeling. The question this game addresses is whether a hard-line or a soft-line approach to problem-solving is best.

2. Objective—To negotiate peace or to win a war.

3. Before the Game—Gather posterboard and six soft-drink bottles for each team.

Read through this outline and start thinking about how you can make this meeting effective with your group.

There are different ways to conduct this game. Here are three ideas:

● Divide your group into teams of four or five. You'll need an even number of groups for this exercise. Have the teams go to different members' homes. Two teams have each other's phone numbers. The negotiating takes place with the telephone as the only means of communicating.

● If your church has two or more phones (or an intercom system), use them to separate the teams.

● If you can't separate the teams, place a large sheet of posterboard in the middle of a table. Have the two negotiators sit opposite each other with the posterboard between them.

Use other sheets of posterboard to make a "nuclear poker board" for each team that looks something like this:

ARM	DISARM
◯	◯
◯	◯
◯	◯
◯	◯
◯	◯
◯	◯

Each team gets six soft-drink bottles. These are nuclear bombs. Obviously, each team can't see the other's bombs.

Have each group choose a negotiator, the only person who can talk with the opposing group. The remaining team members should divide into two smaller groups of "advisors": those who want a hard-line approach and want to win and those who want a soft-line approach and want peace.

Nuclear Simulation Games continued

4. The Poker Game—Have the hard-liners and soft-liners within each of the groups meet to discuss strategy. Each team may place its bombs anywhere on its nuclear poker board to start.

The negotiators of the two teams are to talk back and forth trying to get each other's bombs disarmed (moved into the "Disarm" side of the posterboard). Neither can see what the other is doing. The negotiators may either lie or tell the truth, depending on their team's strategy.

During the negotiations, the teams can advise the negotiators any way they feel like, providing the soft-line and the hard-line groups play their respective roles.

Each team has a referee who observes the action and keeps time.

The teams have seven minutes to start and finish the negotiations. When the time is up, both teams must show or tell each other where their bombs are placed.

If all the bombs on both sides are in the "Disarm" position, then there is peace. If one team ends up with more bombs "Armed" than the other, it wins the nuclear war and the other side dies. If both teams have the same number of bombs "Armed," then the sides are considered at a standoff.

5. Debriefing Time—Get your whole group back together and ask these questions:
- How did the negotiators feel during the game? the hard-liners? the soft-liners?
- Which of the smaller groups seemed to win out: the hard-liners or the soft-liners? Why do you think one group won over the other?
- If one group "won," how did the winners feel? How did the losers feel?
- What were the issues or problems the teams faced during the negotiating?
- Why was it hard or easy to trust the other team?
- What approach is the United States now using in nuclear negotiations—hard, soft or somewhere between the two?
- What makes disarming so difficult?
- Did any group remove the posterboard barrier, or somehow try to find out where the other team's bombs were positioned during the game? How would knowing what the other team is doing or thinking affect the negotiations?
- Read James 4:1-3. What are the root causes for conflict? How does being a "peacemaker" get into action in disarmament talks between superpowers?

THE SURVIVOR

1. Purpose—To give your young people a feel for the various problems that survivors of a nuclear war would face and to help them think about what skills are necessary to rebuild a society. This is a variation of several well-known simulation games.

2. Objective—To decide which survivors will be provided adequate food and supplies for further survival and the rebuilding of a society.

3. Before the Game—Gather some newsprint, a marker, a paper and pencil for each person and 3×5 cards with skills written on them (see "Skill Cards").

4. The Opening—Young people should sit comfortably, but somewhat spaced apart, around your meeting room.

Read to them the following world situation:

The date is July 1, 1999.

Due to terrible harvest and crop productions and the failure of the worldwide economic situation, the Third World nations in Africa and Asia have developed nuclear weapons to blackmail the superpowers.

One of the small Third World nations decided to launch missiles to force response. This terrorist country warned that more retaliation would come if it didn't receive food. The two superpowers failed to reach an agreement on what to do and the Third World nation launched a full attack on the United States and Russia.

One of the areas hit is your city. All food and water supplies are contaminated and the "dirty" nature of the nuclear bomb has forced severe shortages in all housing, food and water.

You are in a civil defense shelter with enough uncontaminated food and water for only half of those in your group.

5. The Survivor Game—Give everyone a blank sheet of paper and instruct each group member to list 10 qualities that he or she possesses (for example: loving, caring, compassionate, gets things done, etc.).

Group members should work together to list on newsprint the qualities and skills they feel are necessary for survival in a post-nuclear-attack society. Remind them they are planning for a future society; they might want to first list farming skills, medical knowledge, building skills, etc.

Group members should rank the items on their list

from most important (#1) to least important.

Distribute the skill cards, one to a member. Tell your group members: Your card lists the skills you have. Silently compare how your skill measures up with the list on newsprint. On the paper you used to list your personal qualities, write a paragraph of reasons why you should be chosen to survive and help rebuild society. Rate your chances of the group deciding that you will live; secretly write on your paper: good, poor, almost none or none.

Have each person read to the group his or her skill card and paragraph saying why he or she should be chosen to survive.

The whole group should vote for the persons who will survive. (If there are 10 group members, five will be chosen to survive.) Use sheets of paper for a secret ballot. Tally the ballots and list on newsprint the persons who are selected and their skill/society title.

6. Debriefing Time—Discuss these questions with your group:

● How did your secret rating of your survival possibility compare with the group's selection? Were you surprised, angry, pleased, what?

● What kind of society have you constructed? Do the people you've selected have both the skills and values needed to construct a viable society? Would the society you made have a real chance of survival in a post-nuclear-attack age? Explain. How did prejudice affect your selections?

● How did your faith affect your voting? Select one of the following and explain:

"My faith was the primary criterion for selecting."

"My faith played an important role in selection."

"My faith had some influence in my selection."

"My faith did not enter into the selection process."

● Did you vote for yourself? If yes, did that vote reflect:

1. High self-esteem?

2. The knowledge that your skill was necessary to the society?

3. Your personal desire to stay alive?

If no, did it reflect:

1. Low self-esteem?

2. The knowledge that your skill wasn't necessary for society?

3. Your willingness to give your life for others to live?

● Have each group member complete this sentence: The most important thing I learned in this game was . . .

—*Larry Keefauver*

SKILL CARDS

Business executive
You have been the vice president of a large corporation with offices around the country.
You are white and conservative.
Male and elderly.

Medical doctor and professor
You are a family doctor who can do basic surgery; you're also a professor.
You have strong socialist and communist beliefs.
Female and elderly.

Politician
You have been elected to a number of major offices and are an expert in law.
You are a white Protestant.
Female and elderly.

Psychologist
You have excellent skills in human relations and marriage counseling.
You are European and an atheist.
Male and elderly.

Social worker
You have worked in many welfare and United Fund agencies.
You are white and politically moderate.
Female and middle-aged.

Priest
You are a Roman Catholic priest who strongly favors a traditional church.
You are a poor Haitian refugee.
Male and middle-aged.

Homemaker
You have excellent skills in parenting, cooking and property maintenance.
You are an Asian Buddhist.
Female and middle-aged.

Nurse
You have worked in intensive care, gynecology, and pediatrics.
You are a white, middle-class liberal.
Female and middle-aged.

Building contractor
You have excellent skills in all kinds of construction.
You are a black Muslim.
Male and middle-aged.

Farmer
You are an expert in growing food and understanding agriculture.
You are a migrant worker.
Male and middle-aged.

Mechanic
You are an expert in car repair and also have good skills in appliance repair and electrical work.
You are a Ku Klux Klan white Protestant.
Male and young.

Day laborer
You have worked a lot of day labor pools and are considered a handyman. You have spent a lot of time unemployed.
You are Hispanic and poor.
Male and young.

Water treatment specialist
You have expert skills in cleaning and purifying water. You also have plumbing skills.
You are an Asian Hindu.
Male and young.

Computer programmer
You have skills in programming computers and adapting them to support ways to serve people.
You are a black Baptist.
Female and young.

Dentist
You have super skills in dental work and have side interests as a dietician.
You are an Orthodox Jew.
Male and young.

AFTER THE FIGHT

1. Before the Bible Study—Gather a pencil, Bible and copy of "Fights 'n' Friends" for each person. Provide paper plates, crepe paper, yarn, newsprint, construction paper, scissors, staples and tape.

2. Take a Stand—Take a couple of minutes and have the kids work through the "Fights 'n' Friends" handout at right.

3. Continuum—After the youth complete the exercise, designate an invisible continuum line across the room. Make one end "always" and the other "never." Encourage kids to stand where they marked their X. Talk about their responses.

4. Discuss—Form small groups of four and have members share their responses to the "Fights 'n' Friends" pie. Ask small group members to share one discovery about themselves and fights.

5. Bible Study—Read Matthew 5:23-24. Ask your young people about a person they recently argued with. Have they gone to that person and talked about it? What made that easy or difficult? If they haven't talked to that person, encourage them to set a time and goal to do so. Now read Matthew 18:15. Discuss ways to individually approach him or her (by phone, in person, with a note). Ask: Which way is most helpful? Why? If someone's angry with you, which approach do you prefer?

6. Armor Making—Read Ephesians 6:13-17. Pair up and have partners share the piece of armor they feel they need most. Provide paper plates, crepe paper, yarn, newsprint, construction paper, scissors, staples, tape, etc. Then have partners create the necessary "armor" for each other. As a worship celebration, begin reading Ephesians 6:10-13. Have each person dress his or her partner with the needed armor and say, "(Name), I give you the armor of _____ because _____. Be bold in sharing the Good News." Continue around the circle until everyone has received his or her armor and blessing. Close by reading Ephesians 6:23-24.

FIGHTS 'N' FRIENDS

Mark an X at the point on each of the following lines that best describes you.

Seems like I'm . . .
always in   never in
conflict _____ conflict

Arguments are . . .
always my   never my
fault _____ fault

Finding ways to solve problems with my friends are . . .
always on   never on
my mind _____ my mind

Think of someone you've recently had an argument with. Then complete this sentence: "After our fight, I felt . . ." Place as many answers as you can inside each pie piece.

Get to the bottom of your feelings by writing *why* you felt the way you did. Put your answers in the appropriate circles.

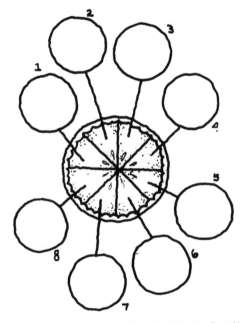

FRIENDS

Friendships.
  Relationships.

They're an integral part of our Christian faith and life.

Since it's the beginning of another school year young people face a special opportunity to make new friends and deepen relationships with old friends.

This Bible study brings together our human need for making friends with the concept of discipleship as friend-making.

1. Objectives—Participants will learn:
● how they become a friend.
● how they share with others their friendship with Jesus.

2. Before the Bible Study—Gather newsprint, paper, markers and pencils for each small group. Follow these hints:
● The numbered activities 3-9 are structured for small groups of six or seven people.
● Print activities on a chalkboard or newsprint to encourage small group participation.
● Use other materials to provide mini-lectures. The following books on friendship are good resources for further study:
The Friendship Factor by Alan Loy McGinnis, Augsburg.
Real Friends by Barbara Varenhorst, Harper and Row.
Friend to Friend: How You Can Help a Friend Through a Problem by J. David Stone and Larry Keefauver, Group Books.

3. Opening—Say to your young people: Introduce yourself using only your middle name. If you don't have a middle name, choose one that has some meaning for you. If you were given your middle name for some special reason, share this with us.

4. Identify—Ask each person to identify a different person for each of the following categories:

An acquaintance:
Name: _____
Word or phrase: _____
Someone you enjoy being with:
Name: _____
Word or phrase: _____
A close friend:
Name: _____
Word or phrase: _____

Then have each person choose a word or phrase which describes his or her relationship with that person. As small group members share, have one for each group list words and phrases on newsprint under the heading "Characteristics of Friendship."

5. Bible Verses—Have members of each small group look up the following Bible verses for additional insight into the characteristics of friendship. As group members share verses, have the recorders add the characteristics to the newsprint listings. Proverbs 17:17; 18:24; Matthew 25:40; Mark 12:31; John 13:1; 34-35; 15:13-15; Romans 13:10; 14:13, 19; 15:7; 1 Corinthians 13:4, 6-7; Galatians 5:13; Philippians 2:3-4; James 2:8.

Friends continued

6. Friendship—Have each small group share its newsprint list with the total group.

Continue by saying: Friendships are important to our personal well-being, but they're also at the heart of our faith-life. By looking at scripture, we'll explore how God made us his friends.

Ask a person in each group to read aloud each of these verses from the Good News (TEV) translation:

- Colossians 1:20-22 (God made us his friends.)
- Acts 2:42 (Jesus' disciples became a fellowship of believers.)
- 2 Corinthians 5:11-21 (Christ changed us from enemies to friends.)

Encourage group members to talk about how God made us friends and explore what God expects of his friends.

7. Compare—Relate scripture to personal life by saying: Recall which persons in your life helped you recognize Christ as your friend. What did they do? Encourage participants to share responses in small groups.

8. Five Rules—Write the five rules for deepening friendships on newsprint for all to see.

Five Rules for Deepening Friendships

1. Assign top priority to your relationships.
2. Cultivate transparency.
3. Dare to talk about your affection.
4. Learn the gestures of love.
5. Create space in your relationships.

Introduce and explain them by saying something like this:

Research indicates that most people become aware of Christ through a friend. For many of us, the friend has been a parent or relative. How about you? Were friends the "door openers" to Christ?

Alan Loy McGinnis, in his book **The Friendship Factor**, identifies five rules for deepening friendships. These rules also apply to our making friends for Jesus.

First of all, if we give top priority to our relationship with Jesus, our other relationships will grow. Likewise, we'll desire to include others in this friendship.

Rule two encourages us to be open in our relationships. Jesus modeled this openness in the midst of his disciples. He says in John 15:15, "No longer do I call you servants . . . but I call you friends . . ." Openness

encourages others to be a part of our life. Openness about our values and faith invites others to "try out" our beliefs.

Rule three challenges us to speak about our love for one another. Saying how much we care isn't easy. Yet daring to talk about our love is important in developing friendships.

Rule four speaks of the ways we demonstrate our love. In his book, McGinnis speaks of rituals, gifts and kindness as particular gestures of love. Hugs and handshakes are rituals that demonstrate our affection for one another. Prayer and other worship practices demonstrate our love for Jesus.

Rule five, as proposed by McGinnis, suggests that relationships which try to dominate, control or judge will fail. Successful relationships allow friends to be free. Christ frees us from sin in order that we can become friends. Others need the freedom to choose Christ as a friend too.

One way to make friends for Jesus is by sharing with others how our lives are linked with Jesus' life. Roy W. Fairchild, in his book **Lifestory Conversations**, calls this "linking our story with His story."

As a beginning step in sharing our lifestories,

Fairchild suggests the following themes:
- joys and high points,
- life-shaping influences,
- troubles and hurts, and
- transitions and transformations.

Reflect on the meaning and direction in your own life, using these steps as a starting point.

9. Timeline—Have each person make a timeline. Say: Indicate the high and low points of your life by drawing them on newsprint. Label the significant events with dates and notes about each situation. When everyone in your small group is finished, each of you can share your timeline. If possible, tell how your relationship with Christ was or wasn't a part of your experiences.

10. Insights—Get together as a total group and talk about the insights gained from the Bible study. Depending on your group members' response, discuss how their Christian faith-life surfaced in their life-story conversations (timelines). Ask: As you recall sharing in your small group, what stands out for you? Be sensitive and affirming.

11. Closing—Share a story about how God was particularly close to you in your life. End with a brief prayer.

An alternative closing is a circle prayer. Have group members hold hands and each offer a sentence prayer. A squeeze of the hand indicates that an individual wishes to pass.

—Dean Dammann

BEAUTIFUL PEOPLE BIBLE STUDY

Leaders: Use this Bible study with your youth group when you know there's pressure at school with class elections, homecoming, choosing team captains, etc. Invite each group member to do the Bible study with a partner. Make a copy of "The Beautiful People" and give one to each person.

Encourage those two to become prayer partners for the next three months. Give ideas of special things they could do for each other. Suggest surprise notes in each other's lockers, a cupcake by their coat after youth group, or other ways to celebrate little personal victories. Plan to keep in touch with what's happening between the "Beautiful People" partners. Every so often, remind them of their commitment to each other.

THE BEAUTIFUL PEOPLE

Use this personal Bible study to explore the concept of "beautiful people." Compare your ideas with God's.

1. List the names of five "beautiful people" at your school:

2. Look at the names and think about why you consider them "beautiful." Are they in the "popular" crowd—athletes, homecoming candidates, cheerleaders, class officers, student body president? Are they in your close circle of friends? Are any of them teachers, janitors or cooks? How did you define a "beautiful" person?

3. What makes someone beautiful in God's eyes? Read Colossians 3:12. What does this say about God's "selection" process? What are God's criteria for loving someone? Do you qualify?

4. Do you think God considers *you* one of the "beautiful people"? Why or why not? Read Psalm 139:1-18; Isaiah 43:1; Ephesians 2:4-9; and 1 Peter 2:9-10 if you have any doubts.

5. Colossians 3:12-17 gives a few hints about living. Being one of God's "beautiful people" calls you to a unique lifestyle. It's one that draws attention to God—not yourself. (Read Ephesians 2:10.) How is that different from what many people consider "beautiful"? To whom does Colossians 3:17 point us?

6. Choose one "beautiful" quality from Colossians 3:12-15 that you want to develop. Write it here:

Pray that you and God, together, will bring that beautiful quality into your life.

Being a Christian during youth group meetings and on Sundays is easy for most young people. But living the Christian life as a high school student is something else. Life in high school is not a right-and-wrong affair. There are few simple and clear answers.

So how do you help young people cope with the issues, the difficult times, the questions—even the victories— they face on their high school campus? Things might be easier if you could walk with them through each school day, helping them solve problems and guiding them in the decisions they have to make.

But you can't. And you shouldn't.

The High School Game is designed to help your young people tie what they experience in their youth group with the lives they lead as high school students. The activities help them see that it is possible to be a Christian and thrive in high school.

The High School Game is a 90-minute meeting made up of three major elements, all easily organized and set up for your group:

1. "The High School Exam" on pages 157 & 158 is a self-test. Young people complete it individually and bring it to each of the centers, where their answers become part of the session.

54
THE HIGH SCHOOL GAME

2. The five learning centers are simple for you and interested young people to set up and run. They cover these areas:

● "Real Friends" helps young people to improve themselves as friends.

● "Me!" encourages young people to see that they are special.

● "What Do I Do Now?" explores various dilemmas young people face at school.

● "Beat 'Em, Bust 'Em, Readjust 'Em" takes a look at Christians and competition.

● "Are You Busy Saturday Night?" encourages young people to look at dating from a biblical perspective.

3. The closing worship caps the entire meeting off with volunteers summing up what they've learned and being part of a positive worship experience.

ALL ABOUT THE HIGH SCHOOL GAME

Here are bits and pieces of information to help you create a memorable learning experience for your group:

1. Involve Your Young People—Now is a perfect time for recruiting interested young people to help you set up this activity. Gather your young people together and give them copies of this outline. Read carefully through the steps for setting up the experience and making it happen.

Then divide your young people into teams of three or four. Give each team one of the five learning centers, the closing worship or "The High School Exam" to set up or lead.

After the assignments are made, follow up on the various teams to help them with any problems. Encourage them in their efforts.

PHOTOGRAPHY/LAUREL WATSON

2. About the Sessions—Each of the five learning centers contains the following elements:

● *Objectives*—What each young person who works through the center will accomplish or experience.

● *Materials needed*—Here's a list of the basic materials needed to give your group a quality, lasting experience. Everything listed is available either around the church, in your young people's homes or in stores around your community. Add to this list as you come up with creative special touches.

● *Set up*—Simple instructions on decorating and setting up the learning center.

● *Assignments*—Each learning center needs no leader. Instead, an "Assignment" gives the teams of three young people instructions on what to do at that center. All this leaves you and other adult leaders freedom to be part of a team or to float from team to team.

HOW TO GET STARTED

Here's a process to follow in setting up **The High School Game**:

1. Read through these instructions carefully. Then reread everything, thinking of your group and your meeting room. Jot notes and questions you may have.

2. Bring interested young people together and explain the concept of the game. Let them read through this outline. Then divide the responsibilities.

3. Publicize this event well. Design a simple letter on notebook paper using local school logos. Or send out a mock report card with details of the meeting. Or send a secret note from study hall to everyone.

4. Picture your meeting room in your mind. Sketch a diagram of the room on a sheet of paper. Visualize how the centers would look and how they should be placed. You'll be dividing your group into teams of three to experience the centers together. Place the centers far enough apart to allow the groups to complete their activities.

For instance, a typical rectangular room might be set up something like this:

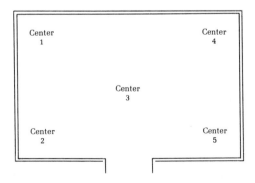

5. Collect the materials needed for each center. This is a great way to involve your young people. Encourage them to come up with additional ways of bringing their own special touch to the centers.

6. Collect large pieces of posterboard and several markers. Write the "Assignment" for each center on separate sheets of posterboard. Find someone in your group with an artistic flair to add colorful, fun artwork to the directions.

7. Make enough worksheets or handouts as the centers require.

8. Bring all the pieces together the night before the meeting or at least two hours before the meeting starts. Set up your meeting room using the following ideas:

● Prepare the "Set Up" ideas for each center.

● Use streamers, yarn or a chalk line drawn on the floor to section off the learning centers.

● Set up the learning centers like miniature classrooms.

● Use carpet remnants to distinguish one center from the others.

● Use school books to fashion a path from one center to another—like a school hallway.

● Make newsprint posters like the ones you see in school for elections, sporting events, etc.

● Write the names of different subjects and school activities on balloons to hang around the room.

9. Set up the centers using the items listed in the instructions. Feel free to add your own ideas to customize the centers for your group.

THE HIGH SCHOOL GAME NIGHT

1. When the time for this meeting arrives, the room should be decorated in high school style, the learning centers set up and the handouts prepared and the closing worship session planned. As people arrive, give them each a pencil and a copy of "The High School Exam." Ask them to take the exam as a "class" when everyone has arrived. Provide scissors, paper and glue.

2. Introduce the meeting as experiences and activities that will help them think through their roles as Christians in their high school.

3. Divide into teams of three and assign each team to one of the centers. It's okay if you have a small group and don't use all of the centers at the same time. If you have a larger group, it's okay to have more than one team at each center.

4. Explain how the centers work. Each team will visit each center during the evening. There's no special order to the centers. For the typical 90-minute meeting, the time breakdown could look something like this:

● Introduction and "The High School Exam"   5 minutes
● Each learning center (15 minutes)   75 minutes
● Closing worship   <u>10 minutes</u>
    90 minutes

The High School Game continued

Watch the time carefully. Keep teams aware of how much time they have if it appears they're taking too much time on any one activity. Use a cowbell, kazoo, duck call, pan and spoon or other noise maker to signal the end of each 15-minute period during the learning center time. Allow ample time to complete the closing worship.

5. Randomly assign teams to a center and begin. Remind your young people to take their "High School Exams" with them. If questions or problems come up, include your young people in the problem-solving. Their insights are valuable. The centers are flexible. Adapt or change them to meet your group's specific needs.

6. At the end of 80 minutes, bring everyone together for the closing worship session. Either prepare to lead the activities yourself or enlist capable youth group members to provide a positive ending for this learning and faith-building experience.

REAL FRIENDS

Objectives

In this center each person will:
- discuss a portion of "The High School Exam."
- design a "friendship shirt" for other team members.
- read Bible verses concerning friendship.
- choose one friendship quality to improve (and pray about).

Materials Needed
- a grocery bag for each person
- ribbon, yarn or string
- Bibles
- markers
- scissors
- glue or tape
- magazines
- other fun "stuff" to be creative with!

Set Up

Decorate this center with a Home Economics or "clothing" flair. Hang letter sweaters, jackets, a chemist's robe, cook's apron, sports uniforms or other clothing associated with school. Hang them from a coat rack, over chairs, on tables or tape them on the wall.

Assignment

1. Design a fun "friendship shirt" for one of your partners from grocery bags. Cut a long opening on one wide side of the sack. Also cut a neck opening and arm holes. Decorate the "shirt" with pictures, drawings and words that symbolize the friendship qualities you appreciate in that person.

2. Discuss answers from the "Real Friends" portion of "The High School Exam." Show which animal head you cut out and explain why it shows what

you're like as a friend.

3. Read the following Bible passages. On your shirt write all the qualities of friendship you discover in these verses: John 13:34; Romans 12:10-13; Galatians 5:22; Ephesians 4:32.

4. Choose one quality from the ones you just listed that you most need to work on when you're at school. Circle that quality.

5. Share the quality with your partners and explain why you chose that one.

6. Remember each of the qualities your partners chose to work on. You'll need them for the worship prayer time. Don't forget to wear your new shirts to the worship!

ME!

Objectives

In this center each person will:
- discuss a portion of "The High School Exam."
- read Bible verses concerning self-image.
- make an "I'm a Gift" box.

Materials Needed
- magazines
- scissors
- glue
- egg carton for each person
- tape
- markers
- pencils
- Bibles

Set Up

Create a relaxing atmosphere that promotes time for individual reflection. Provide soft background music and decorate with words and pictures that express specialness. Use colorful banners and posters that say "I'm a Gift!"

Set this area apart with crepe paper streamers and balloons.

Assignment

1. Discuss answers from the "Me!" portion of "The High School Exam."

2. Look through magazines and cut out words and pictures that best describe you and illustrate what makes you unique.

3. Glue them on the cover of an egg carton. This is your "I'm a Gift" box.

4. Read the Bible verses listed. While you're reading, look for words that are special for you. Write those words on your gift box. See if you can find a dozen! Psalm 139:1-6, 13-15; Luke 15:4-7; John 3:16; Romans 8:16-17; 1 Corinthians 12:4-7; 1 Peter 2:9-10.

5. Take your "I'm a Gift" box with you to the closing worship.

WHAT DO I DO NOW?

Objectives

In this center each person will:
- discuss a portion of "The High School Exam."
- read and offer solutions to tough problems.
- use scripture passages to aid in the decision-making process.
- arrive at solutions for problems.

Materials Needed

- 3×5 cards with tough problem situations copied on them
- tray labeled "tough problems"
- paper
- pencils
- Bibles
- paper plates
- tape

Set Up

Design this center like a cafeteria. Supply a table and chairs. Label a lunch tray "tough problems" and place "tough problem" cards face down on it. If you have more than six teams, make duplicates of some of the problems so that each team will have a card. Put all other supplies in the center of the table. How about supplying a snack tray filled with fruit, popcorn or other munchy treats?

Assignment

1. Discuss answers from the "What Do I Do Now?" portion of "The High School Exam."

2. Draw a card from the tray labeled "tough problems."

3. Ask the person whose full name has the most letters to be your recorder.

4. Together think of as many solutions to the problem as you can. The recorder should write down every idea—no matter how crazy it seems!

5. Read the Bible verses supplied with each problem.

6. With scripture in mind, agree on the solution you all feel is best. Remember: Everyone must agree!

7. With tape, attach the "tough problem" card to a paper plate. Write the problem's solution around the plate.

8. Bring the plate to the closing worship.

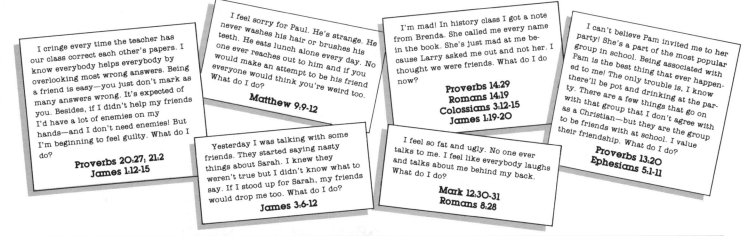

I cringe every time the teacher has our class correct each other's papers. I know everybody helps everybody by overlooking most wrong answers. Being a friend is easy—you just don't mark as many answers wrong. It's expected of you. Besides, if I didn't help my friends I'd have a lot of enemies on my hands—and I don't need enemies! But I'm beginning to feel guilty. What do I do?

Proverbs 20:27; 21:2
James 1:12-15

I feel sorry for Paul. He's strange. He never washes his hair or brushes his teeth. He eats lunch alone every day. No one ever reaches out to him and if you would make an attempt to be his friend everyone would think you're weird too. What do I do?

Matthew 9:9-12

Yesterday I was talking with some friends. They started saying nasty things about Sarah. I knew they weren't true but I didn't know what to say. If I stood up for Sarah, my friends would drop me too. What do I do?

James 3:6-12

I'm mad! In history class I got a note from Brenda. She called me every name in the book. She's just mad at me because Larry asked me out and not her. I thought we were friends. What do I do now?

Proverbs 14:29
Romans 14:19
Colossians 3:12-15
James 1:19-20

I feel so fat and ugly. No one ever talks to me. I feel like everybody laughs and talks about me behind my back. What do I do?

Mark 12:30-31
Romans 8:28

I can't believe Pam invited me to her party! She's a part of the most popular group in school. Being associated with Pam is the best thing that ever happened to me! The only trouble is, I know there'll be pot and drinking at the party. There are a few things that go on with that group that I don't agree with as a Christian—but they are the group to be friends with at school. I value their friendship. What do I do?

Proverbs 13:20
Ephesians 5:1-11

BEAT 'EM, BUST 'EM, READJUST 'EM

Objectives

In this center each person will:
- discuss a portion of "The High School Exam."
- play "The Frisbee and Ladder Game."
- discuss feelings concerning competition.
- rank areas of competition at school.
- read scripture verses that deal with attitudes toward competition.

Materials Needed

- ladder
- Frisbee
- masking tape
- 3×5 cards
- pencils
- Bibles
- slips of paper

Set Up

Give this center the look of a gymnasium. Place sports equipment and other items that reflect games and competition around the area (scoreboard, basketball hoop, trophies, etc.). Prepare "The Frisbee and Ladder Game" by marking each rung of the ladder with masking tape. Starting from the bottom, number each rung with the numbers 2, 4, 6, 8 and so forth. Measure a throw line approximately 10 feet back from the ladder. Mark the line with masking tape so team members can stand behind it when they throw the Frisbee.

Assignment

1. Play "The Frisbee and Ladder Game." Directions: Each person stands behind the throw line. Toss the Frisbee through the rungs of the ladder to gain the most points. After six throws, add your total score.

2. Compare scores and talk about your feelings. How did you feel if you won or lost? When are you most competitive? What's your usual response to competition?

The High School Game continued

3. Discuss your answers from the "Beat 'Em, Bust 'Em, Readjust 'Em" portion of "The High School Exam."

4. List eight areas in your school where you experience competition. Write each area on a separate slip of paper.

5. Rank the areas from most to least competitive. You all must agree on the order.

6. On the ladder, tape the eight slips of paper in rank order: the lowest rung being least competitive, continuing up the ladder.

7. Have each person read one of these passages: Galatians 5:25—6:4; Philippians 2:1-4; James 3:16-18.

8. Explain how each passage can help you deal with competition.

9. Choose one area in school that you struggle with the most. Write it on a 3×5 card and bring it to the closing worship.

ARE YOU BUSY SATURDAY NIGHT?

Objectives

In this center each person will:
- read "The Dating Story" portion of "The High School Exam."
- take a "Rate a Date" report card.
- discuss qualities admired in the opposite sex.
- read a Bible passage that expresses our relationship with the opposite sex.
- write a God-view description of dating.

Materials Needed
- paper
- pencils
- Bibles

Set Up

This center should look like a hallway. With rolls of newsprint design "locker-looking" walls. For fun, hang red construction paper hearts from the ceiling and add any other decorations to make the center appear fun.

Assignment

1. Choose a volunteer to read his or her version of "The Dating Story" from "The High School Exam."

2. Together make a "Rate a Date" report card. Divide a sheet of paper in half. Write "guys" on one half and "girls" on the other.

3. On one half write five qualities that you think girls admire most in guys. On the other half write what qualities guys admire most in girls.

4. Circle any qualities on your list that are similar.

5. With your partners, share answers to these questions:
- Which quality do you admire most in the opposite sex? Why?

- Which quality do you think the opposite sex admires most about you? Why?
- Does the atmosphere at school bring out these qualities in people? Why or why not?

6. Read 1 Corinthians 11:11-12. What does this say about our relationship with the opposite sex?

7. With the scripture verses in mind, write a three-to-five sentence description of dating. Combine God's view and your view.

8. Bring your dating description to the closing worship.

CLOSING WORSHIP

Gather the group in a circle. Remind group members to wear their friendship shirts. Ask each three-person team to place their paper plates with the problem solution in the center of the circle. Form plates into the shape of a cross.

Begin by having volunteers share what they discovered about themselves.

Use the "composite people" they designed in "The High School Exam."

Focus your attention on the cross in the center while someone reads 2 Corinthians 5:21. Say: Jesus came to free us from sin and the things that control us. As a way to show that we give our struggles to him, one by one, share the area that you struggle with the most at school. As participants fold their papers with the struggle written on them, encourage them to share their struggle aloud. Or they can simply place their papers in the center on the paper plate cross.

Say: In our struggles at school—or anywhere—we can be sure that we're never alone. Remember Jesus' promise: "I am with you always, to the close of the age." God is with us and he has placed people in our lives to assure us of his love. Together we celebrate the gifts people can bring.

Ask each group to read the descriptions they wrote in the dating center.

Distribute slips of paper to everyone. Ask them to write a positive word or sentence that reflects what they appreciate about each person in the group. As participants finish writing the good words, have them place the slips of paper in the appropriate "I'm a Gift" box for each person to take home.

Next join hands and say a prayer of strength and friendship. Have partners pray for each other. Keep in mind the quality of friendship that that person chose to work on at the friendship center.

Say: With the Spirit's help we are strengthened to face all situations and relationships. Let these words give you encouragement as you live each day.

Read Ephesians 3:16-21.

Close with a giant group hug.

THE HIGH SCHOOL EXAM

Take this self-quiz and discover more about you and your high school world. Notice that each section has a "creature" choice. After you complete each section, cut out the picture that best describes who you are. Glue them all together on a piece of paper. By the end of the quiz, you just might be surprised to see who you and your friends have created!

Me!

TRUE	FALSE	
T	F	God accepts me the way I am right now.
T	F	I'm more critical of myself than other people.
T	F	I feel comfortable talking about my good qualities and strengths.
T	F	Other people like me.
T	F	I live each day to my fullest potential.

Mark an "x" on the line that describes how you feel:

Most of the time I feel . . .

Great
about myself _____ Down on myself

Loving myself is . . .

The hardest
thing I know _____ Easy as can be!

Learning about myself is . . .

Exciting
and fun _____ Really scary

I'd best describe myself as a . . .

turtle   penguin   monkey

Cut out the body you chose and glue it to the sheet of paper.

Real Friends

1. Complete these sentences:

● To be a friend you must share the same . . .

_____

_____

● I work the hardest at being friends with . . .

_____

_____

● When it comes to forgiveness, it's most difficult for me to . . .

_____

_____

2. It's really hard to be friends with . . .

☐ teachers
☐ school administrators
☐ kids that aren't in my class

3. When it comes to friends . . .

☐ I choose them
☐ they choose me

4. The best place at school to make friends is . . .

☐ in the cafeteria
☐ in the parking lot
☐ during class

5. Most of my friends are . . .

☐ givers
☐ receivers

6. As a friend, I'm most like a . . .

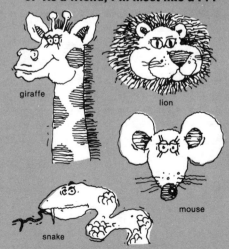

giraffe   lion   mouse   snake

Cut out the head you chose and glue it to the sheet of paper with the body.

The High School Game
continued

Beat 'Em, Bust 'Em, Readjust 'Em

1. **Design your own trophy about yourself:**

I'm the world's
GREATEST
_____

I'm the world's
WORST
_____

2. **Complete these sentences:**

● Competition is/isn't Christian because . . .

_____

● Losing is/isn't easy because . . .

_____

● Winning is/isn't easy because . . .

_____

● The area where I feel most competitive is . . .

_____

3. **As a competitor, I'm most like the legs of a . . .**

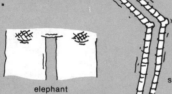

frog

elephant

stork

Cut out the legs you chose and glue them to the sheet of paper with the rest of your new body parts.

What Do I Do Now?

1. Decisions would be a lot easier if . . .

2. I hate making decisions when . . .

3. **When faced with a tough problem, I . . .**
____run away as fast as I can
____jump in and face it immediately
____analyze and look at all the angles . . .
Other:

4. **When friends come to me with their problems, I feel like . . .**
____a teacher
____a janitor
____a coach
____a student

5. **I prefer to face tough problems . . .**
____alone
____with one other friend
____with lots of friends
____with my family
____with God

6. **Create a problem/solution formula:**
____ + ____ = tough problem
____ + ____ = solution to the problem

7. **When it comes to tough problems, I'm most like the feet of a . . .**

tiger

duck

chicken

Cut out the feet you chose and glue them to the sheet of paper with the rest of your new body parts.

Are You Busy Saturday Night?

1. **Fill in the blanks and complete this story:**

THE DATING STORY

My friends and I usually run around together—but tonight's different! I have a date! A real, live date! It's the first time I've ever gone out with _____ and I feel _____. I don't know why, but any time I go out I worry about _____.

I wish I wouldn't be so concerned about what *other* people were thinking. I know I'll see my friends there and they'll be thinking _____. My parents are another story. They don't mind me dating. In fact I think they're glad about it. But it never fails, when I leave the house they always remind me _____. Our youth group talks about dating and relationships with the opposite sex, and whenever we do, we most often discuss _____. I guess a date affects more than the people on the date.

Now that I think about it, I'm looking forward to getting to know _____. I'm confident that I'm a person who has good things to offer, such as _____, _____ and _____! I've always wanted to become friends and date a person who is _____, _____ and _____.

Well, I'd better get ready for this big date!

2. **When it comes to dating, I'm most like the arms of a . . .**

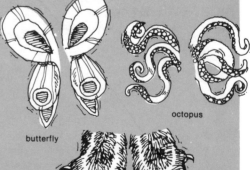

octopus

butterfly

bear

Cut out the arms you chose and glue them to the sheet of paper with the rest of your new body parts.

55

FRESHMAN SURVIVAL NIGHT

THE HORRORS OF FRESHMANCY

Anyone who can remember his or her freshman year can probably recall at least one instance where being an underclassman meant being at an embarrassing disadvantage.

It's forgetting which locker is yours, or getting to your locker and finding everything missing. It's getting lost in the school on the first day, perhaps after being given directions by an upperclass person: "Go down the hall, make a left, go up the stairs. When you hit the pool, go down the elevator." Then you discover there is no pool. Nor is there an elevator.

If you still don't recall what it was like, Nickie Bowers, a 14-year-old high school student from New Jersey will refresh your memory:

"I have to walk across the highway at the bus stop to get my bus," she explains about one of her first days as a freshman. "I'm a little late coming down. I see the bus coming, and my friend Victoria's yelling, 'Come on, Nickie! Come on!'

"There's 20 million cars going back and forth, so there's no way I can cross the street. I'm totally embarrassed. The bus has one freshman other than Victoria on it, and everyone else is laughing at me. So, five minutes later I cross the street!

"I'm trying to be confident and calm and cool. I get on the bus. I go to shut the door and my whole lunch falls out onto the road. So I pick up my lunch. It was really embarrassing."

HOW ONE YOUTH GROUP HELPS

Millions of nervous or overwhelmed teenagers go through similar woes each year in this country—minor instances which are, or at least appear to be, major traumas for the fledgling frosh. Probably, a few weeks or months later, experiences like Nickie's are instances to look back on and laugh about. But in the meantime . . . !

Enter Geri Braden. She is youth minister for St. Mary Catholic Church in Colt's Neck, New Jersey, a rural area with about 850 families in the parish. Students from those families attend one of seven high schools: three Catholic and four public.

After visiting with her young people and talking about their needs (both spoken and perceived), Geri planned a special Freshman Survival Night.

"I decided to have an evening for upperclass teenagers to tell about their freshman experiences and how they got through it," she explains. In advance, Geri enlisted several upperclass people to make the freshmen feel at ease. She met with them to help them determine what they were going to share about

Freshman Survival Night continued

their freshman year.

At first, the planned get-together was a great unknown. Would the kids come? Would they warm up to each other? Would they benefit from the night in the long run?

FRESHMAN SURVIVAL NIGHT

Eight young people came. But Geri's discouragement over low numbers was quickly replaced by her amazement at how rapidly the young people took to the fellowship.

"I was really surprised that freshmen and newer people who didn't know each other were very open," she remarks. "I wouldn't say they shared their deepest, darkest secrets, but they had no problem."

The kids enjoyed Freshman Survival Night.

"We had a chance to be with friends we hadn't seen from our old school that don't go to the new school," explained one freshman. "You could see them and get encouragement."

"It helped me feel more confident about meeting other people," agreed 14-year-old Karyn McCormack.

"It gave us a chance to talk to other people in the same situation as we're in," added Victoria Abba-

tiello, also 14.

Freshman Survival Night opened with two crowd-breakers. Then, after a brief explanation of the evening, each person received a three-section survey sheet to complete.

The first section dealt with "a difficult part about being a freshman." The second asked, "Down deep inside, I am . . .," providing continuums of extreme character descriptions (introvert to extrovert, easygoing to hyper, etc.). The third section consisted of multiple-choice "personality" questions ("Around people I don't know, I'm usually . . ."). The teenagers split up into small groups of four to work on and discuss the survey.

Then the upperclass people told their stories about their freshman year. The freshmen then talked together, using the discussion starters based on the stories. Part of this time also was spent brainstorming "Freshman Survival Tips," a light-hearted list of suggestions such as these:

► Always hide an extra pair of clothes so that when yours are stolen while taking a shower after gym, you will still have something to wear.

► Always turn the gym sneakers in your locker up-

Survey Sheet

A difficult part about being a freshman is:
(Circle your answer. Y = Yes; M = Maybe;
N = No.)

1. Not having all my friends go to my high school.   Y M N
2. Being the "low person on the totem pole" again.   Y M N
3. Being in new surroundings and not sure where everything is.   Y M N
4. Being taken advantage of by upperclass people.   Y M N
5. Always having to be cautious, so as not to do something "stupid" and be laughed at or joked about.   Y M N
6. Memorizing a new locker combination.   Y M N
7. Adjusting to the new cafeteria.   Y M N
8. Being with new people on the school bus.   Y M N
9. The first test in each subject.   Y M N
10. Getting used to all new teachers.   Y M N
11. Not being able to drive while upperclass people can.   Y M N
12. Other (add your own) _____   Y M N

Down deep inside, I am: (Place an "X" on the spot on each continuum that indicates your answer.)

1. easygoing _____ hyper
2. listener _____ talker
3. driver _____ rider
4. optimist _____ pessimist
5. loner _____ grouper
6. leader _____ follower
7. doer _____ thinker
8. giver _____ receiver
9. player _____ spectator
10. introvert _____ extrovert

Around people I don't know, I'm usually:
(Circle two.)

a. super cool   e. goofy
b. nervous   f. confident
c. quiet   g. clumsy
d. outgoing   h. (add your own) _____

In new situations, I usually feel: (Circle two.)

a. frightened   e. painfully shy
b. comfortable   f. relaxed
c. awkward   g. tongue-tied
d. excited   h. (add your own) _____

When it comes to making a tough decision, I generally: (Circle one.)

a. struggle for days
b. make a snap decision
c. wait to see what someone else decides
d. ask for advice
e. hope it will go away
f. take myself on a long walk
g. (add your own) _____

side down, so that when your locker is powdered your sneakers will still be clean.

►Never follow directions given by an upperclass person.

►Write your name phonetically so it won't be murdered by teachers.

►For your protection, tell everyone you have a brother who's a senior and on the wrestling team.

There were many others like these—and a lively conversation about them.

"We followed the discussion with a slide show," says Geri, who takes slides at all the youth activities. "Kids love to see themselves," she adds, "and it's a good reminiscing kind of thing, too.

"For the slides, we played contemporary songs for background music. Then we ended it with a kind of prayer, although the kids wouldn't call it that. We just said, 'It's okay! We're going to make mistakes, and we're all learning, and it's okay. It's nice to be with people who understand you. That's why we get together.'"

Freshman Survival Night ended with refreshments.

IT WORKS! SEE FOR YOURSELF

The first Freshman Survival Night was such a success that a second one was held only a few months later, for which attendance doubled. A third one was then requested by the teenagers.

On the second night, Geri notes that the young people were more ready to get started than she had expected, and one crowdbreaker instead of two would have been enough.

"The kids really just wanted to talk. They simply wanted a sounding board. We didn't even have to ask questions! They just popped right in and started sharing their stories—funny, comical, here and there serious.

"We saw people making new friends," she adds, "and a broadening of already-existing friendships. Some of the guys have asked some of the girls out too."

Based on her two Freshman Survival Nights, Geri has the following pointers for other youth leaders:
● Plan your Freshman Survival Night for late summer, before school starts. Then, if your kids want, schedule another after the first month of school.
● Have a set program, but be flexible.
● Don't overstructure the crowdbreakers.
● Keep it as casual as possible.
● Put the night mostly in the hands of the upperclass people.
● As a leader, moderate the discussion to minimize tangents.
● Keep discussion light.
● Expect sophomores to be more interested upperclass people than juniors and seniors. Sophomores have recent memories of their freshman year.

● Do as much publicity as you can. Ask local high schools to announce the night; at least have your own group members spread the word. Use the phone and personal visits to advertise too.
● Consider inviting youth groups of other churches to participate.
● Don't be discouraged by a small turnout the first time.
● Deal with it as a special project. Don't assume that all freshmen who come will want to come back to all of your other youth group activities, though some might.

Remember, the freshmen you help out now will be sophomores next year (hopefully!). And they'll help you next year with words of encouragement for the next freshmen, such as those offered by sophomore Stephanie Donahue:

"You are only going to be high school freshmen once in your lives. So don't be intimidated by seniors, juniors or sophomores. But on the other hand, don't be a 'know-it-all.'

"Enjoy your frosh year and relax, because it will be over before you know it."

In the meantime, Geri Braden is doing all she can to make that frosh time fly by pleasantly.

—*Paul Baker*

FRESHMAN SURVIVAL NIGHT AT A GLANCE

1. Crowdbreakers
2. Reason for this evening
3. Survey sheet for all to discuss in small groups of three or four
4. Stories by upperclass people about their freshman year
5. Discussion starters based on the stories
6. Survival tips and discussion
7. Slide show
8. Refreshments

DISCUSSION STARTERS

1. Which of the upperclass people's stories would you most fear happening to you? Why?
2. Which of the stories was the funniest? saddest? most harmful? Explain.
3. What are some pressures freshmen face? Explain.
4. Whom do you think you can go to for help during your first few weeks of high school?
5. Read Jeremiah 1:4-10. What kinds of problems did Jeremiah have as a young person? What or who helped him?

56
WHAT'S YOUR TRUST FACTOR?

1. Before the Meeting—Gather a blindfold, pencil and copy of "What's Your Trust Factor?" for each person. You also will need equal amounts of red, green and yellow construction paper. Prepare a brightly colored poster with large block letters that spell "TRUST."

2. Play Trust Games—Begin by playing one or more of these trust games:
● *Trust walk*—Get in groups of two and blindfold one person in each pair. Have the seeing person take the "blind" person for a walk.
● *Trust fall*—Pairs stand close together facing the same direction. Trade off having one partner catch the other as he or she falls. Gradually partners step farther apart, but continue catching each other each time.
● *Pass the bod*—Have group members take their shoes off, sit on the floor and form a circle. Make sure all feet come together to form a close, tight circle. Have one person at a time stand in the middle of the group's feet. Have the center person cross arms in front, stand erect and fall into the outstretched arms of the group. The group then passes the person around the circle as long as possible without letting him or her fall.
● *Trust line*—If your group has 20 or more people, have everyone choose a partner and line up facing the partner, side-by-side. Have group members remove all watches and rings, and firmly grasp their partners' lower arms. This should look like a ladder, with the arms being the rungs. Then have one person carefully jump onto the rungs at one end of the ladder and get bounced down to the other end.

3. Circle Sharing—Bring the group together in a circle. Ask each person to share: What have you learned about trust through these games? Share a special person you can always trust and tell why. Think of someone you can't trust; don't reveal any names; tell why you can't trust that person.

4. The Trust Test—Give each person time to complete the "What's Your Trust Factor?" handout on the following two pages.

5. Colored Paper—When everyone is finished, distribute equal amounts of red, green and yellow construction paper to the group; give each person one color and form groups of three with all three colors in each triad.

6. Trust Talk—In groups of three, have kids share an "always" light from the test, a "sometimes" light, and finally a "never" light. Finish sharing by having kids write their names on their colored paper and exchange the sheets in their group of three.

7. God-Qualities—Discuss with the group: What Godlike qualities must we capture to be trustworthy and faithful in our friendships? Close with prayers asking God for the courage and strength to be trusted friends. Encourage group members to say a special prayer for the person whose colored paper they have. As each personalized prayer is said, tape the colored paper around the word "trust" on the wall.

—*Joani Schultz*

WHAT'S YOUR TRUST FACTOR?

DIRECTIONS: Place an "X" on the traffic light that best answers each question.

When a friend reveals personal information, do you immediately tell others what your friend just told you?

When a friend shares personal information, assume that what's said is meant for you alone.

In trust, Brian told Jill he thought his dad had a job offer. It meant their family might be moving across the country. But Brian's dad didn't get the job, and for weeks Brian battled the rumor of his move. Understandably, Brian was hurt that Jill had shared what he considered a secret.

If people want others to know about themselves, they will take the responsibility of telling. If you feel a strong need to relay information ask permission from the source.

Do you find yourself complaining and saying negative things about others?

Constantly casting a dark shadow on conversations reflects what kind of person you are. Most often people will trust those they know who "put the best construction" on everything. If you're a person who has the reputation of forgiving, listening and offering the benefit of the doubt, you'll be like a magnet. Those positive qualities will attract others to share themselves with you.

In conversations, do you stretch the facts to make stories juicier and more exciting?

If a friend says, "Mike is *so* cute," do you send Cupidlike rumblings saying your friend really likes Mike and wants to go out with him? It won't be long before the word is out: You're someone who blows things out of proportion. Before people confide in you again, they will hesitate because you might exaggerate whatever they say.

Do you jump to conclusions without carefully listening?

Assumptions can get you into trouble. Feelings can be easily misunderstood. Restate and check what you're hearing. Don't be afraid to ask your friend what you think she's just said. Simply ask, "Do I hear you saying . . . ?" and she can correct you if you're wrong.

Accurate communication is crucial for building trust.

When talking with friends, do you often whisper and exclude others from your conversations?

If your friendly lunchroom conversations turn to touchy subjects, learn to reserve them for more private settings. Shifty glances and hushed voices signal mistrust. Others begin thinking: "Maybe they're talking about me. I wonder why? What did I do to make them talk about me?" Even though they might be mistaken, it's easy for others to jump to unhealthy conclusions about you and your trust if you act that way.

When coming home late, do you sneak around and cover up your whereabouts?

Parents will treat you more like an adult when you build trust with them. Two or three times of your parents' discovering whom you *really* were with and where you *really* were will shatter the delicate foundation of parental trust.

Darlene learned the hard way. She started hanging around a group of friends who were into drinking and partying. Darlene knew her parents wouldn't let her go to Friday night's party, so she told them she was doing something else. Later her parents found out she'd lied. Their trust level sank.

Be honest with your mom and dad. They'll appreciate and celebrate your maturity. If you feel like you must be secretive at home, ask yourself why. Re-evaluate your behavior and be honest with yourself. Are you secretive because you're doing hurtful things? Let your sneakiness be a signal for potential personal change.

When asked about certain things, do you fib and tell little white lies?

People grow in trust when they learn that you're honest and not afraid of risking the truth. But lies have a way of haunting you. When people discover contradictions and falsehoods, they have the distinct impression that you can't be trusted. Practice being honest, straightforward and open.

When you're with someone, do you think he or she mistrusts you?

Making assumptions about mistrust breeds mistrust. If you wonder about and question people's motives for friendship, you sow the seeds of mistrust.

Friends *will* trust you if you truly love and care for them. Because of your love, they'll know you always want the best for them and never want to hurt them unnecessarily.

Trust grows out of love. Relationships bound in love automatically create trust as a byproduct.

Do you find it difficult to care about friends who confide in you?

Believe in your friends. Accept the fact that they're confiding in you. The more you feel that your friends trust you to keep their secrets the more you'll do just that! Knowing they're counting on you helps you be a more faithful friend.

Now count the "never" traffic lights. TOTAL:

If you have all (or almost all) "never" lights, congratulations! Keep up the good work! You're a trusted friend and someone people will seek out.

Count the "sometimes" traffic lights. TOTAL:

If most of your lights are "sometimes," re-read the questions. Think about some of the times you said and did these things. Is there a pattern to these situations or are they isolated instances? Work at changing any caution areas in your life.

Count the "always" traffic lights. TOTAL:

Warning! If all (or almost all) of your lights are "always," you may discover your friends abandoning you because they can't trust you. Carefully work on these behaviors. Be aware of your actions and pray for God's special help in building trustworthy relationships.

4 DAYS IN A NURSING HOME

Sleeping bags and pillows carpeted the church parking lot. The church bus—and everybody—looked ready to go.

But Perry wasn't.

The whole idea of spending four days in a nursing home didn't feel right.

"I was thinking of all those feeble, hard-of-hearing old people. Would they be mean? Would they be hard to talk to?"

His thoughts raced to past nursing home visits. They were not something to look forward to.

Was he crazy? Were all 17 youth group members out of their minds? Why would anyone *choose* to spend four days in a prison for dying people?

Yet something had drawn Perry to the unique idea of spending time with people who were four, five, even six times older than he. Maybe he could bring a sparkle of hope to them.

Maybe. Just maybe.

Perry and the other youth group members from First United Methodist Church, Bainbridge, Georgia, were headed for a unique retreat. They planned to stay—day and night—in a nursing home. The youth group was about to live, work, eat and play with some of Magnolia Manor's more than 500 elderly residents.

THE IMPACT OF A NURSING HOME RETREAT

The extended retreat experience wasn't a new concept for Magnolia Manor. The sprawling nursing home in Americus, Georgia, has offered the program for several years.

In the two years the youth group has done this, group members have cleaned and oiled wheelchairs, done yardwork, dusted and cleaned apartments, groomed the nature area, scrubbed and waxed the nursing home bus, and done a number of other chores. And they've done much more. This special group of teenagers grew in Christian servanthood and giving; they appreciated the elderly in a new way; and they gained a fresh perspective on life.

Perry's initial apprehension was understandable. Plenty of hard work and questions lay ahead. But what he and the others found during the experience

4 Days in a
Nursing Home continued

actually changed their concept of the elderly.

"Older people can be just as friendly and outgoing as any other human being," found Perry Hight, a teenager who has gone on the trip both years. "All these people want is someone to visit with."

"The contacts between the young people and the residents are tremendously therapeutic," says Rev. Brooks Partain of the Magnolia Manor staff. "Just by putting on nail polish, writing letters or doing other things for the residents, the young people mean more than the work they accomplish."

After spending so much time with the elderly, the young people gained new insights.

Marcia Willis, another youth group member, learned: "Even though they're in wheelchairs, the elderly can still do a lot of things. And all old people aren't helpless and mean.

"One day when we were cleaning the residents' windows, I walked in and this old woman looked really mean. But when we started talking to her, she was a nice, sweet old lady who shared a lot with us."

Chris Trice, a teenager who's gone on the retreat both years, says, "You would think that most people there would be 'old,' but there are a lot of people who are young at heart.

"For a long time I was scared of growing old," Chris continues, "but in looking at Magnolia Manor, it changes your mind."

THE RETREAT EXPERIENCE

A retreat with an impact such as this takes hours of planning and preparation. Associate pastor L. Glenn Martin remembers the pre-retreat plans. "We contacted Magnolia Manor's public relations person and he really made it happen. Then we secured the dates after our youth council approved the idea."

Next, youth and adult sponsors signed up. Everyone was oriented for the nursing home stay, prepared with sleeping bags, pillows, tools and all other necessary items.

"We had an interesting scene loading the bus. I wouldn't let one guy take along his giant portable radio," recalls Pastor Martin. "They had to realize they'd have to adapt to the lifestyle of a retirement home."

After the project got under way, Magnolia Manor housed and fed the youth group in exchange for the members' services. That helped cut the cost of the project.

As for the actual experience, Rev. Partain emphasizes two aspects: the importance of having plenty of work planned and a flexible schedule to allow time for building relationships.

The youth group completed all sorts of inside and outside tasks. But working in the residents' rooms enabled direct contact with the elderly. Young people held conversations and developed close relationships.

In addition to the work projects, the group had fun. The members swam in a local pool one afternoon, went sightseeing, and took a trip to town for hamburgers one night.

To round out the retreat, the group gathered each evening to discuss the day. "We talked about our experiences—we tried to help each other understand and grow through what we were experiencing," says Pastor Martin. "Then our adults led a closing devotional."

By blending work, play, young and old, the Bainbridge youth group lived four unforgettable days.

YOUR GROUP CAN DO THIS TOO!

Any size group, anywhere, can arrange a nursing home retreat similar to those done by the Bainbridge group. Following these steps will aid you and your group in preparation and actual involvement:

- Find out if your young people want to do a nursing home retreat. At all points, get the young people involved. They must feel ownership. In the same way, you shouldn't try to do everything yourself.
- Ask: Is there a need for a project such as this?

What nursing home would cooperate with a retreat of this nature?

● Contact the nursing home and begin making arrangements.

● Line up adult sponsors. When you've done so—delegate planning responsibilities. Involve sponsors as much as possible.

● Meet with the nursing home staff to:

1. set the date of your stay.

2. establish the number of youth and adult participants from your church.

3. make sure the elderly will be informed of your visit.

4. check with the kitchen staff and arrange meal times so the group members can mingle with the residents.

5. coordinate lodging details such as sleeping arrangements, showers and other facility use.

6. have maintenance people and other staff members prepare a list of duties for young people. (Some suggestions include having walls washed, windows cleaned, knickknacks dusted, clothing mended, hair permed, nails polished, letters read or written, favorite books or the Bible read.)

● Select the work projects to be done and collect any tools or supplies the group should bring.

● Arrange for transportation.

● Write out announcements of the planned event and keep the congregation updated.

● Write a form letter informing the parents of departure and return dates. Fully outline what the youth will be doing at the nursing home. If your church requires written parental permission, send these forms at the same time.

● Make a written list of responsibilities for the adult sponsors. They need to know, specifically, what is required of them, not just during the planning stages, but at the nursing home as well.

● Prepare the young people for some inconveniences: less-than-plush sleeping arrangements, bland food, hushed atmosphere, unpleasant smells, fearful residents, etc.

● Plan to use the "Conversation Starters" and "I Promise" forms.

● Arrange for a nursing home representative to attend the youth group and talk about aging. This person also can prepare the young people for their unique retreat experience.

● Formalize rules and regulations with the group members. These should be developed in conjunction with the needs and setup of the nursing home. Consider respect for the elderly, their possessions and the facilities; moderation of voice; no radios; no complaints about food, living conditions or health of the residents.

● Consider making a financial contribution to the nursing home. Ask the young people and let them

make the decision and plans to raise the donation.

● Keep in touch with the nursing home, calling to make sure both the facility and group are kept up-to-date.

● Arrange musicians and instruments to go from room to room singing.

● Plan recreational opportunities for the group. Welcome breaks include swimming, bowling and visits to fast-food restaurants.

● Give a checklist of what to bring: sleeping bags, towels, washcloths, Bibles, spending money.

● Have the adult sponsors help with a final check. Ask: Has a final call to the nursing home been made to assure arrangements? Are the kids packed and prepared? Is the transportation ready? Do the parents know when you're leaving and returning?

● Enjoy your one-of-a-kind retreat!

—Sandra Wilmoth

I PROMISE

Before the retreat, print this form and have young people fill in the following pledge:

"I Promise"
"Whenever you did this for one of the least important of these brothers of mine, you did it for me!"

—Matthew 25:40

Three things I hope to gain from this experience:

1. _____

2. _____

3. _____

Three things I hope to give:

1. _____

2. _____

3. _____

I promise to work willingly and joyfully in a true servant manner. I realize I am going to work, and that my work will be important. I count. I will be giving of myself—in my labors and in my communications. I will listen more than talk; I will reach out; I will smile; and I will have a helpful word.

Name _____ Date _____

SPLUNGE

On a hot August day, teenagers Tim and Mark stand at a bus stop in the shadows of massive city skyscrapers that seem to overpower them. Neither has ridden a city bus before; however, their goal is to get from where they are to a restaurant located elsewhere in the city. This restaurant will eventually link them to others from their youth group who are in the same situation.

summer program called SPLUNGE (**S**pecial **P**eople **L**iving a **U**niquely **N**ourishing **G**rowthful **E**xperience).

SPLUNGE, sponsored by a group of Denver Catholic youth ministers, makes the inner city come to life once a year for suburban youth. The teenagers experience a variety of activities that confront them with the issues of poverty, justice and lifestyle inner-city dwellers struggle with every day.

On the city streets, SPLUNGE participants learn valuable lessons about life.

Exhaust fumes belch from the downtown morning traffic and police sirens scream through the streets. Businessmen and women clutch their briefcases with one hand and an umbrella in the other, and walk briskly past as if Tim and Mark weren't even there.

"Life in the city sure is strange," Tim mumbles.

"Yeah, it sure is," sighs Mark in agreement.

As they stoop to read the posted bus schedule, both are wondering: How will we get to the restaurant? Which bus should we take? And . . . what if we get lost?

For many teenagers the first bus ride in the heart of any big city would be shocking. But, that's exactly what some suburban Denver teenagers purposefully did last year as part of a week-long, urban-based

"Youth see SPLUNGE as a fun, exciting learning adventure," explains Bill Jaster, the program director and youth pastor of St. Rose of Lima Catholic Church. "It's not a tourist trip. SPLUNGE helps youth develop their Christian responsibility to life's poor and oppressed, and sharpen their awareness to be 'other-centered' through observing, experiencing and becoming actively involved in Christian service."

IT STARTED WITH A "PLUNGE"

The first SPLUNGE happened several years ago and was designed by Bill Jaster and Bryon Plumley. Bryon, a staff member of the Denver Cornerstone Justice and Peace Center, and Bill were both involved

PHOTOGRAPHY/PAUL HORAN

in a similar project at Notre Dame College called Urban PLUNGE. However, the experience they designed was less intense and considered more of a splash than a plunge—so, the name SPLUNGE evolved.

Bryon and Bill wanted to sensitize youth to inner-city life and show them that the city is more than just a place for morons and murderers. Suburban teenagers sometimes see the city as a concrete jungle they'd rather avoid. SPLUNGE puts their fears in perspective and helps them also see the city as a place of beauty, depth and life.

"I used to be scared of the city and the people living there," says Monica, a high school student. "I went to the city because I wanted to know what I was afraid of. SPLUNGE allowed me to see other people as human and lovable."

The program provides a structured atmosphere for young people to live Christ's teachings as a Christian community while being exposed to the inner-city lifestyle.

"Thirteen high school students attended our first Denver SPLUNGE," recalls Bill, "and, it lasted seven days. What those first 13 kids learned and experienced during that time became such an integral part of their lives that it changed them. In fact, several of them have returned and served as leaders."

SPLUNGE TODAY

SPLUNGE begins with the leaders and approximately 20 teenagers spending three days at a retreat center high in the Rocky Mountains. A typical day includes journaling (writing one's experiences), symboling (forming images of a subject using objects from nature), and role-playing games about justice to prepare the group for the city. A personal "pilgrim journey" deep into the woods and a time of prayer provides each group member with confidence and joy before the trip to the city.

From the peaceful mountain retreat, the group emerges to begin its experience in Denver's inner city.

Adjusting to neon lights and the noise of city life is difficult at first. However, after the group settles down in the basement of a church near downtown, anticipation and excitement replace any fear or hesitation.

The remaining four days consist of various activities and learning experiences.

Group members visit a nursing home for senior citizens and hear them tell stories of "how it used to be"; the teenagers are touched when the elderly admonish them not to forget older people. To gain insight into the lives of the needy, group members stock food, sort clothing and help with interviews at local emergency centers. Then they visit with city and county officials to see government's role for the cause of justice in the lives of the poor. The kids ob-

serve a court session and have lunch with a city judge to ask questions regarding our judicial system.

But for many, the most memorable occasion comes at the Catholic Worker House, where the youth group prepares and serves food in the soup kitchen. "When we went to the soup kitchen and served the hungry, I felt I was involved and helping in a more tangible way," says Jim, a youth group member. "I never thought there were so many hungry people right in my own back yard. I thought starving people were only in Ethiopia."

Jennifer, another youth group member, adds: "After serving food to people in the soup kitchen, we sat down and talked with them. We asked them questions like how long they'd been in the streets, did they live a different life before, and what were some of the struggles and joys of street life. This experience made me think more about the poor and homeless and their importance as a people."

Group members play basketball or volleyball at a recreation center, spend the afternoon at an amusement park or have a picnic in a city park to see what city kids do for leisure and entertainment. Finally, the week concludes with prayer, discussion and reflection.

One teenager sums it up well: "SPLUNGE made me realize many things about myself and others. We take too much for granted living in the suburbs and are too selfish."

Bill Jaster feels honored and privileged to help design the program every year. He says: "SPLUNGE is an excellent opportunity to help youth realize and attain their potential of influence in the world where they live. I'm just glad to be a part of it."

YOU CAN DO IT, TOO

Could your group use a good "SPLUNGE"? Would group members welcome a trip to a nearby city, for a time of learning? If so, here's how to do it:

1. **Organize your leadership team.** Include staff members and adult volunteers to implement the program. Since SPLUNGE doesn't have to be limited to just your group, involve pastors or leaders from other churches. Agree on the dates SPLUNGE will be held, and find a place to stay in the city.

2. **Decide on places to visit and things to do.** Some places to visit:
● Nursing homes. Have kids prepare questions regarding the moral support the elderly receive from family members, friends, community, government, etc. Group members could also prepare questions about what a typical day is like, favorite memories, different places the elderly have lived, etc. Have kids give a "mini-service" including a short sermon or Bible story and songs.

SPLUNGE continued

- Where "street people" walk. Divide group members into small groups of five or six with adult supervision, and walk down the city's "skid row." Have kids observe the people on the street. Prepare questions for later discussion.
- City emergency centers. Help with food, clothing, interviews.
- City and county buildings. Have kids prepare questions to ask officials about the judicial system and government's role regarding the poor.
- Recreation centers. Play sports with inner-city youth.

This wall map helps SPLUNGE participants get their bearings on Denver.

Things to do include journal writing about experiences, praying together about needs observed, role-playing games about inner-city lifestyle issues, making collages of images of city life, creating skits, having group discussions, picnicking in a city park, meeting with an inner-city youth group for a pizza party or talent show, serving in a soup kitchen or coffeehouse.

3. Decide on themes for each day. The themes will help group members see order in the varied experiences. The structure will aid their learning and understanding.

4. Prepare a daily outline and a detailed daily schedule. Decide on the details of visiting places and doing other things. Include when you will do them, who will be in charge, food arrangements, discussion questions, etc. Schedule the activities according to each day's theme.

5. Create a registration form and brochure outlining the program. Describe the purpose of SPLUNGE, what it is, dates it will be held, places you will visit, things you will do, costs for the week.

SUGGESTED DAILY THEMES

Day	Theme	Highlights
1	Day by Day	To the retreat center; orientation and overview; community building
2	On the Willows	Learning journaling; practicing quiet time; studying about peace and justice; role playing to prepare for the city
3	Prepare Ye	Finding symbols of God's presence; departure for the city; in pairs, use buses and trains to find way to eating place; settle in church basement
4	Exploring Jerusalem	Exploring the city; visits to institutions, emergency centers; have inner-city youth group show way around
5	All Good Gifts	Finding the good in the city; interviews with shopkeepers; visits to developmental projects, churches; picnic in city park; fun at recreational facilities
6	A Day With Lazarus	Visiting the handicapped, elderly, alcoholics and drug abusers, juvenile offenders; courtroom visit and lunch with judge; walk down "skid row"
7	Salt and Light	Christian service; helping in soup kitchen or coffeehouse; creating collages and skits to help process and debrief experiences; returning home

6. Enthusiastically introduce the program. Introduce SPLUNGE to high school students, freshmen through senior high. Distribute the brochures; make phone calls; do a mailing. Involve no more than 30 from suburban and rural churches.

For more information regarding SPLUNGE, contact Bill Jaster, St. Rose of Lima Catholic Church, 1320 West Nevada Place, Denver, CO 80223, (303) 778-7673.

—Bob Valleau

⦀59
"MY SARI IS SLIPPING!"

People who visit this unique camp think they're in India. They wear awkward Indian clothing, eat strange food and struggle with life-and-death issues. Visitors to this unusual village sometimes forget all this is happening in Wisconsin.

How do you tell kids in your group who cruise the streets of their towns and cities that there are people in the world who walk 30 miles just to find good drinking water?

● How do you explain to the teenager who works at the local McDonald's that there are people whose only meal for the next three days will be a bowl of rice?

● How do you tell someone who's just pumped five quarters into a video game that the same amount of money could feed five hungry children in Northern Ethiopia for one day?

Youth leaders struggle with difficult questions like these. How *do* we sensitize our young people to the needs and concerns of those living in cultures different from our own? One way is to travel to a faraway country, talk with the people and share their food, homes, clothing and other daily experiences.

But for most of us, the journey into another culture is impossible. So now what? The second choice: If you can't go to the country, bring the country to you!

That's exactly what the staff at Wapogasset Lu-

theran Bible Camp has done.

Foreign cultures come to life in the forest near Ox Lake, Wisconsin. With a program of "you-are-there" learning experiences, young people spend three to seven days living as though they are residents of India. A multitude of experiences and activities force them to struggle with the issues of poverty, justice and lifestyle.

GETTING INTO IT

A typical day in the Indian village becomes a not-so-typical experience for its participants. Just imagine . . .

● feeling self-conscious and strange wearing a sari (18-foot-long cloth) if you're a girl or a lungi (nine-foot-long cloth) if you're a guy.

● challenging your taste buds to a strange, exotic-sounding Indian dish you've prepared over an open fire.

● fetching water from a nearby stream, only to find you can't use it until it's boiled for purification.

171

"My Sari Is Slipping!" continued

A hut for a home? Constructing an Indian mud hut was a challenge these campers will remember for a long time.

- sweating to construct a crude, mud hut that becomes your shelter.
- exchanging cultural questions with a visiting Indian who speaks broken English.
- drifting off to sleep with the subtle hum of mosquitoes and sounds of a nearby herd of goats.

These experiences, plus discussion and Bible study, work together to bring a mental and spiritual awakening—a sharpening of who we are as God's people in the world.

This spiritual "sharpening" doesn't come easy. A group of high schoolers from North Minneapolis grumbled as they left their tape recorders and radios behind. Saying goodbye to the comforts and luxuries of home wasn't easy. Complaints of mosquitoes and strange new foods were only a couple of the antici-

The scent of burning wood fills the air as Isaac Moon (left), a pastor from Vellore, India, helps a camper learn the ways of Indian open-fire cooking.

pated aggravations.

One week later an exciting transformation had occurred. Returning from the cross-cultural village to the regular camp, the dozen-plus joined 140 other kids. That night they enthusiastically shared the impact of their week spent in the Indian village. That "pretend" place prompted a deeper understanding of others and themselves. "We're selfish," one young person said sadly. "We eat too much. We use too many resources."

Their week brought a heightened fellowship within their own youth group and a sense of fellowship with the world as they returned home.

There are touching, inspirational moments of learning. And then, there are those unforgettable funny ones. Before the Indian village installed port-a-potties, a group of girls made an unexpected discovery one day. When told to fetch some water, they obediently trouped down a well-worn path in the woods. To their surprise, instead of being on the river bank, they found themselves on the edge of the bathroom "pit."

CROSS-CULTURAL EXPERIENCES MOTIVATE GLOBAL CONCERN

The cross-cultural experience doesn't stop with the experience. The strength of a program such as this is that it motivates campers to consider ways they can live more responsibly as global citizens.

Loren Tieg, the camp director, reflected on his past African journey realizing it had changed his life. "I went hoping to win the world for Christ. But it was a humbling and learning experience. I found out that it was me and my culture that needed to be changed. Through this village I want to help people become more aware. Too often we're talking out of ignorance."

The camp experience stretches people to see that the body of Christ is much greater than the local youth group; it encompasses their community, their country, their world. Participants learn that though "the poor have always been with us," they *can* change their attitudes and lifestyles to help them; they can make a difference!

After an intense experience such as this, individuals discover they're not as afraid to reach out and talk to people visiting from a different culture. Physical kinds of help, like taking part in special foreign projects, becoming aware of political structures, and making financial contributions all make a difference. Even the idea of spending a portion of one's life in another culture becomes more of a natural thought.

One teenager put it this way: "I feel that I should look at my needs rather than just my wants, and not do compulsive buying. And everyone should be conscious of what they use: It's everybody's—not just theirs."

Misunderstanding. Questioning. Learning. Together, campers search scripture for Christian perspectives on Third World concerns.

With a bit of creative energy and resourcefulness, you can produce an experience that enlightens and motivates your young people to global awareness. Choose from this wide variety of suggestions. From simple to elaborate, these ideas can aid you in building a similar learning experience. If you have any questions, contact Lake Wapogasset Lutheran Bible Camp, Route 3, Amery, Wisconsin, 54401-9520.

1. Choose a country. This alone can be an interesting process. Decide with your young people which country you will focus on. Check with your church denomination for mission emphasis. Ask for literature pertaining to that particular mission effort. Use your local library for investigating further information.

2. Find key people. Hunt for resource people who have lived in the foreign country of your choice. Talk to folks who have visited there. Ideally, these people will be Christians who can lead discussions and studies from a Christian perspective. Check with your denominational headquarters for people possibilities.

Check out nearby universities, other churches, schools and personal contacts. You might be pleasantly surprised to find people eager to share insights into foreign countries. They could make helpful suggestions concerning how your group could make a difference.

Another people idea: Include all ages—children, teenagers, young adults, parents, grandparents. Families add a broader dimension to learning experiences.

3. Scout out resources. Use movies, library books, foods, crafts or other creative possibilities. Find out what people in your focus country normally wear and try on those kinds of clothes. Page through ethnic cookbooks and stir up a special recipe together. Discover what games the children play. For fun, learn and play some games. Listen to records; learn phrases of the language; dance to native folk songs; join together to create a typical craft item from that culture. The possibilities are unlimited. Let your imagination run free.

4. Look for various settings. Plan a weekend retreat or an entire week of camping. Transform your church basement into another land. Set up interest areas for learning and make a day of it—invite the whole congregation! Turn the church parking lot into a marketplace. Set up a tent or build a mud hut. Encourage people to visit it and learn how they can care and contribute to that culture. Use a Sunday school room or youth room for a simulated home or living room from another country. How about having young people of your church create an international village for the children's vacation Bible school? Invite parents, youth groups, other churches, the whole community.

5. Prepare simulation games, Bible studies and discussions. Any experience, no matter how great or small, can be the beginning of a better understanding of people in other cultures. Through these discussions, set group and individual goals. Find ways you can tangibly do something to make a difference.

Helping young people gain awareness of global issues is possible! By taking some risks, opening up, looking beyond and stretching your imagination, you can begin an adventure that could make a profound difference in the lives of your young people.

RESOURCES

BaFa-BaFa (simulation game) and others, SIMILE II, 218 12th Street, P.O. Box 910, Del Mar, CA 92014. Phone (619) 755-0272.

The Compassion Project by J. Hancock and R. Van Pelt, Compassion International, Box 7000, Colorado Springs, CO 80933.

Cry Justice by Ronald J. Sider, InterVarsity Press.

Everyone Everywhere (film), Augsburg Publishing House, 426 South 5th Street, Box 1209, Minneapolis, MN 55440. Phone 1-800-328-4648.

Rich Christians in an Age of Hunger by Ronald J. Sider, InterVarsity Press.

World Relief, P.O. Box WRC, Wheaton, IL 60189. Write to the Audio-Visuals Coordinator for a brochure describing their films and filmstrips.

World Vision International, 919 W. Huntington Dr., Box 0, Monrovia, CA 91016. Write to the Special Programs Department for a brochure describing their films.

60

49 WAYS TO HELP YOUR GROUP REACH OUT

trip through the world of missions is to help them see a need. Then list different options for meeting that need and choose which of those options to implement.

Here are a number of ideas to get your group involved in reaching out to others:

• Design and put on a worship program for the people in a rest home or convalescent hospital.

• Invite people from local drug-abuse or treatment agencies to speak about drug abuse in your area.

• Have interested young people prepare a short debate on Bible smuggling.

• Invite teenagers who've grown up with missionary parents to talk about their experiences in foreign cultures.

• Help rebuild or repair an elderly or poor person's home.

• Take part in an organized work or outreach experience.

• Let a local disaster or emergency relief agency train interested youth group members.

• Plan and conduct a vacation Bible school in conjunction with an inner-city church.

• Encourage young people to develop long-term relationships with the elderly by "adopting" grandparents.

• Ask organizations for the handicapped how your group can get involved.

• Set up a babysitting service at a local mall.

• Get involved in your church's vacation Bible school.

• Check with your denominational office for short-term missions opportunities.

• Visit hospitals; ask the chaplain which patients don't get any visitors and visit them.

• Collect clothes for foreign ministries.

• Organize fund raisers for world-hunger organizations.

"**I** feel guilty. I know my group should be more involved in missions, but I spend more time and energy preparing for our socials and special events than I do for anything even closely related to missions."

"The thought of outreach projects bores my kids. It even bores me."

"Good programming is built on meeting kids' felt needs. Topics such as dating, self-image, family relationships and peer pressure should dominate youth group meetings."

Any of these comments sound familiar? Have you said, thought or heard comments like these?

Reaching out to others—"missions"—often gets pushed back into the youth ministry closet along with last summer's church camp materials and the Bible study course that didn't work.

Yet, with the low priority some of us put on missions, young people are increasingly spending time, energy and money searching for opportunities to do something important to help others.

Now is a great time to build on that interest and meet that need to help others by getting your young people involved in outreach projects.

The first step in getting young people to start their

PHOTOGRAPHY/WILL AND ANGIE RUMPF

● Invite speakers from a local Hospice organization to meet with your group.

● Help new residents move in and get settled.

● Collect food for local outreach agencies.

● Take part in a 30-hour fast for hunger awareness and fund raising.

● Visit a children's hospital.

● Volunteer your services to a rescue mission for a series of weekends.

● Sponsor a child through a Christian relief agency.

● Collect money, food and toys for needy families.

● Weatherize an elderly person's home.

● Visit a native American reservation to do whatever's needed. (See accompanying box of ideas.)

● Take a trip to an orphanage. Discuss in advance types of things your group could do to become involved instead of just observe.

● Volunteer your services to the Salvation Army.

● Send cards, flowers, gifts, and books to people in your church who are ill or shut in.

● Run errands, fix food, clean up the home or catch up on chores for the sick.

● Set up supervised recreation times for youngsters in local parks.

● Set up an exchange program with a church from a different culture or race.

● Visit a prison and conduct a worship service.

● Start a letter-writing ministry to people in prisons.

FOREIGN MISSIONS

Expose your young people to missions by involving them in the learning process. Three steps needed to link youthful thirst for adventure with overseas missions are:

1. Make the time spent on missions active.

2. Incorporate missions concepts into all topics.

3. Make provisions for students to experience missions firsthand.

Making traditional foreign missions presentations more active requires creative thought and energy. The idea is to expose your young people to some aspect of overseas mission work. For example, missionaries visiting your church from South America could describe the conditions as they exist in their field (culture, youth needs, youth culture, schools, what kids do in their spare time). Your group could help design a strategy for reaching the young people in that area. Through the missionary's eyes, your young people should be able to imagine what it would be like to relate as Christians to their peers in other cultures.

There's no better way to show kids what missions are all about than to give them direct hands-on experience. Getting your young people involved in projects in your area is great, but don't limit your group's experience possibilities.

Youth groups that travel hundreds of miles on short-term mission projects usually return with changed thoughts about missions. When counting the cost, the effort to raise the funds and to prepare for the trip may seem high, but the results are invaluable.

CONSIDER THESE ACTIVE MISSIONS IDEAS

Care Package—Everybody loves a "homestyle" gift package. After checking some of the customs regulations with the missionary's home office, prepare a bundle of goodies for the missionary's personal or family use. It's super if you know actual sizes for new clothing and can send useful items. Be creative.

Radio Review—Have your group make a cassette tape of singing, short stories, and brief words of encouragement to Christians that can be played over the airwaves or used in a worship service. Let your group's personality shine.

Update—Help a missionary stay current by sending a magazine subscription. Also send a bulletin, church newsletter or your youth group news.

Furlough Service—Contact a missionary family in your area and help make their time here in the States more refreshing. Clean or paint their house, provide baby-sitting, help them move or pack or just make yourselves useful.

Field Reps—Most mission boards have representatives who are well traveled and aware of needs in the areas they serve. Involve them in your youth meeting by having them present some project ideas or career options.

Communication Games—Language barriers make it difficult to share God's love. Games that require non-verbal communication can help make your young people aware of this.

Missions Dinner—When a missionary visits, have your group organize a dinner with an international flavor. Have them interview the missionary about food and customs surrounding mealtimes and then put this information to use for the meal.

Teaching Material—Youth can sort out used Sunday school curricula to determine what would be useful in another culture, then mail it out. Be sure to send only selected items since the expense is worth it only if the literature will be used.

Short-Term Projects—Coordinate a service trip through a missions organization. Plan ahead and take all your young people who meet whatever requirements you establish. The trip can be a motivational incentive; God can really use the experience to change lives.

—*Jim Burns and Steve Greggo*

REACHING OUT TO NATIVE AMERICANS

When we think of reaching out to other groups of people we often overlook our own neighbors. There are many native Americans in our country who could use our support and encouragement. Recently, I found out about a "reservation" of native Americans within a day's drive of our church. Of the 5,000 people who lived there, over 1,000 were teenagers. I was shocked to find out that no youth group had ever offered encouragement to the churches there.

Since my group's involvement with the native Americans, we've come up with several ideas. Here are five:

1. Many native-American pastors can use help in building churches and meeting halls. They can also use help at times in remodeling, maintenance and cleaning.

2. Instead of planning youth group parties and socials for just your group members, why not plan a party that includes the young people of the reservation?

3. Many of the native-American churches plan week-long camp meetings with special programs for all ages. Check with the churches about the dates of the meetings. Then volunteer your group to help.

4. If you have a well-trained youth-worker staff, assist the native-American pastor by training local volunteers to carry out an ongoing ministry with youth.

5. Challenge the young people to a ball game or to a tournament of some kind. Better yet, divide into teams and play crazy games. Provide refreshments for everyone afterward.

Our youth group will never forget our experience there. Most of us agree that we ended up receiving much more than we gave. For names and addresses of native-American pastors, contact your denominational headquarters.

—*Robert Crosby*

TO RUSSIA WITH LOVE

Bring love with action. Stimulate world consciousness in the minds of your young people. Send greetings to a Christian prisoner, who has been imprisoned for his faith, or to the prisoner's family. It's a tangible way to bring joy to the heart of each person who receives your love note. Pick out some meaningful, colorful, religious cards. Get your group together and start writing! Here are some basic guidelines to follow:

1. It's okay to write in English. Most Russians know enough English or know of someone who does—but watch the penmanship.

2. Keep it short.

3. Copy a Bible verse and give the reference. This is precious "bread" to a prisoner with no Bible.

4. Mention that you are praying (then be sure you do).

5. Address the envelope *by hand* and mark it AIR MAIL. Put on the correct postage—40¢ per one-half ounce from the United States.

6. Don't expect an answer. It is difficult to get a letter past the strict censorship.

7. Try your hand at Cyrillic (the Russian alphabet). You might want to copy down some of these phrases.

МЫ ВАС ЛЮБИМ
We love you.

МЫ МОЛИМСЯ О ВАС
We pray for you.

АЛЛИЛУИЯ
Hallelujah!

8. For addresses of prisoners and their families, write to: International Representation for the C.E.B.C. of the S.U., Inc., Georgi P. Vins, Box 1188, Elkhart, IN 46515-1188; or, Word to Russia, P.O. Box 846, Sacramento, CA 95806.

—*LeAnne Trozan*

PART FOUR:
SPECIAL
OCCASIONS

61

VALENTINE'S DAY IDEAS

"HEARTY" PIZZA PARTY

Tell group members to bring their favorite pizza ingredients (mozzarella cheese, pepperoni, mushrooms, etc.). Provide a batch of homemade pizza dough, tomato sauce and baking pans. Pair up group members and have partners shape pizza dough into a heart, then add their favorite pizza toppings. While the pizzas are baking, have a group Bible study on 1 Corinthians 13 or John 15:11-17.

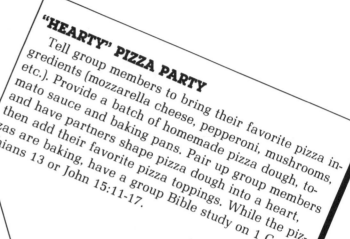

LOVE YOUR NEIGHBOR

Invite everyone to come to the youth group meeting with this requirement: Each person must bring a sack of clothing and a box of canned food to give away. As a group, deliver your "goods" to the nearest helping agency, church or other outlet for food and clothing distribution.

PHOTO FUN

Travel to the nearest quick-photo booth or arrange to have instant-print cameras and film. For a cost of $.75 to $1.25, each youth group member can have self-photos taken to present to parents. Have young people sign their photos, and add something they appreciate about their parents.

REMEMBER WHEN?

Invite group members to recall what life was like when they were little. Ask: What made you feel loved? What gave you feelings of love and appreciation?

Have members write down what they remember. Then encourage them to write about those feelings. Discuss discoveries.

CANDLELIGHT DINING

Plan a dress-up candlelight dinner for the youth group. Transform one of the church's rooms into a candlelight dining area, complete with small tables, candles, fresh flowers and soft music. Find a few parents who would be willing to serve a potluck dinner while the group members enjoy talking and dining. It's a "lovely" chance to dress up in special prom dresses and suits young people wear only once in a while.

APPLE FUN

Provide apples, ribbon and notes. Have group members think of three "everyday" people who've taught them something important in their lives. Give each young person three apples, one for each person chosen. Have them tie a ribbon around the apples' stems with an attached note, "You've taught me . . . and I love you (or appreciate you) for that!" Deliver the apples to the "everyday" people.

LOCKER SHOCKER

Ask youth group members to help collect junk: string, felt, cloth, glitter, cotton balls, colored paper, contact paper, streamers, balloons, ribbon, pipe cleaners. Provide tape, scissors, glue and pins.

Have young people choose one or two friends they'd like to surprise with a little "locker shocker." Then, let them dive into the junk! Give suggestions: create a long, skinny "bananer" banner to hang on the front of the locker door; create a clever heart pocket filled with messages or a place for notes (even sticks of candy); design a "locker shocker" that says "I love you" in those words or in unexpected, creative ways.

Make sure members take their "locker shockers" to school and display them as a special surprise for their friends.

GARAGE DOOR SURPRISES

Have a garage banner-making party where youth group members create huge "I love you, Mom and Dad" posters to display on the family garage door. Use giant old cloth sheets or newsprint as a background for the colorful messages of love, designed with permanent colored markers, bright tempera paint, etc.

Valentine's Day Ideas continued

MIRROR MESSAGES

Have young people sneak into their parents' bedroom or bathroom and write "I love you" on the mirror. They can use soap (if they promise to wash it off after Mom and Dad have been pleasantly surprised).

LOVING PARENTS

Have your group members design a family contract in which they and their parents agree to spend one night a week together. Explain the only stipulation: You and your parents must do something together: watch a TV program and talk about it, go to a movie, play a game, whatever. The object is to share a fun activity and create opportunities to talk.

GRANDPARENTS AND LOVE-MEMORY JARS

Gather old-fashioned canning jars with lids. Give one to each group member. Supply plenty of paper and writing utensils. For starters, have members write down as many special memories they can think of that have to do with their grandparents. Help them think of at least 20 things by suggesting family traditions, ordinary activities that mean a lot to them, special smells, tastes, sights, sounds and touches. (For example: the smell of baking bread in Grandma's kitchen, the secret candy hiding place, the games you used to play with Grandpa, the sounds of your family laughing over family jokes.)

Remind everyone to write large and legibly, one memory per paper. Members should then fold each piece of paper and place it in their jar. Have members deliver the love-memory jars by mail or in person, if possible. If some young people don't have grandparents, have them choose another special elderly person. Supply wrapping paper to prepare the jars for mailing.

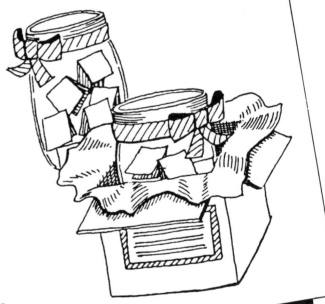

62

IT IS FINISHED

The drama and the beauty of time's greatest story can be poignantly recreated by your group at your Good Friday or Easter service.

The program requires no props, no costumes, no special lighting, no music.

You need only you.

Your voices alone will touch your audience with the message of Jesus Christ. A choral reading uses the individual and collective voices of your members.

You do not need to memorize the script. You'll be behind your audience where you'll be heard, not seen. The script should, however, be well-rehearsed. Your polished inflections and pauses will bring the Passion story of 2,000 years ago to life.

What follows is a script to be carefully studied by all of your members. Rehearsal and sincerity will breathe life into the words.

Each / indicates a pause. When // appears, a longer pause should be used. It is very important that you heed these pauses.

Do not rush through the script. Make sure everyone reads in unison during the group parts.

PHOTOGRAPHY/DAVID STRICKLER

It Is Finished continued

GIRL 1: When evening came/he sat down with the 12//And as they were eating/he said . . .

BOY 1: One/of you/here tonight/will betray me.

BOY 2: It couldn't/it couldn't/be me, Lord//could it?

BOY 3: Lord/it's not/me//is it?

BOY 4: Oh Lord/is it me? Lord?

BOY 1: The Son of Man is soon going/as the scriptures say/But the man who is to betray him/it would be better for that man/if he never/had been born.

BOY 5: Lord/Lord?/It's not/me/is it?/Lord?//Lord?

BOY 1: Yes/Yes/Yes, Judas.

GIRL 2: As they were eating, Jesus took some bread, blessed it, broke it and gave it to his disciples, saying . . .

BOY 1: Take this/eat it/This is my body.

GIRL 2: Jesus then took a cup of wine/gave thanks/and gave it to his disciples saying . . .

BOY 1: All of you drink/this is my blood/poured out for everyone/to forgive their sins.

GIRL 3: Later/Jesus and his disciples went to Gethsemane.

BOY 1: I am so grieved/I/I am almost dying. You stay here/and stay awake with me//Father/if it is possible/please/let this cup pass from me//But/it will be as you want/not as I want.

GIRL 3: Jesus then came back to the disciples/and found them asleep.

BOY 1: Couldn't you stay awake for just an hour?

GIRL 3: Jesus went to pray twice again/each time his disciples fell asleep.

GIRL 4: (faster) Then/with a crowd, Judas came through the darkness.

BOY 5: The one I kiss/he's the one/get him//Good evening, Master.

GIRL 1 and BOY 2: The others came up/grabbed Jesus/and arrested him.

GIRL 1: A man with Jesus grabbed his sword/Jesus said . . .

BOY 1: Put it back/All who take up the sword/shall die by the sword.

GIRL 1: The crowd came closer.

BOY 1: You came here with swords/with clubs/as if I were a robber//Day after day/I would sit in the temple/teaching/and you never arrested me//But/now/all this has come to pass so that what the prophets have written would come true.

GIRL 1 and BOY 2: The disciples then left Jesus and ran away.

GIRL 2: Jesus was taken before Caiaphas/the high priest/After Jesus was ridiculed/and beaten/he was taken to Pontius Pilate/the governor.

GIRL 3: Judas Iscariot/meanwhile/realized he had sinned//Judas died//a victim of his own hanging.

GIRL 1 and BOY 2: Jesus stood before Pilate.

BOY 6: Are you the king?/the king of the Jews?

BOY 1: So you say.

GIRL 3: During festival time/it was a custom for the governor to release one prisoner whom the people wanted/Pilate asked the people . . .

BOY 6: Which man shall I set free?//Barabbas/or Jesus?

GIRL 3: Barabbas was a notorious robber.

GIRL 4: Then word came/from Pilate's wife.

GIRL 2: Leave Jesus alone/last night I suffered much in a dream because of him.

BOYS 2 and 3: But the church officials persuaded the crowds to ask for the release of/Barabbas//and to have Jesus/put to death.

BOY 6: Which of these men shall I free?

ALL: Barabbas! Barabbas!

BOY 6: But/what should I do with/with Jesus?

ALL: Have him/crucified!

ALL BOYS: Pilate/seeing he was getting nowhere with the crowd/took water/and/in front of the crowd washed his hands.

BOY 6: I/am not/responsible/for the death of this man.

ALL: His blood/will be on us/and on our children/Nail him/nail him to the cross!

ALL GIRLS: Barabbas/was set free. Jesus was taken by soldiers/beaten/mocked/and led away/to be crucified.

ALL BOYS: They nailed him to a cross/and gambled for his clothes//Then they sat/watching//Above the head of Jesus/they put a sign.

BOY 3 and GIRL 3: This is Jesus/the king of the Jews.

ALL BOYS: Then/they nailed two robbers to crosses/one on each side of Jesus.

ALL GIRLS: Passersby shook their heads/and tossed insults at Jesus.

BOY 4: (faster) You said you could tear down the temple and build it up again in three days!

GIRL 4: Save yourself/if you are really God's Son!

GIRL 4 and BOY 4: Come down from that cross!

ALL GIRLS: The church officials/and the teachers of the Law/also ridiculed Jesus.

BOYS 2 and 3: He saved others/but he can't even save himself/He's the king of Israel?/Let him jump down off that cross/then we will believe in him!//He's

"He saved others but he can't even save himself. Let him jump down off that cross; then we will believe in him!"

put his trust in God/let's see if God wants to save him now!

ALL GIRLS: Even the robbers who were being crucified insulted him.

ALL: (slower) At 12 o'clock noon/darkness dropped over the whole country//The darkness covered the land for three hours//At about 3 o'clock/Jesus lifted his head/and cried out:

BOY 1: My God/My God/why have you abandoned me?

ALL: Some of the bystanders heard Jesus.

ALL GIRLS: He is calling for Elijah!

GIRL 1: One of the men ran to Jesus/with a sponge soaked in sour wine/put it on a stick/and put it up for Christ to drink.

ALL: Wait/leave him be/let's see if God will come to save him.

ALL BOYS: Jesus called out again.

BOY 1: It/is/finished.

ALL: (faster) At that moment/the curtain in the temple was torn in two/from top to bottom/the earth shook/rocks broke apart/graves were opened/and many of God's people were raised from the dead.

ALL BOYS: The soldiers who were guarding Jesus felt the earthquake and saw the other happenings//They were terrified.

BOYS 2 and 3: He really/he really was the Son of God!

ALL GIRLS: There were many women present/watching from a distance//They had followed Jesus from Galilee to help him//Among them were Mary Magdalene/Mary the mother of James and Joseph/and the mother of Zebedee's sons.

BOYS 2 and 3: When evening came/Joseph/a rich man from Arimathea/asked Pilate for the body of Jesus// Pilate ordered it given to him//He wrapped the body in clean linens/and placed it in a grave of his//He rolled a large stone across the front of the tomb//He then went away.

ALL: On the next day/the high priests and the Pharisees met with Pilate.

ALL BOYS: We remember that the liar Jesus once said he would come back to life on the third day// You/sir/must order that the grave be guarded until the third day/so that his followers won't go and steal the body/then say he was raised from the dead//That lie would be worse than the first.

BOY 6: You're right/take a guard/and guard the grave as best as you can.

ALL GIRLS: As the Sunday morning sun was coming over the horizon/Mary Magdalene and the other Mary went to see the grave//Suddenly a strong earthquake shook the area//The Lord's angel came from heaven/rolled the stone away from the tomb/and sat atop the stone//He was as white as snow//The guards were so terrified they trembled/and became like dead men//The angel spoke to the women.

BOY 3: Don't be afraid/I know you're looking for Jesus//He's not here//just as he said/he has risen!//Quickly/go tell his disciples that he has risen from death.

ALL GIRLS: They left the grave/and ran to tell the disciples//Suddenly Jesus met them.

BOY 1: Good morning!/Don't be afraid/Go tell my brothers to go to Galilee//There they will see me.

—*Thom Schultz*

63

TURNING GOOD FRIDAYS INTO EASTERS

Easter—the ultimate Christian victory! In relationship with God, we too, will defeat death and live forever. Sometimes that victory sounds far in the future. But it's not really. Each day we can experience tiny glimpses of God's Resurrection power.

Our Good Fridays come when we feel the pain of a broken friendship, the struggles over self-acceptance, the hurt when someone close to us dies.

And God still surprises us with Easters! Like the experience of forgiveness, the peace in knowing we're loved, the assurance that God is with us.

Leaders: Have your kids use this Bible study, "Christian Victory," to discover the Good Fridays and Easters in their lives.

CHRISTIAN VICTORY

1. Think of times when you've felt helpless, depressed, forsaken or empty. Jot them down.

2. Read 1 Corinthians 15:56. Now look back at what you just wrote. How are those times like dying? How is sin evident in each situation?

3. Read 1 Corinthians 15:57. Notice the word "but." It means we can't escape Good Fridays and hard times. But it also means there's hope—there's more! How do you feel when you hear the word "victory"? Why is it so hard to see victory in difficult times?

4. Read 1 John 5:4-5. What is the key to victory? What part does your faith play in the Easter message?

5. If you're feeling nonvictorious or inadequate, read Ephesians 1:19-20. What does it mean that God's power is working in you? How do you feel when you realize the power working in you is the same strength that raised Christ from the dead?

6. Go back to your list now and think about each situation. Write at least one victory you've experienced or hope to experience through each circumstance.

7. Read Isaiah 25:8-9. Since victories are worthy of thanksgiving and celebration, write a prayer of thanks and praise for God's power in your life.

64
REALLY LIVING

---

1. Objectives—

For group members to appreciate the personal benefits of Christ's Resurrection and show their desire for a new life by "exchanging their filthy rags for a new set of clothes."

PHOTOGRAPHY/DICK KEZLAN

2. Before the Bible Study—

The activities in this Bible study require these supplies: old newspapers, brightly colored tissue paper, markers, Scotch tape, Bibles, paper and pencils.

This study works best with one or more groups of six to eight persons. If your group is larger than this, split into small groups.

Choose small group leaders; the person with the newest shoes in each group will be the leader.

The leader should keep the group moving through the Bible study and encourage everyone to participate. The leader may also function as a timekeeper so that each group member has the same opportunity to share (two or three minutes in each activity).

Group members should know they have the freedom to "pass" if they don't want to share their experiences.

3. Getting Started—

Give each person a sheet of newspaper. Ask group members to tear it into the shape of an article of clothing that best describes them. See if people can guess each other's article of clothing and why it would describe that person. Place all newspaper "clothes" in the center of the group.

Have small group members discuss the meaning of the phrase "That's really living!" They should identify some activities that they consider "really living."

4. The Study—

Have each small group leader read aloud Colossians 3:1-17. Each small group should complete this sentence: "According to Colossians 3:1, Christ's Resurrection has given us hope for . . . "

Say to your group: In Colossians 3:2-3, Paul speaks of keeping your mind on heavenly things and not on earthly things. Challenge each small group to produce a list of earthly things according to verses 5-9. Have all small groups present their lists.

5. Making It Personal—

Say to your group: Because of Christ's victory over sin and death we can "put off the old self with its habits and . . . put on the new self" (verses 9 and 10). (Have group members take all the newspaper "clothes" and throw them away.) At Eastertime the custom of wearing new clothes symbolizes this putting on a new life. Although for some people this custom has become a simple display of vanity, it can be full of real Resurrection meaning.

Encourage small group members to compile together a list of "clothing" we can put on as the people of God (verses 12-17). Have all small groups present their lists.

Ask your group members to imagine they are planning an Easter parade and they may each wear three new items of clothing. Have each group member read verses 12-17, alone, and select three of the "heavenly qualities" to wear. Small group members should share their choices and reasons with each other.

Instruct small group members: Use the tissue paper to create colorful articles of new "clothing" for each other. Help one another by "dressing" each person in fun, colorful attire. With markers, write on the new clothes the three heavenly qualities that person chose. Wear your new clothes to the closing celebration.

6. Closing—

Instruct each small group to choose a Psalm or song that expresses thankfulness to God. Let the small groups take turns leading everyone in a time of praise and thankfulness to God for giving us the chance to "really live" through the Resurrection.

—*Dean Dammann*

65 EASTER IDEAS

H ere are six ideas for putting more life into your Easter celebrations. Let these ideas spark and generate other creative ways for you and your group to celebrate the Resurrection!

EASTER CAROLING

"Jesus Christ Is Risen Today" and "I Am the Resurrection and the Life" are songs that fill the air with celebration. Gather your youth group together for an Easter caroling party. Share your lively tunes with shut-ins and those in nursing homes. You might even want to bake and decorate a batch of Easter cookies to give your listeners.

Easter caroling might just have an advantage over Christmas caroling—it's warmer weather!

EASTER GIFT-GIVING

Easter's a day for celebrating the gift of life! Have young people think of various Easter "gifts" to give the congregation on Easter morning.

Have them decide what would best symbolize new life and celebration. How about contacting a local florist to see if you could buy fresh daisies at a low cost (or free)? Your group could hand out seeds or plant cuttings. Decorate eggs with Christian symbols—or paint "Resurrection" rocks to symbolize the stone that was rolled away. You could distribute butterfly pins, "He's alive!" buttons or helium balloons. The list goes on!

Have the youth group hand out the gifts as people are leaving the church Easter morning. Encourage them to shake hands and exchange the greetings "He's alive!" and "Jesus lives!"

EASTER DEVOTIONAL BOOKLET

Here is a way for young people with a flair for writing or drawing to share their gifts with the congregation.

Ask group members to contribute to the booklet poems, prayers, personal insights, stories or scripture readings that are meaningful for them this Easter season. Set a realistic time line, using Easter Sunday as the day for distribution. Set deadlines for each part of the booklet. After you've received the writers' contributions, type and prepare them, leaving space for artwork. Then ask your youth group artists to illustrate each devotional thought. Have copies made by a local printer, your church's mimeograph or copy machine. Make the Easter devotional booklets available for the entire congregation.

Another twist to this idea would be to design, print and sell Easter cards for your church members to send.

Easter Ideas
continued

BAND TOGETHER

Discover who plays musical instruments in your church. Then find someone who will work with your musical group and put together a rousing instrumental accompaniment for the Easter Sunday hymns.

If you have quite a few musicians, create an Easter orchestra! Check with a local junior or senior high band instructor who could direct and adapt the music to the ability level of your musicians (you'll need music that uses the instruments available). Use your judgment in knowing whether you will need to pay the director or can expect him or her to volunteer time.

ALLELUIA SURPRISE

Here's an idea for a special surprise during Sunday school or the worship service.

Decorate a large box that has a lid (this will be the container for your "Alleluia" banner). Then tie string to colorful helium-filled balloons. Attach the balloon strings to the banner and put the balloons and banner inside the box. When the box lid opens, the balloons will float the banner! Remember: Fill the helium balloons immediately before you plan to use them so they won't lose their lift-power.

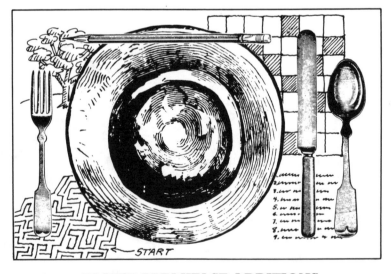

EASTER BREAKFAST ADDITIONS

Many youth groups provide Easter breakfast at their church. Add an extra touch to the morning's meal by designing Easter place mats.

Imagine them "Pizza Hut" style. Fill them with games, crossword puzzles, word scrambles, etc. Have youth group members come up with clever and creative ways to express the Easter story. Regular 8½ × 14 paper would work fine (your church may stock that size). Supply pencils or crayons on each table.

Not only will the breakfast eaters enjoy the food and fellowship, but they will also think about the Easter story in a new way.

KITE FLIGHT

1. Before the Bible Study—For this springtime study, gather for each student a pencil, Bible, copy of "Kites 'n' Colossians," tissue paper, six drinking straws, glue or tape, string and scissors. You also will need markers and bow-tie shaped name tags cut from construction paper. Draw or cut a giant colorful kite for the wall.

2. Getting Started—As kids arrive, give them each a construction paper bow tie. On the ties, have kids write their names and complete the sentences: A time I felt really free . . . and A kite is a symbol of freedom because . . . After each person shares his or her "name tie" have group members place them on the wall. Read John 8:36.

3. Bible Study—Have kids complete the Bible study, "Kites 'n' Colossians." Share responses.

KITES 'N' COLOSSIANS

Use this kite as a symbol of Christian freedom. Do this personal Bible study and write your answers in the appropriate kite sections. Discover the joy of being set free!

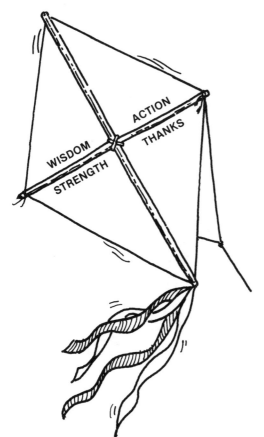

● **Wisdom.** Read Colossians 1:9; Proverbs 2:2-6; 9:10. Complete: God's Spirit fills me with understanding when . . . The key to wisdom and understanding is . . .

● **Action.** Read Colossians 1:10; James 2:18, 22, 26. Complete: Good deeds help me grow in the knowledge of the Lord by . . . List three times when your faith has come alive through your actions.

● **Strength.** Read Colossians 1:11; Ephesians 6:10-18. List three things you do to maintain a strong faith. Complete: One thing I'm not already doing that I can do to strengthen my faith is . . .

● **Thanks.** Read Colossians 1:12; Philippians 4:4-6. Complete this sentence five times: I'm thankful for . . .

Now look at your freedom-kite. Let the cross piece in the center remind you of the importance of having Jesus in the center of your life. Because of his death on the cross, you can be free!

Read Colossians 1:13-14 and Romans 6:6-8 and complete these two sentences: Because of Jesus, I'm free from_____

_____

Because of Jesus, I'm free to _____

_____

Offer a prayer of thanks for the freedom Jesus gives.

Kite Flight continued

4. Kite Making—Have participants follow these instructions and make their own colorful kites.

CONSTRUCT·A·KITE

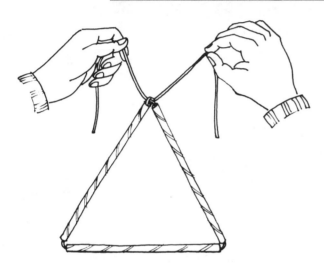

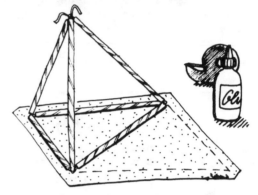

● Create a triangle by threading and tying string through three straws. Leave extra string at one end.

● Make an upright pyramid by threading and tying the remaining three straws, one at a time, to the triangle base. Join the peak last.

● Using the straw frame as a pattern, cut a diamond shape of tissue paper that covers two sides. Glue or tape the paper to the kite frame.

● Create a tail by attaching two-inch-wide strips of tissue paper to the bottom end of the kite. Attach kite string as shown.

You're ready! Go fly a kite!

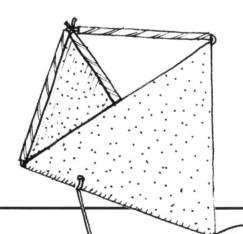

5. Kite Flying—Spend the rest of the time together flying your new kites. For an added touch, sing "freedom" or "wind" songs. Have the group think of as many serious or silly songs they can that mention wind or freedom.

62 SUMMER MINISTRY IDEAS

Summer is a great time for youth ministry! Group members don't have school responsibilities—and do have lots of free time. The weather is perfect for outdoor activities. General enthusiasm and energy run high.

It seems like there's so much your group can do. But somehow the ideas don't always flow when you most need them.

In search of summer youth ministry ideas, we checked around the country with dozens of phone calls to places such as Billings, Montana; Grand Haven, Michigan; Garden City, New York; Columbia, South Carolina; Omaha, Nebraska; Long Beach, California; and Cincinnati, Ohio.

Of the hundreds of ideas we collected, here are 62 we think you can use:

62 Summer Ministry Ideas

continued

1. Set up a sports camp led by group high school athletes. Invite third- to fifth-graders, for a week, to bring sack lunches and attend afternoons of getting tips on their favorite sports and hearing some sports-related object lessons.

2. Plan a reunion for youth group alumni who are back in town. Sing the old favorite songs; show old high school photos; tell funny stories and reminisce about the good old days.

3. Celebrate together with a midweek sunrise worship service at the beach, the mountains or a park.

4. Raise money with a volleyball marathon. Have group members collect pledges for each hour of playing.

5. Create a roller rink in the church's parking lot. Find an old roller rink to donate skates for a tax write-off. (Be sure to check your church's insurance policy for coverage.)

6. Make friends. Invite preschool or disabled kids, or senior citizens to go with you to a picnic, a zoo or a farm.

7. Visit patients at a children's hospital once a week.

8. Invite other local churches to compete in The Challenge of the Churches in a city park. Have a tug of war, a human pyramid contest, an obstacle course, pie-eating and egg-toss contests, two-person wheelbarrow races and others.

9. Do a clown car wash! Everyone dresses as clowns. Sell helium balloons and cotton candy.

10. Sponsor a weekly backyard Bible club for younger kids in group members' neighborhoods. Feature puppets, songs, crafts, Bible stories, clowns, etc.

11. Rent the student union of a college or university for a lock-in. Student unions are generally equipped with a snack bar, chapel, video games, pool tables, ping pong tables, giant televisions, fireplace, theater, lounge area and more.

12. Have a lock-in at a YMCA. Swim; use the gym; show rented videos or movies. Or rent the YMCA for a Family Fun Day.

13. Surprise church members or neighbors by washing their car windshields or mowing their lawns.

14. Conduct a worship service at a camping/trailer park for campers who aren't familiar with area churches.

15. Learn a musical cantata and tour with it.

16. Bike for fun. Have a bike rally; earn money with a bike-a-thon; go on bike trips; bike to breakfast at a fast-food restaurant.

17. Create a carnival on the church grounds. Give pony rides; have clowns, balloons, games; sell hot dogs and snacks; play carnival music.

18. Celebrate summer with a Tom Sawyer Day. Go fishing, rafting, picnicking.

19. Welcome new youth group members with a breakfast party! Invade their bedrooms with the breakfast all ready, sit down, and all eat together—right there. Or sneak into their rooms, play reveille on a French horn and then kidnap them for breakfast out.

20. Enroll in life-saving courses.

21. Set up a St. Francis Table at your church. Invite church members to donate garden surplus—or to help themselves to the food there, whichever their case may be.

22. Create the ultimate obstacle course. Use tires, logs, swinging ropes, etc. Group members can work all summer at getting the best record.

23. Grow a flower garden. Get permission to clean up and use a vacant lot; take turns tending the garden; give flowers to nursing homes and/or sell bouquets to church members.

24. Sponsor an intergenerational church progressive dinner—cookout style.

25. Play "statues" at a shopping mall. Have one person at a time get in a statue pose—and hold it. Others should watch, inconspicuously. See who can be a statue the longest. Take photos of people looking at your "statues."

ILLUSTRATION/JUDY ATWOOD

26. Brainstorm ideas for the coming year. Meet at advisors' homes and get to know them better.

27. Produce a candid-camera video.

28. Pretend you're all in second grade again. Go to the park and play children's games (remember "Ring Around the Rosie!"); eat animal cookies and name the animals; enjoy the playground equipment.

29. Challenge the adults in the church or another youth group to a game of softball.

30. Sponsor a Colonial Craft Day. Have an instructor teach interested church members how to make candles, soap and paper.

31. Do barbeque Bible studies. Everyone brings a Bible and some meat.

32. Kites! Make kites together, then go to the park and have a kite-flying contest.

33. Choose a hot summer day to go out and pretend you're caught in the "Blizzard of '84." Bundle up in warm, bulky clothes; sing Christmas carols; drink hot chocolate.

34. Rent a city pool and challenge another youth group to compete in Crazy Water Olympics.

35. Experience stress camping or solo camping. Write to Christian Camping International, 388 E. Gundersen Drive, Carol Stream, IL 60187, for information.

36. Dress up and go together to a big city for a show.

37. Rise very early on a Sunday morning and write cheery chalk messages on the sidewalks by the church to greet worshipers.

38. Have a lock-in at a bowling alley. Move in with your own food, games, etc.

39. Go to the beach or a lake for a Water Bash. Have water-balloon fights; play water-balloon volleyball (using sheets to catch the balloons); have an ice-block melting contest; have crazy swim races.

40. Stage a soapbox derby. The losing team should prepare/serve a meal to the winning team.

41. Rent a houseboat for a week of Houseboat Camp. Waterski, swim, etc., and have water-related devotions each night.

42. Combine group members' popular sports with Bible studies or prayer groups. Have a weekly "Tennis and Talk," "Pool and Parables" or "Track and Prayer."

The next 20 ideas use the object lesson "formula," but count on your knowledge of your unique location. Take an ingenious look around and brainstorm with your group. Transform nearby "places" into giant, interesting object lessons.

43. Meet at the cemetery. *(See John 11:25-26.)* Do grave rubbings: Place paper over a tombstone's lettering and rub over the letters with a crayon; the words will appear on the paper. Share what it means to die. Ask: What does the Resurrection mean for us? Talk about death and what Jesus has to do with our death.

44. Find a dry creek bed or river. *(See Revelation 7:14-17.)* Imagine what it would be like to have water flowing through the creek bed. Compare that to having faith. Ask: What is "life-giving water"? How are lives made different because of the life Jesus brings?

45. Journey to a wheat field. *(See John 6:25-59.)* Ride the combines, grind some wheat, make a loaf of bread. Discuss what Jesus meant when he said, "I am the Bread of Life."

46. Go to a zoo. *(See Galatians 3:21-29; 5:1.)* Take your trip near Independence Day and talk about freedom. Observe the cages and other attempts to keep the animals imprisoned. Discuss the purpose of "the Law." Ask: What does it mean to be slaves of sin? What keeps us "caged up"? What does freedom mean to you? How has Christ set you free?

47. Meet in a playground. *(See Matthew 18:1-5.)* Allow plenty of time for play. Then talk about what Jesus meant when he said, "Unless you become like a child."

62 Summer Ministry Ideas

continued

48. Go to a garden. *(See Luke 8:5-15; 1 Corinthians 3:5-9.)* Plant seeds, weed, or harvest produce from the garden. Compare faith to the plants in the garden. Ask: What are the "weeds" in your life? How can your faith produce more fruit? Or talk about ways to "stretch" food for those less fortunate. Discuss what can be done for those who can't grow their own gardens.

49. Stake out a deliveries-only pizza place. *(See Psalm 50:15; Matthew 7:7-11; 21:22; Mark 11:24.)* Talk about prayer. Ask: Do you think of God as a delivery person? Why or why not? Is prayer like instant service? Why or why not? After your discussion, spend time in prayer—alone and as a group. Then order out for pizza!

50. Visit a sheep farm. *(See John 10:1-16.)* Talk about Jesus as our Good Shepherd. Ask: What qualities do sheep have? How are we like sheep? What is the relationship between the shepherd and his sheep?

51. Meet in a cornfield or wheat field after harvest. *(See Matthew 9:35-38.)* Have the group glean the field and collect all the grain that's fallen to the ground. Bring it to a granary; send the money to a world hunger organization. Share what it means to believe in the "Lord of harvest." Ask: Is witnessing "harvesting" for the Kingdom of God? Why or why not? What does Jesus mean when he says there are few workers to gather in the harvest?

52. Go to a local restaurant. *(See Philippians 2:1-11.)* Interview the waiters and waitresses. Ask them what it's like to do what they do. Find out what makes their job worthwhile, fun, a drudgery. Ask them why they do it. Then discuss what Jesus meant about being a servant. Ask: How can we have a servant attitude all the time? What makes our lives worth living? What are ways you can become a better servant?

53. Hold an entire meeting on a sidewalk. *(See Matthew 7:13-14.)* Play hopscotch or other sidewalk games. Talk about the narrow gate and hard road. Ask: Why is faith the "hard road"? Why is a Christian's choice "narrow"? Have kids choose favorite Bible verses that help them in the "narrow and hard" times. Then write the verses on the sidewalk with white or colored chalk. (The chalk will wear off.)

54. Walk through a wooded area. *(See Matthew 12:33-37.)* Get in touch with nature, the trees, the leaves. Talk about how people are like trees. Ask: What should we be "rooted in"? What are signs of a healthy tree? What are signs of a person living the Christian life? What is "good fruit"? "bad fruit"? What "good fruit" should a Christian exhibit daily?

55. Browse through a shopping mall. *(See Matthew 6:24-34.)* Windowshop. List all the things you *want* to have. Then list all the things you *need* to have. Discuss possessions and what's really important. Ask: Do you worry about food and clothes? If so, why? How does God want us to view possessions? What makes that so difficult?

56. Visit a library. *(See Psalm 119:105; 2 Timothy 3:16; 2 Peter 1:21.)* Find book titles that describe each group member. Check out a favorite story and read it to the group. Talk about the Bible as the "good book." Ask: What importance does the "good book" have in your life? What questions do you have about the Bible? Give away daily scripture reading guides provided by the American Bible Society, Box 5656, Grand Central Station, New York, NY 10163.

57. Wander through a dump or auto graveyard. *(See Psalms 38:1-8; 189:1-15.)* Talk about what it means to be thrown away, worn out, crushed. Share times you felt useless and unwanted. Ask: Why are we valuable? Can people bring value to themselves? Why or why not? What causes people to lose their sense of value? What makes you valuable?

58. Stop at a local print shop. *(See Psalm 139:1-15.)* Watch them make hundreds of copies. Mention how each person in the group is an "original." Discuss what it means to be a "one and only." Challenge group members to come up with each person's qualities that aren't "carbon-copied." Talk about peer pressure. Ask: What makes us want to be like everybody else? What does God require of us?

59. Walk along the beach. *(See Genesis 22:15-19.)* Play in the sand; make sand castles. Talk about when God promised Abraham as many descendants as grains of sand along the seashore. Ask: What does that mean? How does it feel knowing you're connected with so many other people? What part do you play in God's plan? What's the difference between a grain of sand and an entire beach of sand?

60. Gather at a site that's under construction. *(See 2 Corinthians 4:16-18; Philippians 2:13; 1 Thessalonians 2:13.)* Discuss hope and growth. Ask: What times have you felt "under construction"? What hopes and dreams do you have? Are Christians always "under construction"? Why or why not? How are you becoming God's person?

61. Gather under a street sign or traffic sign. *(See Psalm 119:33-40.)* Talk about direction in your life. Ask: How do you get it? What kind of plan does God have for you? How do you know you're going in the "right direction"? What are signs in your life that say you're following Jesus? Does God have such "clear cut" signs for us to follow? Why or why not?

62. Stop at a used car lot. *(See 2 Corinthians 5:17-21.)* Volunteer your group to wash all the car windows—free! Focus on being made new. Ask: What does it mean to be "used"—then made new? What does newness say about forgiveness and redemption? How does Jesus accept us as "second hand"? What image do you have of "used" cars? How are you like a used car? In God's eyes are you "used" or new?

10 SUMMER MINISTRY TIPS

Youth groups have a variety of approaches to summertime. Many highlight mission and service projects that they've planned for all year; some emphasize travel and group growth experiences; others plan to simply take it easy and "hang around" together.

Whatever your group's style, keep in mind that summer provides many opportunities for ministry that don't exist any other time. Here are tips to help make this summer a special experience for your group:

1. Welcome back high school graduates and college students who are home. Including them as counselors in summer activities gives current group members a sense of the group's rich history.

2. Be flexible with scheduling. Since young people aren't in school, almost any time is a good time. And unless many work early shifts, you can plan longer and later evening activities.

3. Have more socials and congregational activities to which group members will want to bring their friends. Friends attracted now to the group may return in the fall.

4. Designate a weekday for each grade, if your group is large. Have Tuesdays be ninth-grade day; Wednesdays, 10th-grade day; etc. Knowing they'll get together "every Tuesday afternoon," even if it's just for tennis, increases young people's loyalty to the group.

5. Give young people more responsibility and opportunities to develop organizational skills. Be available to guide and assist, but let *them* plan the midweek trip to the amusement park, the roller skating party or that additional cookout they want.

6. Plan new, fun, creative activities. Spice up the summertime schedule with special events, such as a rafting trip, to keep maximum interest and involvement in the group.

7. Encourage one-on-one time between adult sponsors and group members. Nurturing quality, in-depth relationships builds solid foundations for ministry.

8. Consider travel opportunities. While young people aren't free to travel much during the school year, they are eager and available to do so in the summertime.

9. Work with other youth groups in the area to arrange big projects, such as sponsoring and promoting a Christian concert, youth rally or all-church picnic and party in the park.

10. Plan for the coming year. Recruit adult sponsors and provide leadership training; let interested young people also be involved. They can help "initiate" sponsors and give good ideas for the coming year.

SPOOK INSURANCE

Last Halloween, did your neighbors and friends have trouble with ghosties and goblins? Did they wake up in the morning to find their windows soaped, their yards covered with trash, rotten tomatoes on their cars?

This year, why doesn't your youth group protect these unfortunate people and earn some money at the same time?

"The Jack O. Lantern Insurance Company" will sell "a piece of the pumpkin" to individuals who want to insure their dwelling, automobile, property, or all three. Prices vary according to the type of policy.

"Jack O. Lantern" policies guarantee that your group will clean any damages caused as a result of "spooks" on Halloween night, provided they are reported by the specified date.

Here's how one group set up its policies:

Coverage A—dwelling . . . . 75¢
Coverage B—automobile . . . . 75¢
Coverage C—property . . . . 75¢
Coverage D—all perils $2

This coverage includes any act in which the following are used: eggs, soap, tomatoes, watermelons, shaving cream, marshmallow cream, toilet paper, or trash.

This coverage does not include and specifically disallows vandalism and malicious mischief meaning only the willful and malicious damage to, or destruction of, the property covered. (Examples would be burning, painting, broken windows, etc.)

Claims must be reported by November 2, before 6 p.m.

All cleaning or clearing will be done by midnight, November 2.

To report claims, call one of the following phone numbers.

Start with your congregation, and make sure everybody is offered a policy. Then, each of your members should go door to door in his or her neighborhood selling policies.

Your mimeographed policy should have spaces for the insured's name and address and the type of policy desired. Use a carbon, making a copy for the insured and for your group.

Then, have teams of two or three kids who can be dispatched to the houses reporting "attacks" from Halloween tricksters.

This is a fun fund raiser, and your only expenses are the mimeographed policy fliers and a couple bottles of cleanser. Plus, you're providing a very useful service!

You may even want to buy some insurance yourself.

FAVORING THE OLD FOLKS

Halloween also can be a special event for elderly people. A number of good activities can be planned at a local rest home for the enjoyment of the residents.

Don't be afraid to consider organizing a costume party for the oldsters. They may surprise you with their originality and enthusiasm.

Also, some of the old-timers will have some dandy spook stories to tell around a dim candle.

OCCULT DISCUSSION

The Halloween season offers a good opportunity to discuss Christianity and the occult. Your discussion may be a part of your regular meeting, or it may follow a fun social activity. Here's a discussion guide to get you going.

1. Is Halloween a holiday of the devil? Should Christians observe Halloween? Why or why not?

2. Do you know any Christians who are followers of astrology? Is there a conflict there? Explain.

3. Read Deuteronomy 17: 2-5 and Isaiah 47:13-14. Do these passages speak to astrology?

4. Have you ever gone to a fortuneteller? Read Deuteronomy 18:10-14 and react. Also read Acts 16:16-18.

5. Read Matthew 6:25-34. Should Christians become worried about the future?

6. Does the devil manifest himself in individuals, such as illustrated in today's horror movies? Read Mark 5:9 and Matthew 12:43-45.

7. Why has occultism been undergoing a revival lately? Should Christians be concerned? What can be done? What can your group do?

ALTERNATIVES

DEATH DISCUSSION

Halloween and death seem to go together. Here's a group discussion guide that may broaden your feelings about the "Last Great Unknown."

If you want to feel what death means to you, take a look at your favorite death fantasies. How do you most frequently see yourself dying?

Who died the way you expect to die?

What habits may dictate your style of dying? (Smoking, drinking, commuting, worrying, sky diving?)

When will you die? Who are other people you know who died at this age?

Why are you going to die? Is death a failure? A depletion of energy? A natural conclusion to life? Do you die to make more room for the living? Because your body is worn out? Because you are bored, frustrated, despairing? Because you are satisfied? Explain.

What is your dominant attitude toward death—defiance, acceptance, fear, longing, sorrow, curiosity?

Imagine you died yesterday, and look back on your life. You died with many dreams unfulfilled. What accomplishments, relationships, moments mean most?

What are your regrets? What have you left undone that you wanted to do? What have you done that you wish you hadn't?

Death wears many faces. When the young die death is tragedy; when the old or incurably ill die it is deliverance; when our enemies die it is retribution and justice. What moods and emotions have dominated your experience of the death of others? (Grief, anger, fear, relief?)

Whose death would cause you the greatest sorrow? Whose would give you the greatest pleasure? Who would care the most if you died?

What does the Bible say about death?

Does death conquer you or do you have the ability to conquer death? How was it with Christ?

Read and discuss Psalm 23; Romans 8:38; 1 Corinthians 15:51-57. What is the hope and promise that we have as Christians?

ENTERTAINING THE KIDS

Halloween is a special time for children. And your group can do a lot to make this time memorable for the kids in your community.

Organize a costume party at a local orphanage, handicapped children's center, or children's hospital. You may want to provide pumpkins, refreshments and games. Or perhaps you may want to bring a batch of pumpkins for the kids to have a carving festival.

Some groups have had great success with busing a group of disadvantaged kids to a farm where the kids can pick their own pumpkins. There's a special thrill for picking a pumpkin from the vine and taking it home to become a jack-o-lantern.

Your group can show a positive message of love to your community and its children.

RED PUMPKIN HUNT

Here's a great competition idea for your group. Hide a red-painted jack-o-lantern somewhere in town. It's up to the teams to find it.

Divide the group into teams of four or five. Give everyone a beginning clue. Example: Red pumpkins don't grow in patches, but under ball catches. For the alert Sherlock, this would mean to look under the church's basketball hoop. There he would find another written clue, leading him to another spot in town, where another clue would direct him elsewhere, and ultimately to the red pumpkin.

The first team to find and interpret all the clues and discover the pumpkin, is the winner. The team should then return to the church with the pumpkin.

A time limit should be set so that everyone must return to the church by a set time.

STUFF TO BE THANKFUL FOR

1. Before the Bible Study—Gather a pencil, Bible and copy of "Stuff" for each person. Supply all the makings for mini pumpkin pies (two for each person). Buy pre-made pie crusts and tiny foil tins. You also will need thank-you notes, envelopes, stamps, newsprint and a marker.

2. Being Thankful—Distribute the following handout to the young people. Let the handout kindle more ideas of ordinary things you can be thankful for. Ask the class to help you create your own list of things to be thankful for. Write them on newsprint and post it on the wall.

STUFF TO BE THANKFUL FOR

Here's a thinking-thanking challenge for you: Look for the ordinary, everyday, taken-for-granted stuff that makes life a rich and worthwhile experience. To get you started, here are a few ideas:

Say thanks for . . .
- road signs that tell you where you are and where you've been
- the splashy, carbonated-bubble feeling in your mouth after sipping a Coke
- pipes that carry refreshing water through faucets and showers
- the feel of clean sheets on your bed
- the person who scrapes the plates after hot lunch
- the peculiar blend of orange and blue in the sunrise sky
- being able to breathe without ever thinking about it
- parents remembering to pick you up
- after basketball practice
- the unique sound of an old friend's voice over the phone
- that favorite kindergarten teacher who taught you to print
- the sense of smell that distinguishes between burning leaves and chocolate-chip cookies
- a comfortable room to call your own
- the helping hand that held the door when your arms were stacked with books
- how good it feels when someone says, "I love you"
- an ability to understand a tiny portion of God's love through other people.

---

3. A Pie Surprise—Prepare the pumpkin mix together having each person make two pies. While you are getting the pies ready for the oven, think of people in the congregation who receive little recognition for their behind-the-scenes efforts. Plan to divide up their names and deliver a surprise pie!

4. Thanking God for People—While the pies are baking, hand out thank-you notes, envelopes and postage stamps. Ask kids to think of one person who has especially touched their life. Have them write a surprise note of thanks and address it for mailing. For a closing group activity, ask participants to share whom they've chosen and tell why. Read 1 Corinthians 1:4-7; Philippians 1:3-7 and Colossians 1:3-4. Talk about the value of thanking God for people. Why is that important? How would you feel if people said they thanked God for you? Remember to deliver the pies and mail the thank-you notes. Close with a circle prayer thanking God for the person on your left.

For a snack, eat the extra pumpkin pies at the meeting's close.

SANTA'S WORKSHOP

1. Before the Workshop—Find five or more volunteers from your group who will collect and buy supplies necessary for making all the gifts suggested. Have one person be responsible for each "Santa's Workshop" area. Set up the room with various gift-making stations. Provide tables filled with enough supplies that kids could make a number of gifts if they choose to do so. Introduce this crafty extravaganza by encouraging kids to wander from table to table to work on various gift items. Defray the cost of supplies by having kids donate money to cover each gift's cost.

2. Gift Areas—Let your youth group members try these on for size and see if any fit the people on their shopping lists. Tell the young people about the five gift areas. Use the descriptions below.

3. Prayers and Gifts—Wrap up the meeting by gathering the group together. Place all the completed gifts in the center of the group. Join hands and close with a prayer. Have each person pray for the people who will be receiving the creative gifts.

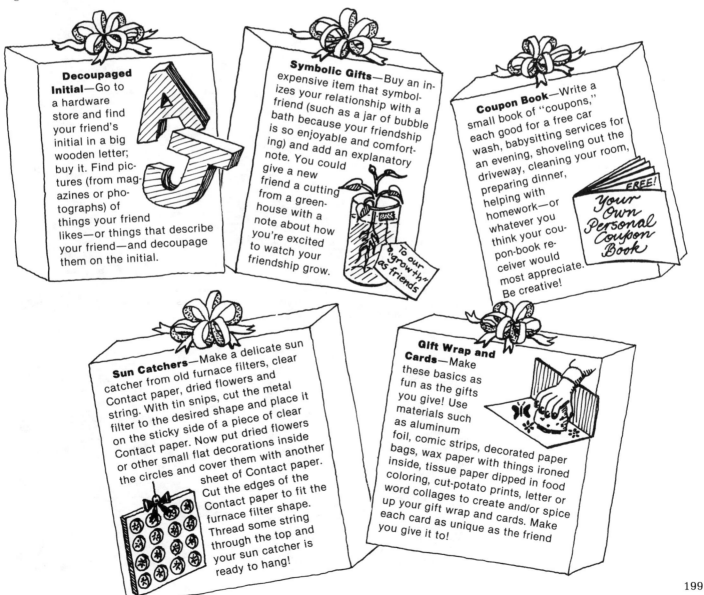

Decoupaged Initial—Go to a hardware store and find your friend's initial in a big wooden letter; buy it. Find pictures (from magazines or photographs) of things your friend likes—or things that describe your friend—and decoupage them on the initial.

Symbolic Gifts—Buy an inexpensive item that symbolizes your relationship with a friend (such as a jar of bubble bath because your friendship is so enjoyable and comforting) and add an explanatory note. You could give a new friend a cutting from a greenhouse with a note about how you're excited to watch your friendship grow.

Coupon Book—Write a small book of "coupons," each good for a free car wash, babysitting services for an evening, shoveling out the driveway, cleaning your room, preparing dinner, helping with homework—or whatever you think your coupon-book receiver would most appreciate. Be creative!

Sun Catchers—Make a delicate sun catcher from old furnace filters, clear Contact paper, dried flowers and string. With tin snips, cut the metal filter to the desired shape and place it on the sticky side of a piece of clear Contact paper. Now put dried flowers or other small flat decorations inside the circles and cover them with another sheet of Contact paper. Cut the edges of the Contact paper to fit the furnace filter shape. Thread some string through the top and your sun catcher is ready to hang!

Gift Wrap and Cards—Make these basics as fun as the gifts you give! Use materials such as aluminum foil, comic strips, decorated paper bags, wax paper with things ironed inside, tissue paper dipped in food coloring, cut-potato prints, letter or word collages to create and/or spice up your gift wrap and cards. Make each card as unique as the friend you give it to!

71

THE MIRACLE

OF GOD

The Christmas season.
Why all the hoopla?

Any Christmas-wise one would reply, "Jesus is the reason." Another could chime, "Yes, let's put 'Christ' back into Christmas." While a youngster might even add, "It's Jesus' birthday party!"

They're right.

But all those "pat" answers go much deeper.

The essence of Jesus' birth-celebration is God taking on human form. "The Word became flesh and dwelt among us, full of grace and truth," as John 1:14 would say. Christmas is God's ultimate sign of empathy and understanding. God came to be with us—learning to talk, walk, laugh, cry, hurt and help.

The Incarnation, God embodied as a person, is an awesome concept to grasp. Yet it's the crux of our Christianity. We marvel and give thanks that God would care so much he'd send his son to live among us.

The miraculous plan of God goes even further. In his divine wisdom, he's become incarnate in each of us. "Surely you know that you are God's temple and that God's Spirit lives in you" (1 Corinthians 3:16). Blessed with the honor of housing God's Spirit, *we* embody the Christmas spirit of service and love.

Use this creative Bible study with your group as an exploration and celebration of the Incarnation.

1. Objectives—In this study, the youth will:
● explore God's Incarnation and what that means for them; and
● affirm God's Spirit in their bodies.

2. Before the Bible Study—Advance preparation for this Bible study involves inviting a man and a woman and their newborn child. In selecting a couple, choose one who'll be open to talk about hopes and fears concerning the child. Make sure the parents won't mind young people holding their baby. Tell them their baby can have a profound effect as your group explores what it meant for God to take on human form.

Other supplies include Bibles, paper, pencils, newsprint, markers and strips of cloth. (Tear 3-inch-wide strips from an old sheet.)

Invite the couple and baby to come, but ask them not to let the group see them till you're ready to introduce them to the group. Their unexpected appearance will help capture the feeling of surprise. Or have them arrive about 15 minutes after the young people. This way you can begin introducing the theme and having group members make name bandannas.

As young people arrive, create a festive atmosphere with Christmas music playing in the background.

3. Getting Started—Explain that you're going to discuss the essence of the Christmas message—God taking on human form. Ask each person to design a name "bandanna" from the strips of cloth provided. As a reminder of Jesus' humble birth, you might want to refer to the strips as "swaddling cloths." Say: "Write your name on your piece of 'swaddling cloth' and complete this sentence three times: God coming to Earth as a baby makes me feel . . ."

After individuals share their "swaddling cloth," they should tie it around their forehead and wear it.

After everyone's finished, write the word "Incarnation" on newsprint. Ask group members what they think the word means. It's possible they might be more familiar with the word, "reincarnation," a non-Christian belief that after death a soul reappears in another bodily form. Make a clear distinction between the two words. Explain that the Incarnation means the Spirit of God literally became flesh. Jesus birth signified God in human form.

Read John 1:14. Talk about how God became a human being—with tiny toes, fine hair, soft skin, the works—to fully understand his creation. Because God came to our world in Christ, *we* can fully understand what life was meant to be, with Jesus as our model.

Tell the group you want to make the concept of the Incarnation especially real this Christmas, so you've invited a special guest. Bring in the parents and their baby at this time.

4. God as a Baby—Have group members sit in a circle. Ask each person to think about what strikes him or her most about a baby. Then begin carefully passing the baby from one person to the next. While the baby is briefly held by each person, have the rest of the group softly sing Christmas carols such as "Away in a Manger" and "Silent Night." (If you group is larger than 12, ask for six or eight volunteers to hold the baby while you sing.)

The Miracle of God continued

After everyone's held the baby, return the child to one of its parents.

Record on newsprint each person's thoughts about the baby. Record everything. For example, someone might say, "It was so helpless, fragile and utterly dependent." Another might say, "It cried and I didn't know what to do about it."

A hint: Take advantage of spontaneous moments. For example, if the baby cries, talk about interruptions and how we deal with them in our lives. Ask: In your life, is God considered an interruption? Does God only fit in when it's convenient for you? Another surprise might be if the baby needs a bottle or a diaper change. Talk about God's need to be cared for. Ask: Do you think of God as forever giving, loving and never really needing to be cared for? Do you think about God's need for you to love him?

5. The Christ Child's Significance— Have the group members stand in a circle. Ask one parent to hold the baby and stand in the center of the circle. Slowly have the parent walk around, showing the baby to each person. With participants focused on the child, have one person read aloud Isaiah 53:2-9.

Have everyone sit down. Then ask: What perspective does that passage bring concerning God's love for you? How does that make you feel? Why was it necessary for God to take on human form? What difference does that make in your faith.?

Divide into three groups. Give each group one of the following Bible passages: Mark 3:33-35; Hebrews 2:9-10, 14-18; Hebrews 4:14-16. Allow about 10 minutes for each small group to read the Bible passages and write its answers to these questions: What was God's purpose and plan for Jesus? What impact does Jesus' humanity have on your relationship with God? How do you view someone after you've spent time together—talking, playing, working? How can that be applied to you and Jesus? How do you feel about Jesus as your brother—a family member? What difference does that make in your relationship with

him? Imagine the baby with you is Jesus. How would your attitude toward that child change? Should it? Why or why not?

After each group has finished bring everyone together. Have members share their recorded responses.

6. God in Us Today— Say: God didn't stop with Jesus. He still comes to us today in human form through each other.

Ask a different person in the group to read aloud each Bible passage: 1 Corinthians 3:16; 6:15; 12:7; 12:27; Ephesians 3:17; Colossians 1:27-28.

Ask everyone to find a partner. Then say: Because God came to us in Jesus and now shows his love *through us,* what does that mean to you? How do you feel about God using *you* to show the world what he's all about?

Give partners time to discuss the questions. Then ask for one or two discoveries from the group.

7. A Closing Celebration—Bring everyone together in a close circle. Join hands. If you'd like, have the group kneel. Have the mother hold the child in her lap and sit in the center of the cirlce. Encourage the group to imagine, for a moment, that the child is Jesus. Sing the first verse of "What Child Is This?"

Have one person read this prayer:

"God, you loved us so much, you wanted to become one of us. Help us grow in understanding of your Incarnation. Thanks for living our life, dying our death and rising to live eternally, so we, too, can live forever. Amen."

One by one, go around the circle giving thanks for each person. Say: "Thanks, God for coming to us through (name)." As the group gives thanks, the named person stands. Continue around the circle. Close with "Thanks, God, for coming to us through Jesus."

For the final touch, make sure nobody leaves without hugging at least six other people.

—*Joani Schultz*

CREATIVE CHRISTMAS CARDS

You and your group members can add spice to Christmas card-giving by creating your own cards. Here are some ideas:

FELT BOOKMARK

Make this functional Christmas card by cutting red felt in the shape of a candle and yellow felt in the shape of a flame. Glue them together. Use green or white liquid embroidery to write on the candle, "Jesus is the light of the world."

CHRISTMAS STOCKING CARD

Cut two back-to-back 8½×11 pieces of red construction paper into the shape of a stocking. Staple or glue together the edges of the stocking, but leave the top open. Cut white construction paper into small 2-inch-by-3-inch squares. Decorate them to look like small packages. Write Christmas wishes on the packages and stuff them into the stocking. Glue wisps of cotton around the stocking top. On the front of the stocking, write the person's name with glue and sprinkle glitter over it. Mail in an 8½×11 envelope.

CHRISTMAS CARD/TREE DECORATION

Cut posterboard into a star, circle, donkey, gift box or other Christmas design. Paper punch a small hole at the top and attach a string, pipe cleaner, reshaped paper clip or regular ornament hook. Design the card using one of these techniques:
- Dip a corner of a sponge in paint or food coloring and apply to the card.
- Wet the end of colored chalk and draw a design and message.

- Brush liquid starch over the card and apply tissue paper in various colors and shapes.
- Make a collage of yarn, material scraps or aluminum foil.

BANNER PRINTS

Cut brown paper bags into banner shapes—5 inches by 12 inches. Carve the flat surfaces of potatoes into Christmas shapes (e.g., manger, angel, star, crown, shepherd's staff). Dip the carved potatoes in bright-colored tempera paint and print your banner cards in mass production. Add a Christmas message with a marker or paintbrush. For easy hanging, attach yarn to the top with tape or glue. Fold to send.

RECORDED CHRISTMAS CARD

Tape record members of your family answering the question, "What is your favorite Christmas memory?" Make copies and send them to your relatives."

DOORKNOB CARD

Cut construction paper into any Christmas shape and leave enough room to cut a doorknob-size hole in the top of the card (or attach string with tape or glue). Use a squirt gun filled with red or green tempera paint to decorate the card. Add a Christmas message with a marker or glued-on construction paper letters. Hang the card on the door of a friend's house, classroom, office, bedroom or car.

8 CHRISTMAS ACTIVITIES FOR YOUR GROUP

Awaiting your action are eight Christmas ideas ranging from outreach to personal reflection, from playful to practical. Enjoy bringing Christmas to life with your group.

COOKIES 'N' CAROLS

Take along sacks of Christmas cookies and candies when your group goes caroling. Give the people a sack of goodies as well as special songs. This is a great act of love and Christmas giving.

Imagine all the fun your group will have when they get together before your caroling party to bake the cookies and candies.

GIFT OF LOVE

Don't limit Christmas gifts of love to the yuletide calendar. Try this as a personal exercise, then with your group for new insights into gift giving all year.

Take a piece of paper. Divide it into four columns from top to bottom. In the first column, list five of your closest friends. Then list three to five family members who are close to you. In the second column, list the actual material gifts you gave these people last Christmas.

In the third column, write a special quality—such as love, patience, kindness or humor—that you'd like to give each person. Think of one quality that would help that particular person the most. Give each of these eight to 10 people a carefully chosen intangible gift.

In the fourth column, list the gift or quality each of these people might give you. Based on their close knowledge of you, what quality would each of these people like to see you have? Maybe their gifts of behavioral or personality change would be similar. If so, it tells you something about yourself, your friends and your relationship with them.

Help other people achieve their goals by giving them what you think they want. Most importantly support them by giving them the year-round gift of love: friendship.

SYMBOLIC GIFTS

Here's an idea for unique and meaningful gift giving. Divide your group into teams of six to eight people. Have everyone hunt around the church, home or wherever you're meeting and find an item that makes a symbolic gift of love to the other people in your group.

Allow plenty of time for the hunt. Encourage everyone to give careful thought to the gifts. Examples: Find paper and cut it into little bits, making confetti to represent joy for a person in your group who needs cheering up. Or, find a telephone book to symbolize your appreciation to a person in the group who phoned you when you were lonely.

After people have gathered all the gifts they intend to give, regroup and sit in a circle. One at a time, group members should give their gifts and explain each gift as it is given. Avoid jokes and gag gifts. These symbolic gifts could be some of the most beautiful gifts your group will receive this Christmas.

TOY TAGS

Ask one person to write names of toys on sheets of paper; one toy for each sheet. Pin a sheet on the back of each person in the group. Make certain they can't see what the tag on their back says.

Have everyone mill around and find out what is on his or her own back. This is done by asking questions that can only be answered yes or no. One person might ask, "Would I fit in your pocket?" or "Am I a Slinky?" All questions must be answered correctly.

When people find out what toy they are, instruct them to take the tag from their back and put it on their front. The game stops when everyone has discovered his or her toy.

CHRISTMAS CARD DELIVERY

For a pre-holiday group activity and cents-saving project, deliver Christmas cards for your congregation free of charge. Here's an outline for making that happen:

1. Set boundaries of the delivery area. Make the church the center of your map. The uniqueness of your area will help determine a workable distance of delivery. If your church is in a city, a one-mile radius may be appropriate. If you're in a rural church it's possible to cover a larger area.

2. Notify the congregation of your plan. Give them a two-week notice of your delivery date. Advance notice enables them to bring their cards in on time. Ask them to include their return address on the envelope in case there are any questions about the address. To make sure the congregation knows the area you'll be covering, draw a map showing the boundaries. Set at least two delivery dates in case you're inundated with mail. Use the two Sunday afternoons before Christmas to deliver all the cards.

3. Decorate a big box for depositing cards. Make it bright, colorful and highly visible. Place it in a convenient location.

4. Divide the Christmas cards according to city blocks or districts, whatever is suitable to your surroundings. Cards that do not fit into the specified boundaries should be returned to the sender. Divide your group into four smaller groups to cover north, south, east and west. Arrange transportation for each area. Assign one person in each car the responsibility of seeing that all their mail is delivered. Encourage delivery to take place in a quiet orderly manner since this is a witness to the neighborhood. Meet back at the church to make sure everyone finished safely.

5. Show gratitude for the workers. Perhaps someone from your church could prepare a supper or snack for the card deliverers. Or some people may want to donate the money they saved on stamps to your youth group or other charitable organization.

HUMAN CHRISTMAS TREES

Have everyone find a partner. Provide a glittering supply of Christmas decorations. Include ornaments, tinsel, garland, wrapping paper and other holiday decor. Give partners a five-minute time limit. Within the time allowed have partners decorate each other with the ornaments.

When everyone is finished, gather in a circle and celebrate. Sing favorite carols; use this as a time to rejoice in the gift of each other.

TREE SANTAS

Bring joy to disadvantaged families in your area with little expense. Visit Christmas tree lots on Christmas Eve and ask the owners to donate their leftover trees to your group.

Your church or local social service agency office can provide a list of those families in your area who can't afford a Christmas tree.

Have a tremendous time as you deliver your special tree surprise to each family you visit.

GROUP GIFT SHOPPING

Meet at the church or some other convenient place. Make sure adequate transportation is available. Then go on a group shopping spree.

It's a great way for group members to spend a day—and their Christmas gift allowances. Encourage them to take advantage of a chance to get family members presents in secret.

74

IF IT'S CH
I MUST BE

1. Before the Bible Study—Have three young people record Christmas music and the following quotes. The music can be from a record or you could involve more young people by recording their singing.

Tape the following Christmas music suggestions to preface the readings. If possible, use soft background music as each person speaks.

Tape "Joy to the World" and "Deck the Halls" as a prelude to the following quote:

- *Depressed? It doesn't make sense. Isn't Christmas the "season to be jolly"? Where did I go wrong? If I really had the Christmas spirit, wouldn't I be ho-ho-hoing and exploding with "joy to the worlds"?*

Tape "Jingle Bells" to precede this quote:

- *Even the youth group caroling party made me feel guilty. What do they mean, "O'er the fields we go, laughing all the way—ha, ha, ha"? Last night I cried myself to sleep because I wasn't invited to Nancy's Christmas party. And that stupid mistletoe hanging in the hall. It reminds me I haven't had a date yet. All my friends are buying gifts for their sweethearts and I'm spending money on presents for my cat.*

Finally, record "Silent Night" for the last quote:

- *"Little House on the Prairie" could just as well be "Little House on the Moon" when it comes to my family. Mom and Dad argue a lot—especially when we're spending so much money on presents. Sometimes I'm afraid they might get a divorce. Grandpa died this year and my brother won't be home for Christmas. Everything's a mess.*

Gather a refrigerator box, tempera paints and wrapping paper. Plan to go Christmas caroling after the meeting to a shopping mall, nursing home or homes of elderly church members.

2. "But I Don't Feel Happy"—Gather the group in a circle and play the first recorded section. Have group members share times when they thought they were *supposed to feel* a certain way, but didn't.

RISTMAS, HAPPY

Tell the kids that many people feel depression during the Christmas season. What we *feel* and what we think we're *supposed to feel* don't match.

3. Helping a Friend—Play the second recorded piece. Then ask each person to find a partner and share how a friend would respond to the person on tape.

When everyone's finished, have another young person read the three suggestions that follow:

● Be honest with yourself and accept your feelings. Don't be too hard on yourself for feeling bad.

● Talk with somebody. Seek out a friend who'll listen, understand and offer support. A warning: Holidays press people's schedules and sometimes it might appear they don't have time for you. If that happens, be patient and understand. Whatever you do, talk with someone.

● And remember: Holiday depression will pass. The time and circumstances will change.

Have each pair join another pair to form a group of four, and discuss which of the suggestions would be the most difficult to do and explain why.

4. Troubled Times—Play the final recording. In the groups of four, have each person complete: A struggle I'm facing right now is . . .

Ask the young people to each do the following:

● Focus on what you *do* have. Zero in on the blessings around you. Read Philippians 4:10-13 and see how Paul felt when his experiences grew dim. Next make a list of your talents, qualities and abilities. Include what you can do, see, hear, smell and touch. Celebrate those gifts!

● Look for the positive qualities in the people around you. What makes your friends your friends? Focus on what your mom and dad have given you over the last few years—not just material things either. After you've thought about those positive qualities, tell them.

Come together as a large group and discuss the discoveries.

5. Discovering God-Qualities—Divide into four small groups. Assign each group one of the following "God-qualities."

● *Unchanging*—Malachi 3:6; Psalm 102:27
● *All-powerful*—Genesis 17:1; Matthew 19:26
● *All-knowing*—Psalm 139:1-4; John 21:17
● *Kind and generous*—Exodus 34:6-7; Psalm 145:9; 1 John 4:8

Have the groups look up the Bible verses and write the God-quality on one side of a piece of paper. On the other side, have them write a false promise of commercialism. Compare the two.

Ask each group to create a brief skit that portrays that quality. Have each small group share its skit.

6. Closing—Read Psalm 50:15 as a closing prayer. Know that God means it. In the good times and the troubled times—you can count on God's love.

7. A Christmas Gift—Another cure for beating the Christmas blues is giving of yourself to someone else. One way to do this is with "Colossal Christmas Cards" from **Try This One . . . Strikes Again** (Group Books).

As a group, design a large, colorful Christmas card from two sides of a refrigerator box. Cut and fold the box to create a card-like effect. Use bright tempera paints and wrapping paper to add pictures and words on the front. On the inside, cut numerous holes for people's heads. They stand behind the card, stick their heads through the holes and sing the special Christmas message.

Pile your group and the colossal card in the back of a van or pickup and drive to the first home. Have one person greet the recipient and explain that your group is delivering a unique Christmas card. Open the card. With everyone behind the card, heads through the holes, sing and share the joyful message of Christ's birth. Continue to the other homes.

—Joani Schultz

75

A PROGRESSIVE CHRISTMAS STORY

1. Before the Story—You've heard of a progressive dinner? How about a progressive Christmas story? This idea works best with small groups because of transportation, but any size group is workable.

Advance planning is necessary to arrange transportation, gather supplies and plan destinations.

2. People Who Walk in Darkness—Meet and begin at the church. Gather in a dark room and explain the plans for your progressive Christmas story. Distribute candles to each person. Have a young person read Isaiah 9:2-3, 6-7. Then light the candles and discuss the contrast of light and darkness. Talk about the contrast Jesus makes in our lives. Then ask each person to choose one of Jesus' names from the passage and explain why that's meaningful to him or her. (Bring the candles with you.)

3. A Trip to Bethlehem—Gather by the exit door and have a young person read Luke 2:1-5. Ask each person to answer, "When I begin a journey, I feel . . ." Have the group members share responses in the vehicle on the way to the next place. Also sing and hum "O Little Town of Bethlehem" on the way.

4. No Room in the Inn—Gather outside—or in—a motel lobby. (Wouldn't a Holiday Inn be appropriate?) Have a young person read Luke 2:6-7. Distribute one matchbook to each person. (If the motel supplies them, use those, otherwise, bring your own.) Have people write their names inside the matchbook cover. Place the matchbooks in the center of your circle. Draw out one at a time and have the person named answer, "A surprise for me in those two verses was . . ." Close by singing "Away in a Manger."

5. In the Fields—Next go to a hillside, park or yard. Huddle in a circle as if you were cold shepherds. (If it's cold, that's okay; it adds to the effect.)

Have a young person read Luke 2:8-14. Sing "Hark the Herald Angels Sing." Have another young person read Luke 2:15. If the weather cooperates, remain outside, otherwise share responses in the vehicle. Ask each person to share one discovery he or she made about that portion of scripture.

6. Worship and Praise—Return to the church and form a circle in front of the altar. Sing "Silent Night." Have a young person read Luke 2:16-20. Have group members share what Jesus' birth means to them personally. As each person shares, light his or her candle and continue around the circle.

Conclude with carols of praise and a circle prayer. Serve Christmas goodies.

ILLUSTRATION/JUDY ATWOOD

76

BETHLEHEM REVISITED

You'll remember this night for a long time.
Nothing appears out of the ordinary when you walk into the church sanctuary. But you're about to be surprised. And you'll love it.

You find a seat, wrestle out of your winter coat and join in the singing of familiar Christmas carols.

Suddenly, a robe-clad man, who looks as though he just stepped out of a scene from **The Ten Commandments** movie, shuffles up and motions for you to follow him.

Your 21-step trip from the sanctuary to the church basement is like sprinting 2,000 years backward through time. Those steps take you from a comfortable, 20th-century church building to an authentic Bethlehem marketplace near the time of Christ's birth.

Before you enter the marketplace, a gruff, no-nonsense old-timey person tells you to sign the census scroll. After all, you are a visitor in a city where most people are outsiders who have returned for the census that Caesar Augustus wanted.

You sign the scroll, walk past a scowling Roman soldier and stop to take in the sights. Children are playing in the street and your sense of smell tells you animals are present. The hustle and bustle of the open-air shops and friendly storekeepers are refreshingly different from today's glass and plastic department stores.

Crowded together in the marketplace are all types of people and things to experience: beggars, wandering "prophets," a rabbi, weavers, tailors, tentmakers, food sellers and an array of shops.

You feel the electricity in the air. Almost every merchant has something to say about recent strange happenings. Rumor has it that a new king has been born. Even the rabbi is gripped in this vise of expectancy. He tells his students, "We've been under Roman rule for many years. But the prophets tell us

CENSUS TAKER

Bethlehem Revisited continued

that our Savior will come soon to rescue us, and crush our oppressors under his heel."

Just then, cold, murderous-looking soldiers appear. They nudge you away from the rabbi. One says loudly, "What's going on here? We Romans are very suspicious. We don't like gatherings and gossiping. Move on, you rabble! We want these streets cleared before nightfall! Get along now!"

Life in Bethlehem isn't what you imagined it to be. It is not the sleepy, friendly town you hear about in the Christmas carols.

You're nearing the end of the marketplace when an excited elderly man approaches you. He stands too close to you for comfort. Someone in your group remarks that this must be Simeon, the old man mentioned in Luke 2:25-35.

He leads your group to a dimly-lighted room where shepherds and a young couple with a baby are celebrating. The young father is ecstatic. He pulls you toward the mother and baby.

The mother is quiet, exhausted. Yet, the glow on her face can't hide her joy. She holds up her child. "He is a special son. God has special plans for him."

It doesn't make much difference how much time has passed since Christ was born. In a small, simple way, you've experienced the same sights, sounds, smells, thoughts and feelings people experienced almost 2,000 years ago.

As you leave the church basement, you pass by a huge Christmas tree covered with homemade ornaments. One of the attendants slowly removes a small ornament and hands it to you with the words, "Remember Jesus."

How could you forget?

TIPS FOR DESIGNING YOUR OWN BETHLEHEM MARKETPLACE

The Bethlehem Marketplace you've just experienced has taken place over the last several Christmas seasons at Gary Memorial United Methodist Church in Wheaton, Illinois. This all-church project includes 52 family units and over 130 people.

Your group can work with other people in your church to develop your own version of the Bethlehem Marketplace. The folks at Gary Memorial United Methodist Church offer the following ideas and tips:

● Start talking and thinking about the project one year ahead of time. Now's a good time to start planning for next year.

● Pick an event to portray. (One group designed a "Bethlehem home" to show what a Bethlehem home might be like.) Then study the scriptures, commentaries and background sources to find what life and people were like.

● Write everything down as you develop your ideas. Then find someone who can communicate those ideas to the entire congregation.

● Start small and do it well. Add ideas and characters yearly.

● Get plenty of interested people involved in the planning process. Then delegate: costumes, publicity, props, job descriptions, scripts, recruitment, photography, animals, newsletters, after-project celebration time.

● Once you know what you want to do, develop scripts and costume ideas.

● Include all ages of people in your project.

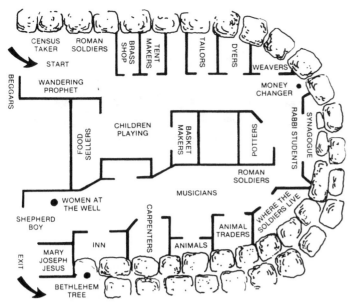

The Bethlehem Marketplace layout looks like this.

- Consider including family units (mother, father, kids) in your project.
- Plan your publicity campaign carefully. Consider using huge banners stretched across streets near your church, local newspaper, bulletin inserts, announcements in church, radio, television, posters and fliers in church and around town.
- Ask people to donate materials and time to keep your budget low.
- Decide on a creative form of admission—canned goods, clothes, toys, etc.
- The Gary Memorial version of Bethlehem Marketplace is open for three hours on one afternoon only. That short viewing period helps in recruiting characters and in focusing attention on the quality of the event.

- Over 1,800 people visited the Bethlehem Marketplace in the three hours it was open last year. If you expect large crowds, be sure your project meets local fire codes.
- Be deliberate in how you recruit. Don't start too early or too late. Gary Memorial United Methodist Church started recruiting members about three weeks before the event.
- When recruiting members, show a detailed plan that gives the type of involvement required, the script, and what's expected of them.
- Consider including musicians and animals if they'll add to the quality of your event.
- If you don't have a great deal of space, consider partitioning off Sunday school classrooms for booths and using the hallway as the marketplace street. Use your space creatively.
- Have booth building and prop parties. Make the nuts and bolts work as fun as you can.
- Have the visitors meet in the sanctuary for carols, hymns, and music as they wait to tour the Bethlehem Marketplace.
- Like the census taker in Gary Memorial's Marketplace, determine a way to control the viewers and their pace through the marketplace. That way, people can experience more of the event.
- A nice tradition established by Gary Memorial Church is that of the Christmas tree. As people pass by after visiting the Bethlehem Marketplace, they are invited to take an ornament from the tree and place it on their tree at home as a reminder of their visit.
- The project will take long hours of hard work. But be prepared to get more from it than you've given.

—Gary Richardson

OTHER IDEAS FOR BETHLEHEM REVISITED

1. Compare—Have your young people read this short article. Then have them read Luke 2:1-40 and compare the scriptural account with Gary Memorial United Methodist's version of Bethlehem Marketplace. How are they similar? different?

2. Simple Project—The Bethlehem Marketplace project described in this article included nearly 130 people and months of planning. Consider taking one booth or one aspect of Bethlehem Marketplace and putting it on for your entire church. For instance, have a census-taking booth with gruff Roman soldiers in the church lobby. Or design a stable scene in the church lobby with Mary and Joseph and shepherds and animals. Or

choose one of the booths to put together. Spend time thinking of all the possibilities. Use some of the presented tips and ideas to help you design a more effective presentation.

3. Stable Birth—Surprise your young people by holding this meeting in a stable, barn, old garage, cattle barn at a local fairground—any place that simulates the stable where Christ was born. Pass around a doll wrapped in a blanket. Tell your group to imagine the doll is the newly born Jesus Christ. Ask how they'd feel if the doll really were Jesus. Discuss why Jesus was born in a stable and the implication that fact has for today's Christians. Talk about humility and why the Bible stresses it.

77

WAITING!

1. Before the Play—Your group members may choose to present this following article in either "readers theater" style or as a drama with costumed characters and props.

If "Waiting!" is done "readers theater" style, explain that readers will mainly read the script aloud with much expression. No around-the-stage movements or gestures are necessary. Ask a sixth person to introduce the play and explain to the audience any supposed actions.

Since "readers theater" relies so heavily on oral interpretation, be sure to rehearse the drama, making the most of each line. Alternating pitch, mood and pace is important. Encourage readers to picture the characters in their minds. To present the drama, the readers may stand or sit, facing the audience.

If you decide to stage the drama, here are a few suggestions:

● Seat the three waiting characters (Hal, Judy and Bill) Center Stage, facing the audience.

● Seat the angels, Gabe and Raph, atop ladders, framing the characters at Center Stage.

● An atmosphere of anxious waiting should characterize the dialogue.

● Additional directions for staging and props are included in the script.

By all means, bring a spirit of fun and play to your production!

"Waiting!" focuses on the waiting we do in life. The Advent days before Christmas are waiting days. This skit cautions us never to be so busy waiting that we miss the glory and importance of the present moment. Use this skit after Thanksgiving or before Christmas.

[Hal, Judy and Sid sit Center Stage, facing the audience. They are waiting.]

Sid: I hope the waiting will be over soon.

Judy: It helps to know that we're on the edge of something great. I just know we are. [to Hal] Wouldn't you agree?

Hal: [has been reading a magazine] Pardon me?

Judy: Wouldn't you say that we're on the edge of something great? Something major, I mean! Something marvelous!

Hal: I certainly hope so.

Judy: You don't sound very certain.

Hal: What if we're not waiting for the same thing?

Sid: That has not been established yet.

Judy: [to Sid] So, tell us, ah-h-h, I didn't get your name.

Sid: You're right. You didn't.

Judy: So, tell us. What are you waiting for?

Sid: Why do you want to know?

Judy: [searching for a response] Well, maybe we can support each other.

Hal: Highly unlikely.

Judy: Oh, be quiet. [to Sid again] Come on, tell us. What do you hope for? On the edge of what great dream do you now stand?

Hal: Oh, brother!

Sid: Applause.

Hal: Applause? What does that mean?

Sid: If you must know, I'm waiting for recognition, for some applause, a bravo, an ovation.

Hal: [stands and claps three times] There. You may go now. [sits back down]

Sid: Sooner or later I'll be recognized. People will take note of me. I will be appreciated.

Judy: A noble objective. You have my support.

Hal: Have you done anything?

Sid: What do you mean, have I done anything?

Hal: What's your contribution, man? Have you done anything to deserve an ovation?

Sid: I am gifted. I am noteworthy. I am destined for recognition.

Judy: Oh, that's *marvelous*. Isn't that marvelous?

Hal: I'm tired of waiting.

Judy: I suppose I'm next.

Hal: Next for what?

Judy: Don't you want to hear what I'm waiting for?

Hal: All right, tell us. I know you want to tell us.

Judy: I am waiting for him.

Hal: Him?

Judy: When *he* comes, you'll know that it's always worth waiting for *him*. Why, on certain great days, when *he* comes, the world is . . .

Hal: [hurriedly] Don't say it . . .

Judy: The world is marvelous! I wouldn't trade anything for days like that. I live for those days. Christmas is coming soon. I love Christmas. It's one of those days. The trees, the lights, the

Judy: It'll be marvelous. [silence]

Sid: [to Hal] I think it's only fair now that you tell us what you're waiting for. After all, we bared our souls.

Hal: It might be more than you can handle.

Judy: Try us. Perhaps it will make you more sociable. We can only hope.

Hal: If you must know, I'm waiting for a way out.

Sid: A way out? Out of what?

Hal: A way out of almost everything! It seems I always get myself into predicaments. Here's a case in point: I'm sitting here with an egomaniac on one side and a holiday cheerleader on the other. People drive me nuts. I can't get away from them. They're all over the place.

Sid: So what are you waiting for?

Hal: Some peace maybe. Who was the guy who said that life is like being in a room with all the doors marked, "NO EXIT"? That's how I feel. So there; now you know. Can't you just give me some peace now?

Judy: Poor man. Perhaps if we'd sing some carols . . .

Hal: Just leave me alone.

[Gabe and Raph (Gabriel and Raphael) enter Stage Left carrying large stepladders. White makeup covers their faces and they should be dressed in white.]

Gabe: We set up right here, Raph.

Raph: Looks good, Gabe. [They set up ladders on each side of the characters seated Center Stage.]

Sid: I beg your pardon, but this happens to be a waiting room.

Hal: Oh, great.

Gabe: Let's see. [pulls out scroll from back pocket, opens it and reads aloud] Orders for Angels Gabriel and Raphael: Pay angelic visit to three human beings waiting on Earth. They carry the names Sid Snyder . . .

Sid: That's my name!

Gabe: Judy Lindstrom . . .

Judy: That's me! Marvelous! Imagine that!

Gabe: And Hal Winston . . .

Hal: All present and accounted for. May we see your wings? [sarcastically] Angels *do* have wings, don't they?

Gabe: No wings called for in this order. Unnecessary, I suppose. Shall we begin?

Raph: Certainly.

[Gabe and Raph climb to the top of their ladders. Raph sits atop his ladder. Gabe remains standing on uppermost rung of his ladder.]

Gabe: Behold . . . I might just mention that angelic messages frequently begin with the word, "behold."

carols . . .

Hal: We get the picture. You're waiting for Christmas.

Judy: And for days like Christmas, you know, the big days, the days that warm the human spirit. Eventually, you know, it will be time for the Big Day. Now that will really be something.

Hal: The Big Day.

Judy: Right. He'll break through the clouds and show his glory!

Hal: And you're waiting for him.

Judy: Hallelujah! Yes!

Hal: And in between? What do you do in between these m-a-arvelous days?

Judy: Why, I get ready for the next one. There's always a next one, and sooner or later will come the Big One, the Grand Finale!

Hal: I suppose you have your Christmas shopping done.

Judy: Months ago.

Hal: And the cards?

Judy: Sent them out the week after Thanksgiving.

Hal: And now all you have to do is sit and wait for the day.

Hal: Just wait a minute. We're supposed to believe that the two of you are angels? Looks to me like you're house painters who held the spray gun the wrong way.

Judy: Hush now. Listen.

Hal: I don't think I can take any more of this.

Sid: Since when do you just show up like this—unexpected, I mean?

Gabe: Since forever. We rarely come announced. Let's see. It's Sid, isn't it?

Sid: Correct.

Gabe: You're the one who's waiting for applause, aren't you?

Sid: I am.

Gabe: Well, then, this one's for you.

Sid: This one what?

Gabe: [clears throat; takes on posture of proclamation]
"The Lord, your God, is in your midst, a warrior who gives victory; he will rejoice over you with gladness, he will renew you in his love; he will exult over you with loud singing as on a day of festival" (Zephaniah 3:17-18a).
I am to tell you that this prophecy is already true. You have the applause of One no less than our Chief, your Lord and Master. He rejoices over you. That should be enough.

Sid: Hold on here . . . what do you mean . . .

Gabe: I'm sorry. No questions. Raph? [sits atop ladder]

Raph: [stands on uppermost rung] Judy, Judy, Judy.

Judy: Here am I. Here am I. Here am I.

Hal: I don't believe it.

Raph: Hear the word of the Lord.
"Behold, now is the acceptable time; behold, now is the day of salvation" (Corinthians 6:26).
Now, Judy, now! I am to tell you that every day is important.

Judy: But I . . .

Raph: I defer to my colleague, Gabriel, for the third and final message. Gabe? [sits atop ladder]

Gabe: [stands on uppermost rung] Hal Winston, listen well. What you seek is in this word:
"Behold, I bring you good news of a great joy which will come to all the people for to you is born this day in the city of David a Savior, who is Christ the Lord . . . (Forgive me if I don't sing) . . . Glory to God in the highest, and on earth peace, good will among men" (Luke 2:10-11, 14).
Hal Winston, peace! Raph, this completes our assignment. [both angels begin to descend ladders]

Hal: Hold on just a second here.

Raph: [after angels fold up ladders] Finis.

Gabe: Well done, I'd say. [both exit Stage Left]

Sid: They can't just leave like that, can they?

Hal: I think they did.

Sid: "You have the applause of One no less than our Chief," he said.

Judy: "Now," he said, "Now is the time."

Hal: He seemed to imply that I could have peace right here, right now. I find that hard to believe.

Sid: Maybe we don't need to wait.

Hal: Don't jump too soon, Sid.

Judy: Maybe we have what we're waiting for *now.*

Hal: It would be a risk to believe that. It's safer to bank on the future.

Sid: I'm not so sure.

Hal: I'm going to wait and see what else happens.

Sid: I don't know. I hadn't thought about an ovation from God!

Hal: I say, wait.

Judy: Maybe we should. For a while. At least until Christmas.

Sid: Unless we can have Christmas *now.*

Judy: Don't be silly. Christmas is December 25. Let's wait a while longer . . .

Hal: Just to see what happens.

Sid: Okay.

[Characters settle back into waiting posture; then freeze; dim lights.]

—Dean Nadasdy

---

2. Follow-Up—Whether you present the play to your congregation or use it as a youth group experience, it's important to give all persons involved an opportunity to determine its meaning for their personal lives.

Use these discussion starters. Hand them out to youth group or congregation members for further thought and reflection.

● Describe in your own words the tragedy of the characters in the drama.

● In what sense is the birth of Christ in human form an ovation for humanity and for every Christian?

● What aspects of Christmas carry throughout the year and make every day significant?

● Talk about what gets settled inside people through the coming of Christ into their lives.

● What are the great things for which you're waiting? What can you do *now* to make these dreams come true?

● Describe a time when you missed something great because your attention was focused on something else.

● With which of the characters did you most identify? Why?

● Complete this sentence: If an angel were to visit me, I'd most like to hear him say . . .

78 HOLIDAY IDEAS

A CHRISTMAS PRAYER SERVICE

In the midst of the holiday busyness, stop. Quietly, simply focus on the Christmas story by using this 20- to 30-minute meditation with your group. Gently, yet powerfully, this service uses contemporary Christian music as a worship tool.

Atmosphere is most important, so prepare the meeting place with soft lighting. Invite your group to sit in a circle surrounding a single red candle. Assign the readings to three well-prepared, articulate young people.

Follow these suggestions: (All songs to be played are found on Amy Grant's, "A Christmas Album," Myrrh Records, 1983.)

Prelude
- Reader One: Isaiah 7-14.
- Play the following songs for quiet meditation: (They're in this order on the album.)
  "Preiset Dem Konig ("Praise the King")
  "Emmanuel"
  "Little Town"

Prophecy
- Reader Two: Isaiah 2:2-5.

Response
- All sing "Hark the Herald Angels Sing."

Prophecy Fulfilled
- Reader Three: Luke 2:1-20.
- Play the song: "Love Has Come."

Prayer
- Encourage participants to offer sentence prayers. Close with the Lord's Prayer.
- All sing "Silent Night."

—Patrick M. Mulcahy

Holiday Ideas continued

UNCONDITIONAL GIVING

Challenge your group members to choose one person—a family member, friend, someone they appreciate or someone with a special need. Encourage each person to give an anonymous gift to the special person of his or her choice. Stress one guideline: The gift must be given without knowledge or clue of the giver's identity. The "unconditional-ness" is made real by giving without expectation of thanks or recognition.

After the holiday season, bring your group members together and talk about their experiences. Discuss their feelings, surprises, insights and personal discoveries.

HOLIDAY CHAIN

Here's an idea that will fill every day of your holiday season. Use a simple paper chain as a prayer reminder and countdown to Christmas. Have each person in your group make a holiday chain to display at home.

Begin by cutting construction paper into strips six to eight inches long. The paper strips need to be about an inch wide, providing enough space to write a few words. Depending on when you begin your holiday chain, cut the number of strips to equal the number of days till Christmas. Open a link a day and pray for the person named, read the Bible verse listed, or do the activity given.

Here are a variety of holiday ideas to write inside the links:

● **Giving thanks for youth group members**. As a group, list the names of youth group members—active and inactive. Don't forget your adult sponsors. Have each person transfer the names to his or her chain.

● **Giving thanks for your church family**. With your group, list tasks—big and little—that are accomplished by your church members. Fill the chain with these tasks and the people who do them. Use the chain as an awareness tool and a way to say thank you.

● **Giving thanks for family and friends**. Have each individual fill the chain with names of personal friends and family members.

● **Using links for personal devotions**. Prepare a list of short Bible readings, one for each link, to be used as daily personal devotions.

Sprinkle these Bible verses throughout the chain links: 1 Corinthians 1:4-9; 2 Corinthians 1:3-4; Ephesians 1:3; Philippians 1:3-11; Colossians 1:3-4; 1 Thessalonians 1:2-4; 2 Thessalonians 1:3.

● **Doing nice things for others**. Create a list of quick activities (phone a friend, say "I love you" to your parents, drop a note to your grandparents, etc.) to do after opening each link.

Watch this paper chain activity "disappear" as Christmas draws closer!

THE GINGERBREAD EXPERIMENT

Put some uniqueness into your New Year's resolutions. Use this gingerbread figure to develop a sense of wholeness and wellness with your young people. Give these instructions to your group:

1. Draw a gingerbread figure and label it like the one at the left.

2. Look at each of the five sections. Jot down some activities in each section that you (or your family) do to give balance to your life.

3. On another piece of paper, draw your gingerbread figure during the past 12 months. Use the portions of the gingerbread man to illustrate proportions of time spent with those activities.

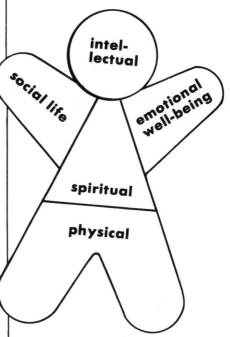

Is it like this?   Or like this?

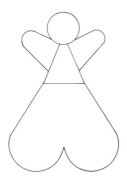 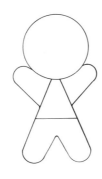

4. Next draw the gingerbread figure as you'd like it to be next year. Design it to reflect the kind of balance you value in your life.

After doing so, evaluate it closely. Is it different from your drawing in #3? If so, how?

5. What can you do this coming year to make your life more the way you'd like it to be? List suggestions and ideas that can make that happen.

6. For extra fun and flavor—bake, decorate and serve real gingerbread people. Use the snack as a reminder of bringing wholeness into your life in the new year.

7. Add this Bible verse, which speaks to your wholeness and well-being: "May the God who gives us peace make you holy in every way and keep your whole being—spirit, soul, and body—free from every fault at the coming of our Lord Jesus" (1 Thessalonians 5:23).

—*Roland Larson and Bob Rathbun*

GOOD PARTY IDEAS

Here are some ideas to help you get started in thinking what you might like to do for a fun party.

● **Create-your-own-pizza party.** Everyone could make different dough shapes and unique topping designs.

● **All-occasion party.** Combine New Year's, Valentine's Day, the Fourth of July, Halloween . . .

● **Color party.** If it's green: eat green food, dress in green, talk like frogs, etc.

● **Video/movie party.** Marathon movies with plenty of popcorn, whether at the theater or at home, guarantee a good time.

● **Instant party.** Call people together, then assign party responsibilities: games, decorations, food. Do them.

● **Fondue party.** For a small group of people, a cheese, oil and chocolate combination is always a winner.

● **Kite party.** Go to the park, make and fly kites. Have contests: which kite looks the best, flies the highest, flies the longest . . .

● **Tree party.** Welcome the spring with a celebration of blossoming trees. Climb trees; build a treehouse; have a bonfire; do crafts.

A HOLIDAY BIBLE STUDY GRAB BAG

Here's a gift for you: Five innovative Bible studies for the upcoming holiday. Have fun as you and your youth group take a closer look at what scripture says about light, gifts, newness and love.

Read through the studies and decide which ones best suit your group. Choose to use one or all of them. Feel free to adapt the studies to best meet your group's needs.

BASKING IN THE LIGHT

1. Objectives—Use this Bible study to:
● find scripture messages of hope, comfort and joy; and
● celebrate the light of God's love.

2. Before the Bible Study—Gather a pencil, Bible and small candle for each person. You also will need one large candle and matches.

3. News of Hope, Comfort and Joy—Assemble group members in a circle. Say: Even as the sun gives life to plant life, so Christ is the light which gives new life to us.

Place a large candle in the center of the circle as a symbol of Christ. Have someone light the candle. Have another person read John 8:12 while the candle is being lighted.

Divide members into five groups; a group can be one person or six or more. Have each group look for "light" messages in its assigned section of scripture.

Use these Bible passages:
● John 1:1-14 (especially verses 5 and 6-9);

● John 3:16-21;
● John 12:32-36;
● Luke 2:22-32 (especially verses 29-32);
● Isaiah 60:1-6.

Ask each group to look for two or three "Good News" messages of hope, comfort and joy in its scripture section. Or ask, "As I sit in darkness, what warm words in this scripture tell me about God's love and care?"

Ask each group to be prepared to share its findings with the total group. Allow time for study and discovery by the five groups.

4. Basking in the Light—As the groups re-form in a circle around the Christ candle, give each person a small candle. Then as each group reports, have that group's members light their individual candles from the center candle as a symbol of spreading Jesus' light into their lives.

Conclude by singing "Pass It On." Have members keep the small candles as a reminder of God's light and love.

ILLUSTRATION/JUDY ATWOOD

PARASOLS THAT SHADE THE LIGHT

1. Objectives—Use this Bible study to:
● explore what it means to "walk in darkness" and "walk in light"; and
● learn what keeps people from enjoying God's light of forgiveness.

2. Before the Bible Study—Gather a large candle, matches, Bibles and a small parasol for each person. (A parasol top can be cut from colored poster paper; use toothpicks or match sticks as handles.)

3. Parasol Passages—Say: Most people don't want to walk in darkness. They want to be respectable. Yet they don't want to walk in the bright sunlight of God's righteousness, either. They're reluctant to let go of certain wrong behaviors or attitudes, and they don't want them exposed to the open light. So people prefer to walk in the shade. It's like carrying a parasol. Keep the parasol concept in mind as you study the following section of scripture.

Give each group member a parasol.

Divide the members into small groups of four to six people. Make sure each group has at least one Bible. Post the following instructions on newsprint or type a copy for each small group.

Instructions: Read John 1:5—2:12. Your mission, Mr. and Mrs. Christian, is to discover who God "manifests" or reveals himself to be in this part of his holy Word.

● Talk about what it means to walk in darkness. Point out verses which particularly show the dark side of people.

● What does it mean to walk in the light? Reflect on your answers. Do your answers offer you hope, comfort or joy? Explain.

● Sometimes we're inclined to describe "walking in darkness" as breaking God's commandments and "walking in the light" as keeping God's commandments. Given only these two options, all of us are without hope, because no one can keep God's commandments.

Read 1 John 1:7; 2:1, 2, 12. Consider this interpretation: "Walking in the light" means to walk in God's forgiveness, and that the sun of righteousness shines upon us to purify us of all dark deeds. Does this thought comfort you or give you hope? Explain. Do you agree with this interpretation? Why or why not? What does this portion of scripture say about who God is and how he relates to us?

4. Walking in the Light—Reassemble all group members in a circle. Place the large candle in the center and light it. Ask small groups to each share a new discovery from the scripture they just read.

Say: A parasol suggests the option of living in semi-darkness. That's where you don't do grossly wrong things, but you still cling to a few behaviors and attitudes that aren't pleasing to God. That suggests living as a "shady character." If God's light is really God's forgiveness, or God declaring us righteous through Christ, then why not soak in all the sun you can and toss away the parasols!

Have members reflect on "parasols" in their own lives. (Everyone has behaviors or attitudes that aren't God-pleasing.) Encourage kids to tell about the "parasols" in their lives right now. Then have them quietly, prayerfully, place their parasols next to the burning Christ candle. Let the tossed parasols be a symbol of commitment to renounce sin and walk in the light of God's forgiveness.

Sing "Walking in the Light," "Now Thank We All Our God" or some other appropriate song. Speak a prayer of thanksgiving for God's never-ending light.

A Holiday Bible Study Grab Bag continued

REFLECTING HIS LIGHT

1. Objectives—Use this Bible study to:
● focus on "light" scripture; and
● understand how Christians are a reflection of God's light.

2. Before the Bible Study—Gather for each person: a Bible, small mirror or aluminum-foil square, small candle and matches.

3. Scripture Reflections—Have group members sit in a circle. Make sure everyone has a Bible. Divide the circle into five segments. Give each segment one of the following passages:
● Matthew 5:14-16;
● John 12:35-36;
● Acts 13:47-49;
● Romans 13:11-14;
● Revelation 22:1-5.
Say: God shines into our lives with his love and mercy. As we, in faith, receive his light we also reflect that love and forgiveness into the lives of those around us. Individually, as a group, and with the help of the scripture, let's focus on reflecting his light.
We'll pause after each scripture reading to allow time for personal reflection and these two questions:
● In what ways have you experienced Christ shining into your life?
● How do you presently reflect his light into the lives of those around you?
Cue each of the five segments to read in unison its section of scripture.

4. Light Reflections—Give each person a candle and matches to light it, as well as a small mirror or aluminum-foil square. Ask each person to complete this sentence: "I reflect Christ's light by . . ."
As group members each make their statements, they should reflect their light: With the mirror or aluminum foil held in the hollow of one hand, they should reflect the light from their candle. It's helpful for you, the leader, to model the sentence completion and reflecting of the light. When the last person has shared, have all the members reflect the light from their candles all at once! Let the lights dance around the room.

5. Final Reflections—Ask: How is this reflection experience like our reflection of God's light? Use the answers to create a closing prayer.

GIFTS THAT REFLECT GOD'S LOVE

1. Objectives—Use this Bible study to:
● review the story of the Magi in light of group members' gifts and talents; and
● see how individual gifts can be used in ministry to others.

2. Before the Bible Study—Gather a Bible, 3×5 cards, pencils, one large candle and matches.

3. The Story of the Magi—Have everyone sit in a circle with a large lighted candle in the center. This candle will represent the light of Jesus.
Ask a volunteer to read the story of the Magi in Matthew 2:1-12 to the entire group.

4. Gifts for Ministry—After the reading, say: The Magi brought the Christ child gifts of gold, frankincense and myrrh. These gifts came from the Earth which God had made. Now the Magi were returning them to God as symbols of their honor and devotion to the newborn king.
God has given you special gifts too. Think for a moment. What do you consider to be your gifts and talents? A *gift* may be a musical instrument; the person may also have the *talent* to play it. Or the gift may be a car, and the talent to drive it. Or your gift may be teaching, singing, listening, tutoring, caring or many others. Make a list of your gifts or talents on a 3×5 card. (Allow time for thinking.)
Ask each person to think of ways to use a specific gift in reaching out to others. Have each person share with someone sitting nearby how he or she plans to use one gift in ministry to others. Have partners suggest additional ways the gifts could be used to serve others.

5. Gift-Prayers—Remain in a circle around the Christ candle. Invite each person to speak a sentence prayer using the following general format:
"Lord, I lay before you my gift of _____;
I ask you to use it for _____
_____."
As each person finishes his or her sentence prayer, the group members respond by saying: "Jesus bless you, ___(name)___, and make your gifts a blessing to others."
Conclude by singing "We Three Kings," "As With Gladness, Men of Old" or other appropriate songs.

1. Objectives—Use this Bible study to:
● recognize areas of participants' spiritual lives that need rejuvenation;
● identify and tell ways their lives can be renewed; and
● be reminded that God is our source of growth and strength.

2. Before the Bible Study—Gather newsprint; markers; Bibles; and, for each person, one stick of chewing gum, a pencil, an envelope, a copy of this study.

Read through the entire Bible study and become acquainted with the passages of scripture.

3. What's "Getting Old" in Your Life?—As young people arrive, give them a few minutes for informal fellowship and sharing. Pass out one piece of chewing gum to each person to chew. Listen to them as they share recent experiences they've had.

Sing some "old favorite" songs for starters. Share pertinent announcements and pray for particular concerns your kids might share.

Say: We speak of things that are no longer exciting or interesting as "getting old" in our lives. Ask for a show of hands indicating kids whose chewing gum has "gotten old." Say: Bad jokes "get old." School, jobs, routine tasks and chores often "get old." Even relationships "get old." Ask group members to each suggest some things that have begun to "get old" in their lives. Give volunteers a few moments to share their answers. Some may be humorous. Others may be serious.

Hand out a copy of the "Spiritual Growth Chart" to each young person. Have individuals map out their spiritual growth over the past year on the left side of this chart. Have them indicate months when they felt close to God or were growing in their faith by drawing a line toward the top of the chart. Those months when they were "in the spiritual doldrums" should be marked with a line toward the bottom of the chart. To help their memories, mention activities (retreats, youth weeks, rallies) in which your group participated over the last year.

Show your own Spiritual Growth Chart to group members to help them understand this activity. Be honest. It's good for young people to see you might have times of "spiritual dryness" as well as "high spiritual points" in your life.

Next, ask your kids to fill in the right half of the chart, indicating how they'd *realistically* like to see themselves grow over the next year. Encourage them to note the times of the year that might be tougher on

SPIRITUAL GROWTH CHART

Name: _____

This Year	Next Year

JAN. FEB. MAR. APR. MAY JUN. JUL. AUG. SEP. OCT. NOV. DEC. JAN. FEB. MAR. APR. MAY JUN. JUL. AUG. SEP. OCT. NOV. DEC.

A Holiday Bible Study
Grab Bag continued

their faith. For example, some may find it harder to get up in the mornings for personal devotions in the winter; others may find their time squeezed out by seasonal athletic teams; others may have to go away from the support of the youth group over the summer.

After members have completed their own charts, have them choose partners and share their findings. Encourage them to describe the activities and background information that helped to lift them up or let them down spiritually over the last year. Also, ask them to share the upcoming events which they anticipate will help in their spiritual growth through the next year. (Be on the lookout for any young person who might be left out. Make a point to be his or her partner yourself or ask another adult.)

4. What Does It Mean to Become Spiritually New?—Divide group members into four small groups. If you have over 24 members, have more than four small groups and assign the same passages more than once. Give each group at least one Bible and one of the following scripture passages:
- Mark 2:1-12 (a crippled man is healed);
- John 3:1-7 (Nicodemus, a Pharisee, meets Jesus);
- John 8:3-11 (a woman is caught in adultery);
- John 9:1-11 (a man is born blind).

On a sheet of newsprint, display the following questions:
- How would you describe the character who met Jesus in your passage?
- What are three feelings your character may have experienced before meeting Jesus?
- What was the new gift Jesus offered your character?
- What new responsibilities (burdens) accompanied that new gift?

Allow time for members to answer the questions as they relate to their passages of scripture. After each group has had sufficient time to finish, ask a volunteer from each group to report the findings.

5. Making a Covenant—Instruct your group members to turn over their Spiritual Growth Charts and complete the Personal Covenant on the back. After they've completed their worksheets, have them find their previous partners and together read and sign each other's covenants.

Give kids envelopes and tell them to place their worksheets in the envelopes and seal them. Have the partners fill in their names and addresses on the other partners' envelopes. Collect the envelopes, and say you'll send them to the partners in three months to serve as reminders to support the friends' decisions made during the study. When partners receive

---

PERSONAL COVENANT
Name: _____

Therefore, if anyone is in Christ, he is a new creation; the old has gone, the new has come (2 Corinthians 5:17).

Yet to all who received him, to those who believed in his name, he gave the right to become children of God (John 1:12).

And he said: "I tell you the truth, unless you change and become like little children, you will never enter the kingdom of heaven." (Matthew 18:3).

Place a check by each of the following areas you feel have "gotten old" in your life and need to "become new."
- ☐ Personal devotions
- ☐ Relationships with friends
- ☐ Relationships with family
- ☐ Christian fellowship
- ☐ Unhealthy habits
- ☐ Worship
- ☐ Bible study
- ☐ Sharing your faith with others
- ☐ Other _____
- ☐ Other _____

Write a New Year's resolution concerning the area you'd like to see renewed.

_____
_____

I agree to personally support you in your decision regarding this area of your life.
Signed: _____

---

the letters, they may call the individual, continue to pray for him or her or write a note of encouragement to show support.

Be sure to follow through and mail the envelopes in March. This will help reinforce the learning.

Form a circle with kids resting their arms on the shoulders of their neighbors. Close in prayer thanking God for the strength and resources that help to cultivate all the new things he gives. Ask him to help everyone present keep their promises and resolutions. Thank him for his constant love.

6. Just for Fun—Create a crazy "old" sculpture using the old chewing gum!

—*Leo Symmank and Ben Sharpton*

More Practical Resources For Your Youth Ministry

Get Real: Making Core Christian Beliefs Relevant to Teenagers

Mike Nappa, Amy Nappa & Michael D. Warden

Here are the 24 Bible truths that Christian teenagers *must* know to survive in an unbelieving world. Included: proven strategies for effectively communicating these core Christian beliefs into the chaotic, fast-paced youth culture.
ISBN 1-55945-708-2

Last Impressions: Unforgettable Closings for Youth Meetings

Here's a collection of over 170 of Group's best-ever low-prep (or no-prep!) meeting closings...and each is tied to a thought-provoking Bible passage! With **Last Impressions** you'll be ready with thoughtful... affirming...issue-oriented...high-energy...prayerful...and servanthood closings—on a moment's notice!
ISBN 1-55945-629-9

Growing Close

These 150 practical, quick ideas help break the ice when teenagers don't know each other and break down cliques that often form in groups. A must-have resource for youth workers, coaches, camp directors, and Christian school teachers.
ISBN 1-55945-709-0

Ready-to-Use Letters for Youth Ministry

Tom Tozer

These 110 already-written letters cover practically any situation that arises in youth ministry. And the included IBM-compatible computer disk makes adapting these letters quick and easy. You'll save hours of administrative time with this handy resource!
ISBN 1-55945-692-2

MORE INNOVATIVE RESOURCES FOR YOUR YOUTH MINISTRY

The Youth Worker's Encyclopedia of Bible-Teaching Ideas: Old Testament/ New Testament

Explore the most comprehensive idea-books available for youth workers! Discover more than 360 creative ideas in each of these 416-page encyclopedias—there's at least one idea for each and every book of the Bible. Find ideas for...retreats and overnighters, learning games, adventures, special projects, parties, prayers, music, devotions, skits, and much more!

Plus, you can use these ideas for groups of all sizes in any setting. Large or small. Sunday or midweek meetings. Bible study. Sunday school class or retreat. Discover exciting new ways to teach each book of the Bible to your youth group.

Old Testament   ISBN 1-55945-184-X
New Testament   ISBN 1-55945-183-1

Clip-Art Cartoons for Churches

Here are over 180 funny, photocopiable illustrations to help you jazz up your calendars, newsletters, posters, fliers, transparencies, postcards, business cards, announcements—all your printed materials! These fun, fresh illustrations cover a variety of church and Christian themes, including church life, Sunday school, youth groups, school life, sermons, church events, volunteers, and more! And there's a variety of artistic styles to choose from so each piece you create will be unique and original.

Each illustration is provided in the sizes you need most, so it's easy to use. You won't find random images here...each image is a complete cartoon. And these cartoons are fun! In fact, they're so entertaining that you may just find yourself reading the book and not photocopying them at all.

Order your copy of **Clip-Art Cartoons for Churches** today...and add some spice to your next printed piece.

ISBN 1-55945-791-0

Bore No More! (For Every Pastor, Speaker, Teacher)

This book is a must for every pastor, youth leader, teacher, and speaker. These 70 audience-grabbing activities pull listeners into your lesson or sermon—and drive your message home!

Discover clever object lessons, creative skits, and readings. Music and celebration ideas. Affirmation activities. All the innovative techniques 85 percent of adult churchgoers say they wish their pastors would try! (recent Group Publishing poll)

Involve your congregation in the learning process! These complete 5- to 15-minute activities highlight common New Testament Lectionary passages, so you'll use this book week after week.

ISBN 1-55945-266-8

Order today from your local Christian bookstore, or write:
Group Publishing, Box 485, Loveland, CO 80539.